Texas Assessment Review & Practice

Biology

Boston, Massachusetts • Chandler, Arizona • Glenview, Illinois • Upper Saddle River, New Jersey

Content Reviewer

Heide Marcum, Ph.D.
Senior Lecturer
Department of Environmental Science
Baylor University
Waco, TX

ISBN-13: 978-0-13-319133-2
ISBN-10: 0-13-319133-8
5 6 7 8 9 10 V069 17 16 15 14 13

Contents

About this Book

This review and practice book focuses on the basic content that may be tested on the end-of-course assessments in Biology. Each Texas Essential Knowledge and Skills (TEKS) is reviewed in sequence. You can use the book in any order, as each TEKS review is independent.

TEKS Ⓐ

Each three-page lesson begins with the TEKS. Readiness standards, which have been identified as those most important for in-depth understanding of a particular topic, are clearly indicated. The content summaries specifically address the concepts called out in the TEKS. The lessons include numerous illustrations to help you visualize and understand the concepts and vocabulary of biology. You should carefully review the illustrations as well as the explanations within the text.

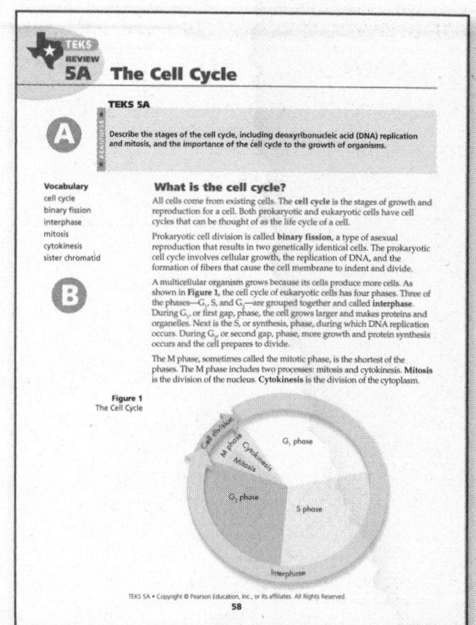

TEKS REVIEW 5A **The Cell Cycle**

TEKS 5A

A **Describe the stages of the cell cycle, including deoxyribonucleic acid (DNA) replication and mitosis, and the importance of the cell cycle to the growth of organisms.**

Vocabulary
cell cycle
binary fission
interphase
mitosis
cytokinesis
sister chromatid

B

What is the cell cycle?

All cells come from existing cells. The **cell cycle** is the stages of growth and reproduction for a cell. Both prokaryotic and eukaryotic cells have cell cycles that can be thought of as the life cycle of a cell.

Prokaryotic cell division is called **binary fission**, a type of asexual reproduction that results in two genetically identical cells. The prokaryotic cell cycle involves cellular growth, the replication of DNA, and the formation of fibers that cause the cell membrane to indent and divide.

A multicellular organism grows because its cells produce more cells. As shown in **Figure 1**, the cell cycle of eukaryotic cells has four phases. Three of the phases—G_1, S, and G_2—are grouped together and called **interphase**. During G_1, or first gap, phase, the cell grows larger and makes proteins and organelles. Next is the S, or synthesis, phase, during which DNA replication occurs. During G_2, or second gap, phase, more growth and protein synthesis occurs and the cell prepares to divide.

The M phase, sometimes called the mitotic phase, is the shortest of the phases. The M phase includes two processes: mitosis and cytokinesis. **Mitosis** is the division of the nucleus. **Cytokinesis** is the division of the cytoplasm.

Figure 1
The Cell Cycle

TEKS 5A • Copyright © Pearson Education, Inc., or its affiliates. All Rights Reserved.
58

Vocabulary Ⓑ

You will need to know the definitions of the vocabulary words listed at the beginning of each lesson in order to answer many of the end-of-course assessment questions. These words are shown in bold type within the topic where they are first defined. Each bold word is accompanied by a simple definition in the text. Vocabulary words are also defined in the glossary at the end of the book. Words that are in italicized type are words that you need to know to understand basic biology concepts. Although you are not likely to be tested on the specific definitions of non-vocabulary words, these words may be used in end-of-course assessment questions.

Study Tip Ⓒ

Each lesson contains a study tip that either refreshes your memory of relevant information that may have been covered in previous science courses or helps reinforce understanding of a particular concept.

End-of-Course Assessment Review Questions Ⓓ

Following each content summary is a set of questions that will help you clarify and reinforce your understanding of the content. Answering these questions will help you gauge your understanding of a particular TEKS. Answers and explanations can be found at the end of all of the reviews.

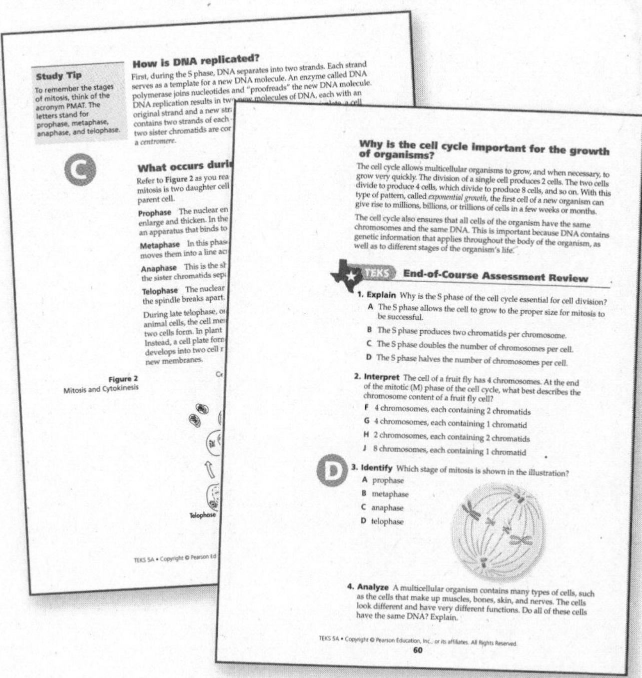

Study Tip
To remember the stages of mitosis, think of the acronym PMAT. The letters stand for prophase, metaphase, anaphase, and telophase.

C

Why is the cell cycle important for the growth of organisms?

The cell cycle allows multicellular organisms to grow, and when necessary, to grow very quickly. The division of a single cell produces 2 cells. The two cells divide to produce 4 cells, which divide to produce 8 cells, and so on. With this type of pattern, called *exponential growth*, the first cell of a new organism can give rise to millions, billions, or trillions of cells in a few weeks or months.

The cell cycle also ensures that all cells of the organism have the same chromosomes and the same DNA. This is important because DNA contains genetic information that applies throughout the body of the organism, as well as to different stages of the organism's life.

TEKS **End-of-Course Assessment Review**

1. **Explain** Why is the S phase of the cell cycle essential for cell division?
   - A The S phase allows the cell to grow to the proper size for mitosis to be successful.
   - B The S phase produces two chromatids per chromosome.
   - C The S phase doubles the number of chromosomes per cell.
   - D The S phase halves the number of chromosomes per cell.
2. **Interpret** The cell of a fruit fly has 4 chromosomes. At the end of the mitotic (M) phase of the cell cycle, what best describes the chromosome content of a fruit fly cell?
   - F 4 chromosomes, each containing 2 chromatids
   - G 4 chromosomes, each containing 1 chromatid
   - H 2 chromosomes, each containing 2 chromatids
   - J 8 chromosomes, each containing 1 chromatid

D

3. **Identify** Which stage of mitosis is shown in the illustration?
   - A prophase
   - B metaphase
   - C anaphase
   - D telophase
4. **Analyze** A multicellular organism contains many types of cells, such as the cells that make up muscles, bones, skin, and nerves. The cells look different and have very different functions. Do all of these cells have the same DNA? Explain.

TEKS 5A • Copyright © Pearson Education, Inc., or its affiliates. All Rights Reserved.
60

Test-Taking Tips E

Test-taking tips provide strategies for answering multiple-choice questions. Accompanying sample questions allow you to practice your test-taking skills.

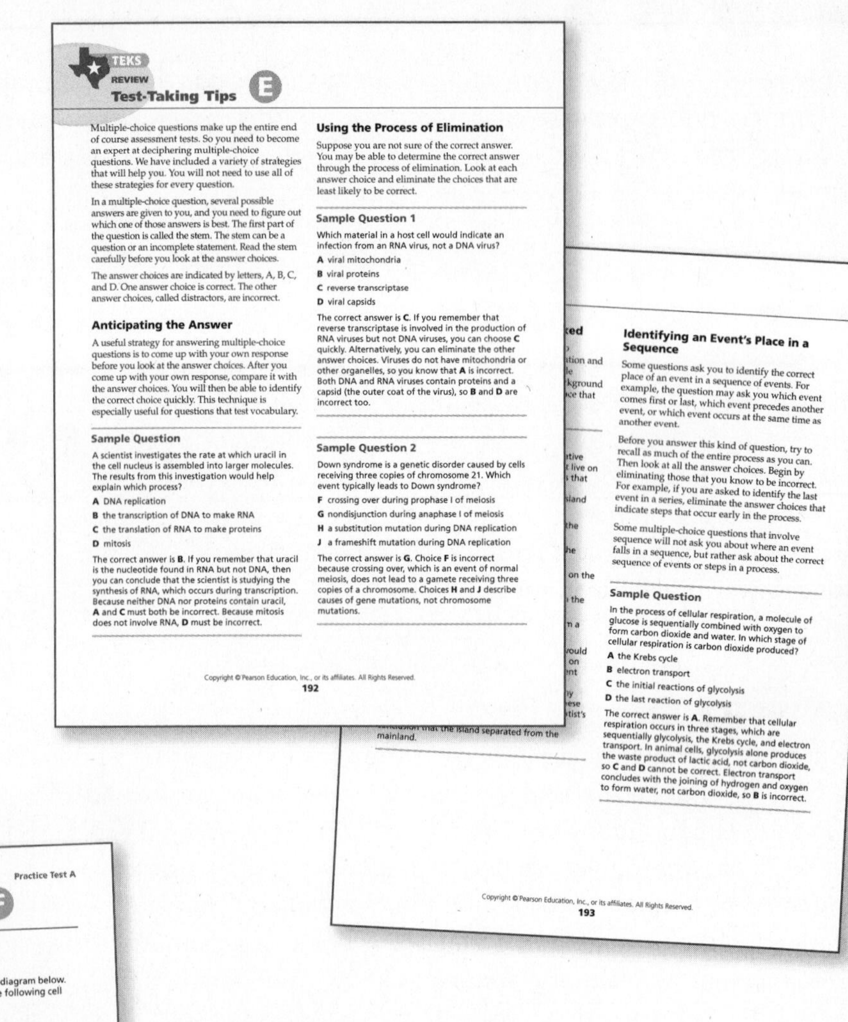

TEKS REVIEW

Test-Taking Tips E

Multiple-choice questions make up the entire end of course assessment tests. So you need to become an expert at deciphering multiple-choice questions. We have included a variety of strategies that will help you. You will not need to use all of these strategies for every question.

In a multiple-choice question, several possible answers are given to you, and you need to figure out which one of those answers is best. The first part of the question is called the stem. The stem can be a question or an incomplete statement. Read the stem carefully before you look at the answer choices.

The answer choices are indicated by letters, A, B, C, and D. One answer choice is correct. The other answer choices, called distractors, are incorrect.

Anticipating the Answer

A useful strategy for answering multiple-choice questions is to come up with your own response before you look at the answer choices. After you come up with your own response, compare it with the answer choices. You will then be able to identify the correct choice quickly. This technique is especially useful for questions that test vocabulary.

Sample Question

A scientist investigates the rate at which uracil in the cell nucleus is assembled into larger molecules. The results from this investigation would help explain which process?

A DNA replication
B the transcription of DNA to make RNA
C the translation of RNA to make proteins
D mitosis

The correct answer is **B**. If you remember that uracil is the nucleotide found in RNA but not DNA, then you can conclude that the scientist is studying the synthesis of RNA, which occurs during transcription. Because neither DNA nor proteins contain uracil, **A** and **C** must both be incorrect. Because mitosis does not involve RNA, **D** must be incorrect.

Using the Process of Elimination

Suppose you are not sure of the correct answer. You may be able to determine the correct answer through the process of elimination. Look at each answer choice and eliminate the choices that are least likely to be correct.

Sample Question 1

Which material in a host cell would indicate an infection from an RNA virus, not a DNA virus?

A viral mitochondria
B viral proteins
C reverse transcriptase
D viral capsids

The correct answer is **C**. If you remember that reverse transcriptase is involved in the production of RNA viruses but not DNA viruses, you can choose **C** quickly. Alternatively, you can eliminate the other answer choices. Viruses do not have mitochondria or other organelles, so you know that **A** is incorrect. Both DNA and RNA viruses contain proteins and a capsid (the outer coat of the virus), so **B** and **D** are incorrect too.

Sample Question 2

Down syndrome is a genetic disorder caused by cells receiving three copies of chromosome 21. Which event typically leads to Down syndrome?

F crossing over during prophase I of meiosis
G nondisjunction during anaphase I of meiosis
H a substitution mutation during DNA replication
J a frameshift mutation during DNA replication

The correct answer is **G**. Choice **F** is incorrect because crossing over, which is an event of normal meiosis, does not lead to a gamete receiving three copies of a chromosome. Choices **H** and **J** describe causes of gene mutations, not chromosome mutations.

Copyright © Pearson Education, Inc., or its affiliates. All Rights Reserved.
192

Identifying an Event's Place in a Sequence

Some questions ask you to identify the correct place of an event in a sequence of events. For example, the question may ask you which event comes first or last, which event precedes another event, or which event occurs at the same time as another event.

Before you answer this kind of question, try to recall as much of the entire process as you can. Then look at all the answer choices. Begin by eliminating those that you know to be incorrect. For example, if you are asked to identify the last event in a series, eliminate the answer choices that indicate steps that occur early in the process.

Some multiple-choice questions that involve sequence will not ask you about where an event falls in a sequence, but rather ask about the correct sequence of events or steps in a process.

Sample Question

In the process of cellular respiration, a molecule of glucose is sequentially combined with oxygen to form carbon dioxide and water. In which stage of cellular respiration is carbon dioxide produced?

A the Krebs cycle
B electron transport
C the initial reactions of glycolysis
D the last reaction of glycolysis

The correct answer is **A**. Remember that cellular respiration occurs in three stages, which are sequentially glycolysis, the Krebs cycle, and electron transport. In animal cells, glycolysis alone produces the waste product of lactic acid, not carbon dioxide, so **C** and **D** cannot be correct. Electron transport concludes with the joining of hydrogen and oxygen to form water, not carbon dioxide, so **B** is incorrect.

Copyright © Pearson Education, Inc., or its affiliates. All Rights Reserved.
193

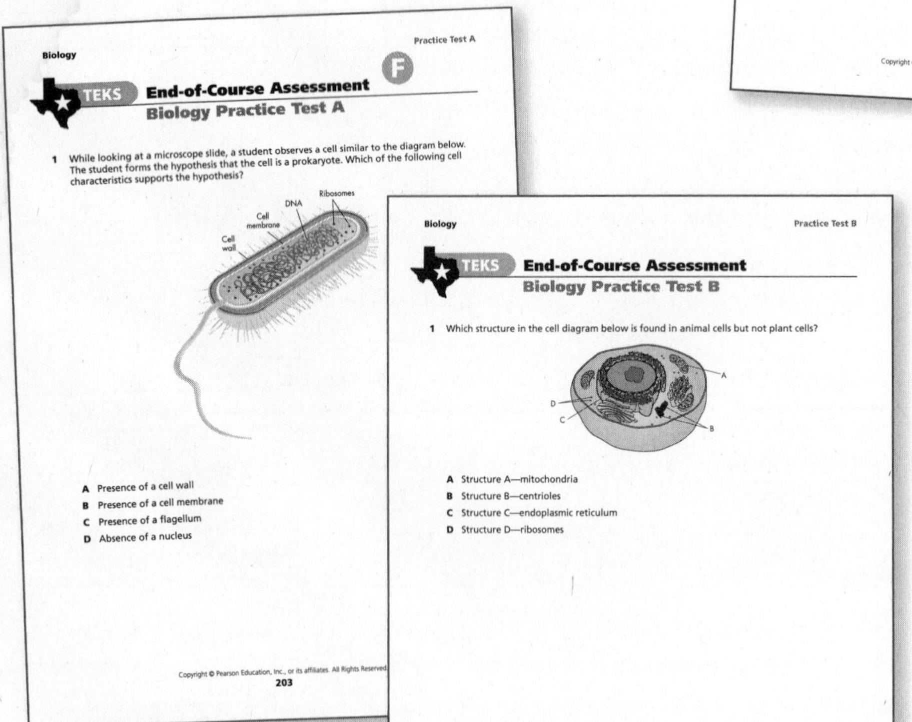

Biology Practice Test A

TEKS End-of-Course Assessment F
Biology Practice Test A

1 While looking at a microscope slide, a student observes a cell similar to the diagram below. The student forms the hypothesis that the cell is a prokaryote. Which of the following cell characteristics supports the hypothesis?

A Presence of a cell wall
B Presence of a cell membrane
C Presence of a flagellum
D Absence of a nucleus

Copyright © Pearson Education, Inc., or its affiliates. All Rights Reserved.
203

Biology Practice Test B

TEKS End-of-Course Assessment
Biology Practice Test B

1 Which structure in the cell diagram below is found in animal cells but not plant cells?

A Structure A—mitochondria
B Structure B—centrioles
C Structure C—endoplasmic reticulum
D Structure D—ribosomes

Copyright © Pearson Education, Inc., or its affiliates. All Rights Reserved.
227

Practice Tests F

Two sample full-length exams mimic the end-of-course test in both format and layout. Following each test is an answer sheet for you to fill in the correct answers.

Texas Essential Knowledge and Skills (TEKS) for Biology

(1) Scientific processes. The student, for at least 40% of instructional time, conducts laboratory and field investigations using safe, environmentally appropriate, and ethical practices. The student is expected to:
(A) Demonstrate safe practices during laboratory and field investigations.
(B) Demonstrate an understanding of the use and conservation of resources and the proper disposal or recycling of materials.

(2) Scientific processes. The student uses scientific methods and equipment during laboratory and field investigations. The student is expected to:
(A) Know the definition of science and understand that it has limitations.
(B) Know that hypotheses are tentative and testable statements that must be capable of being supported or not supported by observational evidence. Hypotheses of durable explanatory power which have been tested over a wide variety of conditions are incorporated into theories.
(C) Know scientific theories are based on natural and physical phenomena and are capable of being tested by multiple independent researchers. Unlike hypotheses, scientific theories are well-established and highly-reliable explanations, but they may be subject to change as new areas of science and new technologies are developed.
(D) Distinguish between scientific hypotheses and scientific theories.
(E) Plan and implement descriptive, comparative, and experimental investigations, including asking questions, formulating testable hypotheses, and selecting equipment and technology.
(F) Collect and organize qualitative and quantitative data and make measurements with accuracy and precision using tools such as calculators, spreadsheet software, data-collecting probes, computers, standard laboratory glassware, microscopes, various prepared slides, stereoscopes, metric rulers, electronic balances, gel electrophoresis apparatuses, micropipettors, hand lenses, Celsius thermometers, hot plates, lab notebooks or journals, timing devices, cameras, Petri dishes, lab incubators, dissection equipment, meter sticks, and models, diagrams, or samples of biological specimens or structures.
(G) Analyze, evaluate, make inferences, and predict trends from data.
(H) Communicate valid conclusions supported by the data through methods such as lab reports, labeled drawings, graphic organizers, journals, summaries, oral reports, and technology-based reports.

(3) Scientific processes. The student uses critical thinking, scientific reasoning, and problem solving to make informed decisions within and outside the classroom. The student is expected to:
(A) In all fields of science, analyze, evaluate, and critique scientific explanations by using empirical evidence, logical reasoning, and experimental and observational testing, including examining all sides of scientific evidence of those scientific explanations, so as to encourage critical thinking by the student.
(B) Communicate and apply scientific information extracted from various sources such as current events, news reports, published journal articles, and marketing materials.
(C) Draw inferences based on data related to promotional materials for products and services.
(D) Evaluate the impact of scientific research on society and the environment.
(E) Evaluate models according to their limitations in representing biological objects or events.
(F) Research and describe the history of biology and contributions of scientists.

Biology TEKS *continued*

(4) Science concepts. The student knows that cells are the basic structures of all living things with specialized parts that perform specific functions and that viruses are different from cells. The student is expected to:	
(A) Compare and contrast prokaryotic and eukaryotic cells.	Supporting Standard
(B) Investigate and explain cellular processes, including homeostasis, energy conversions, transport of molecules, and synthesis of new molecules.	**Readiness Standard**
(C) Compare the structures of viruses to cells, describe viral reproduction, and describe the role of viruses in causing diseases such as human immunodeficiency virus (HIV) and influenza.	**Readiness Standard**

(5) Science concepts. The student knows how an organism grows and the importance of cell differentiation. The student is expected to:	
(A) Describe the stages of the cell cycle, including deoxyribonucleic acid (DNA) replication and mitosis, and the importance of the cell cycle to the growth of organisms.	**Readiness Standard**
(B) Examine specialized cells, including roots, stems, and leaves of plants; and animal cells such as blood, muscle, and epithelium.	Supporting Standard
(C) Describe the roles of DNA, ribonucleic acid (RNA), and environmental factors in cell differentiation.	Supporting Standard
(D) Recognize that disruptions of the cell cycle lead to diseases such as cancer.	Supporting Standard

(6) Science concepts. The student knows the mechanisms of genetics, including the role of nucleic acids and the principles of Mendelian Genetics. The student is expected to:	
(A) Identify components of DNA, and describe how information for specifying the traits of an organism is carried in the DNA.	**Readiness Standard**
(B) Recognize that components that make up the genetic code are common to all organisms.	Supporting Standard
(C) Explain the purpose and process of transcription and translation using models of DNA and RNA.	Supporting Standard
(D) Recognize that gene expression is a regulated process;	Supporting Standard
(E) Identify and illustrate changes in DNA and evaluate the significance of these changes.	**Readiness Standard**
(F) Predict possible outcomes of various genetic combinations such as monohybrid crosses, dihybrid crosses and non-Mendelian inheritance.	**Readiness Standard**
(G) Recognize the significance of meiosis to sexual reproduction.	Supporting Standard
(H) Describe how techniques such as DNA fingerprinting, genetic modifications, and chromosomal analysis are used to study the genomes of organisms.	Supporting Standard

(7) Science concepts. The student knows evolutionary theory is a scientific explanation for the unity and diversity of life. The student is expected to:	
(A) Analyze and evaluate how evidence of common ancestry among groups is provided by the fossil record, biogeography, and homologies, including anatomical, molecular, and developmental.	**Readiness Standard**
(B) Analyze and evaluate scientific explanations concerning any data of sudden appearance, stasis, and sequential nature of groups in the fossil record.	Supporting Standard
(C) Analyze and evaluate how natural selection produces change in populations, not individuals.	Supporting Standard
(D) Analyze and evaluate how the elements of natural selection, including inherited variation, the potential of a population to produce more offspring than can survive, and a finite supply of environmental resources, result in differential reproductive success.	Supporting Standard
(E) Analyze and evaluate the relationship of natural selection to adaptation and to the development of diversity in and among species.	**Readiness Standard**
(F) Analyze and evaluate the effects of other evolutionary mechanisms, including genetic drift, gene flow, mutation, and recombination.	Supporting Standard
(G) Analyze and evaluate scientific explanations concerning the complexity of the cell.	Supporting Standard

(8) Science concepts. The student knows that taxonomy is a branching classification based on the shared characteristics of organisms and can change as new discoveries are made. The student is expected to:	
(A) Define taxonomy and recognize the importance of a standardized taxonomic system to the scientific community.	Supporting Standard
(B) Categorize organisms using a hierarchical classification system based on similarities and differences shared among groups.	**Readiness Standard**
(C) Compare characteristics of taxonomic groups, including archaea, bacteria, protists, fungi, plants, and animals.	Supporting Standard

(9) Science concepts. Science concepts. The student knows the significance of various molecules involved in metabolic processes and energy conversions that occur in living organisms. The student is expected to:	
(A) Compare the structures and functions of different types of biomolecules, including carbohydrates, lipids, proteins, and nucleic acids.	**Readiness Standard**
(B) Compare the reactants and products of photosynthesis and cellular respiration in terms of energy and matter.	Supporting Standard
(C) Identify and investigate the role of enzymes.	Supporting Standard
(D) Analyze and evaluate the evidence regarding formation of simple organic molecules and their organization into long complex molecules having information such as the DNA molecule for self-replicating life.	Supporting Standard

Biology TEKS *continued*

(10) Science concepts. The student knows that biological systems are composed of multiple levels. The student is expected to:	
(A) Describe the interactions that occur among systems that perform the functions of regulation, nutrient absorption, reproduction, and defense from injury or illness in animals.	**Readiness Standard**
(B) Describe the interactions that occur among systems that perform the functions of transport, reproduction, and response in plants.	**Readiness Standard**
(C) Analyze the levels of organization in biological systems and relate the levels to each other and to the whole system.	Supporting Standard

(11) Science concepts. The student knows that biological systems work to achieve and maintain balance. The student is expected to:	
(A) Describe the role of internal feedback mechanisms in the maintenance of homeostasis.	Supporting Standard
(B) Investigate and analyze how organisms, populations, and communities respond to external factors.	Supporting Standard
(C) Summarize the role of microorganisms in both maintaining and disrupting the health of both organisms and ecosystems.	Supporting Standard
(D) Describe how events and processes that occur during ecological succession can change populations and species diversity.	**Readiness Standard**

(12) Science concepts. The student knows that interdependence and interactions occur within an environmental system. The student is expected to:	
(A) Interpret relationships, including predation, parasitism, commensalism, mutualism, and competition among organisms.	**Readiness Standard**
(B) Compare variations and adaptations of organisms in different ecosystems.	Supporting Standard
(C) Analyze the flow of matter and energy through trophic levels using various models, including food chains, food webs, and ecological pyramids.	**Readiness Standard**
(D) Recognize that long-term survival of species is dependent on changing resource bases that are limited.	Supporting Standard
(E) Describe the flow of matter through the carbon and nitrogen cycles and explain the consequences of disrupting these cycles.	Supporting Standard
(F) Describe how environmental change can impact ecosystem stability.	**Readiness Standard**

Demonstrating Safe Practices

TEKS 1A

Demonstrate safe practices during laboratory and field investigations.

Why is preparation important when carrying out scientific investigations?

Good preparation helps you stay safe when doing scientific activities in the laboratory. Preparing for a lab should begin the day before you will actually perform the lab. It is important to read through the procedure carefully and make sure you understand all the directions. Also, review general safety guidelines that may be included with your lab manual or textbook. The most important safety rule is simple: Always follow your teacher's instructions and the laboratory directions exactly.

When you have completed the lab, clean up your work area. Follow your teacher's instructions about proper disposal of wastes. Finally, wash your hands thoroughly with soap and warm water after working in the laboratory.

At some point, an accident can occur in the lab. If an accident occurs, no matter how minor, notify your teacher immediately. Then, listen to your teacher's directions and carry them out quickly. Make sure you know the location and proper use of all the emergency equipment in your lab. Knowing safety and first-aid procedures beforehand will prepare you to handle accidents properly. Other important safety policies are listed in **Figure 1** (on the next page).

Some investigations will be done in the "field." The field can be any area outside of the lab, such as a schoolyard, a forest, a park, or a beach. Just as in the laboratory, good preparation helps you stay safe when doing science activities in the field. There can be many potential safety hazards outdoors, including severe weather, traffic, wild animals, and poisonous plants. Advance planning can help you avoid some potential hazards. Whenever you do field work, always tell an adult where you will be. Never carry out a field investigation on your own.

What is the appropriate use of important safety equipment?

Each person has a responsibility to learn the dangers that may be present while working in the laboratory and the purpose and operation of all emergency safety equipment. Always follow a teacher's instructions in an emergency. The most important safety practice is the proper use of protective safety equipment.

Figure 1

Biology Laboratory Safety Do's and Don'ts

- Notify the teacher of any sensitivities or allergies to chemicals or other substances.
- Do not leave an experiment unattended.
- Never chew gum, eat, or drink in the laboratory.
- Always wear shoes and avoid wearing loose-fitting clothing and dangling jewelry.
- Secure long hair and loose clothing; roll up loose sleeves when working with burners or flames.
- Inspect all equipment for damage prior to use; do not use damaged equipment.
- Keep the floor clear of all objects such as personal items, spilled liquids, and any other item that may cause someone to trip or fall.
- Never point the open end of a container containing biological materials or chemicals at other people.
- Do not touch any chemical with your hands.
- Never pour biological materials or chemicals down the sink drain unless you've been specifically instructed to do so.
- Know the location of all emergency exits in the laboratory and the building.
- Wash your hands with soap and water at the end of each investigation.

Safety Goggles As a rule, safety goggles should be worn at all times in the laboratory and during performance of field investigations. During an experiment, you may use wet or dry chemicals. Safety goggles can help protect your eyes from splashes or particles of those chemicals. Safety goggles can also help protect your eyes from pathogens and organisms you encounter in the laboratory or field.

Safety Gloves It is always appropriate to wear safety gloves in the laboratory and in the field. Whether you are handling biological or chemical materials, it is important to protect your hands. While some biological substances such as pathogens and venom are hazardous to everyone, even apparently harmless biological substances can harm some people. For example, peanuts are harmless to most people, but they can cause severe allergic reactions in other people. Animal saliva causes some people to break out in hives. (Note that regular safety gloves are *not* heat-resistant. You need heat-resistant mitts for protection from heat.)

Fire Extinguishers Not all fires are the same, and no single fire extinguisher works on every type of fire. Fires are designated by type and listed by class. Water extinguishers are never used in the laboratory as they put out only certain fires. Pouring water on fires involving combustible liquids, electrical equipment, or combustible metals may spread the fire or make it worse.

Study Tip

Look for all symbols that represent safety equipment and protective devices in the laboratory. Learn the meaning of the symbols and purpose of each device so that you can act quickly in an emergency.

Safety Shower Whenever the skin or clothing is exposed to a significant amount of corrosive or toxic chemicals, the contaminants must be immediately washed away with large quantities of water. An emergency safety shower is the most effective way to quickly eliminate contaminants on your skin or clothing and avoid injury. In any circumstance in which the use of a safety shower is necessary, it is important to act quickly and remove any affected articles of clothing to avoid further exposure. Once the hazardous materials have been washed away, obtain medical attention immediately.

Fire Blanket If clothing or hair catches fire, *do not* run, because running fans flames. A fire blanket can be used to smother flames. Or, a safety shower can be used if there is one nearby.

Eyewash Fountain Even though the use of safety goggles is required, eyewash fountains are located in all laboratory environments where the eyes may be exposed to hazardous substances. In the event that one or both eyes are exposed to a hazardous substance, an eyewash fountain should be used without delay. Hold the eyelids open, and flush the affected eyes thoroughly for several minutes to ensure the substance has been purged. Then seek immediate medical attention.

TEKS End-of-Course Assessment Review

1. Infer In a biology laboratory, safety gloves would help protect you from

A airborne pathogens.

B hot water.

C irritating plant oils.

D a small candle flame.

2. Identify A student is performing an investigation that requires using an acid. Which of the following types of safety equipment must the student wear during the investigation?

F ear plugs

G heat-resistant gloves

H safety goggles

J None of the above

3. Explain What are two appropriate safety responses to your clothing or hair catching fire in the laboratory?

4. Evaluate A student says that he does not need to wear safety goggles for an experiment because no liquid chemicals are being used. What would your response be to this student?

Conservation of Resources and Proper Disposal

TEKS 1B

Demonstrate an understanding of the use and conservation of resources and the proper disposal or recycling of materials.

Vocabulary
decontamination
biohazard

Why is the conservation of resources important?

Most natural resources are limited. Conservation of these resources will ensure that they are available for future generations. One way to reduce waste is to use the smallest possible amounts of materials, and to use materials that can be recovered or recycled, instead of just being discarded.

What are the proper ways to reuse and recycle materials in the laboratory?

Many materials used in the laboratory can be reused after thorough cleaning and safe removal of chemical residues. These materials include containers and instruments made of sturdy glass, plastic, and metal. Materials that cannot be reused, but can be recycled, should be collected and sent to recycling plants. Recyclable items should always be discarded in containers designated for each type of material.

Before placing items in general recycling containers, care should be taken to make sure they are decontaminated. **Decontamination** is the removal of hazardous compounds. Decontamination should be performed only under the supervision of your teacher or qualified laboratory personnel.

Some chemicals used in the laboratory can also be reused or recycled. Solvents such as acetone, methanol, and toluene are routinely reused because they can easily be purified. Chemicals that cannot be purified in the laboratory may still be good candidates for recycling because of the value of the chemical. Designated containers should always be used for each chemical to be recycled because mixing certain materials can be extremely hazardous.

Study Tip

Think about the lab investigations you performed throughout the year. Recall the disposal methods used for various chemicals and other materials.

What are the proper ways to dispose of materials in the laboratory?

Whenever chemical substances are used in the laboratory, some waste is generated. Because of the potential risks, very little laboratory waste can be disposed of in public waste containers. However, some laboratory consumables —materials that cannot be recycled and were not exposed to chemicals—may be discarded as regular trash. Your teacher will tell you which, if any, of the materials can be discarded in regular trash.

Why is the proper disposal of materials in a laboratory important?

Proper disposal or recycling of waste materials is also essential to protecting human and environmental health. Many biology experiments and investigations involve **biohazards**, biological substances that pose a threat to the health of living organisms, primarily humans. Your teacher will tell you how to handle and dispose of biohazards. Biohazards are labeled with the symbol shown in **Figure 1**.

Figure 1
Biohazard Symbol

Biology experiments may also involve hazardous chemicals. When chemicals cannot be recycled, disposal must follow strict guidelines and comply with local, state, and federal regulations. These regulations were implemented to avoid the health problems and expense caused by pollution and contamination. Hazardous or toxic chemical wastes must be disposed of separately according to proper guidelines for safe disposal. They also must be properly labeled. The recommended disposal method for a substance is provided on its Material Safety Data Sheet (MSDS).

Laboratory workers can discard chemicals such as dilute acids, bases, and certain organic compounds by pouring them down the drain with large quantities of water. Materials that are acceptable for this disposal method are water soluble, have very low toxicity, and, if organic, are readily biodegradable. However, this type of disposal should be performed only with the approval of your teacher and after a thorough review of disposal guidelines. Sometimes, because of pollution concerns, chemicals cannot be poured down a drain. When this is the case, you may see a sign similar to the one shown in **Figure 2.**

Figure 2
Common Laboratory Sign

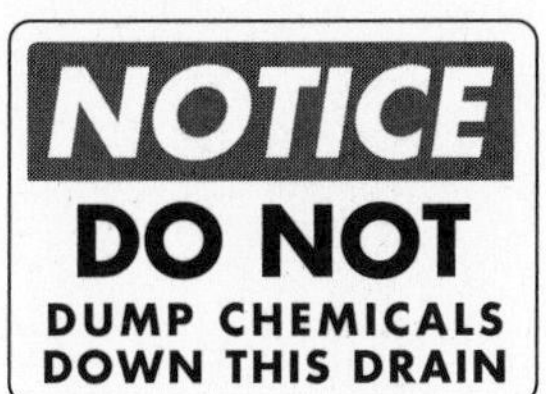

Some hazardous chemical wastes can be neutralized, or made non-hazardous. Wastes that cannot be neutralized must be shipped to a hazardous-waste landfill by a licensed company approved by the Department of Transportation.

Disposal of all hazardous chemical wastes must comply with local, state, and federal regulations. The federal agencies responsible for regulating waste disposal are the Environmental Protection Agency (EPA) and the Occupational Safety and Health Administration (OSHA). Failure to properly dispose of chemical wastes is dangerous and can result in fines and lawsuits.

TEKS End-of-Course Assessment Review

1. **Identify** Which object or material may be discarded safely with the regular trash?

   A a Petri dish used in an experiment on bacterial growth

   B a broken Petri dish that was not used in an experiment

   C a sample of blood from an investigation of blood clotting factors

   D strong acids and bases from an experiment on blood pH

2. **Evaluate** At the end of a laboratory experiment, a student disposes of all liquid chemicals by flushing them down the sink drain with water. Explain what is wrong with this action.

3. **Demonstrate Understanding** During an investigation, Evan spills some compound on the lab table. His lab partner tells him that the compound should be recycled. Evan collects the substance and disposes of it in a container marked for general recycling. Describe two mistakes Evan made.

4. **Infer** Why would a laboratory never have a single waste container for all wastes?

2A Definition of Science

TEKS 2A

Know the definition of science and understand that it has limitations, as specified in subsection (b)(2) of this section.

- **(b)(2) Nature of science. Science, as defined by the National Academy of Sciences, is the "use of evidence to construct testable explanations and predictions of natural phenomena, as well as the knowledge generated through this process." This vast body of changing and increasing knowledge is described by physical, mathematical, and conceptual models. Students should know that some questions are outside the realm of science because they deal with phenomena that are not scientifically testable.**

What is the definition of science?

Science is the use of evidence to construct testable explanations and predictions of natural phenomena, as well as the knowledge generated through this process. In other words, *science* is the study of the natural and physical world using physical, mathematical, and conceptual models.

Scientific explanations must be both testable and falsifiable—able to be proven incorrect. Observation, experimentation, research, and the use of models produce evidence that allows scientists to understand natural phenomena. Scientists study patterns and make predictions about natural phenomena and processes to understand how the world works.

In many cases, because of the use of observation, experimentation, research, and models, scientists can predict the results of a natural process even if they do not have all the information about that process. Many explanations of natural processes are accepted as valid because there is so much evidence supporting them, and because they have been observed and/or tested under a wide variety of conditions. When scientific explanations have been tested and widely accepted, predictions about future events usually end up to be accurate.

Science is not the same as technology. Technology is the application of science, often for industrial or commercial uses. Science identifies *how* or *why* a natural or physical phenomenon occurs. Technology identifies *how to apply* that phenomenon for a practical use.

Study Tip

Remember that scientific concepts must be part of the natural and physical world and must be testable and falsifiable. Concepts that do not fit into these categories are not scientific.

Why study science?

People study science for thousands of reasons. Botanists might study plants to improve crop yields or find sources of new medicines. Meteorologists might study weather patterns to predict hurricanes or tornadoes. Geologists might study natural processes to recognize how events in the past might influence events, such as earthquakes, in the future. Doctors, dentists, veterinarians, nurses, and pharmacists all study science to provide health care to you and your pets. What would you be most interested in studying through science?

What are the limitations of science?

Because science is the study of natural and physical phenomena, science has limitations. Science is not emotion, art, or feeling. Science cannot determine which painting is more appealing or who is the best choice for president. Science cannot answer questions regarding faith or personal feelings. Science can provide information, but non-scientific factors decide how we use science.

Current scientific knowledge is limited to the information presently known about the natural and physical world. This is why all scientific hypotheses and models are subject to change. As we learn new information, current scientific ideas sometimes become outdated. As new information becomes available, new technologies may also arise, making old technologies obsolete.

Figure 1 is an illustration of the modern model of DNA, the molecule that codes for traits in all organisms. For many years, scientists suspected that proteins coded for traits. Then in 1952, the Hershey-Chase experiment confirmed that DNA, not proteins, served this function. Still later, James Watson and Francis Crick determined the double-helix structure of DNA. Later scientists discovered details of the genetic code. Today, with the use of sophisticated technology, scientists can determine the specific atomic structure of a DNA molecule. They also are able to splice sections of DNA and reassemble the pieces.

Figure 1
The Double Helix Model of DNA

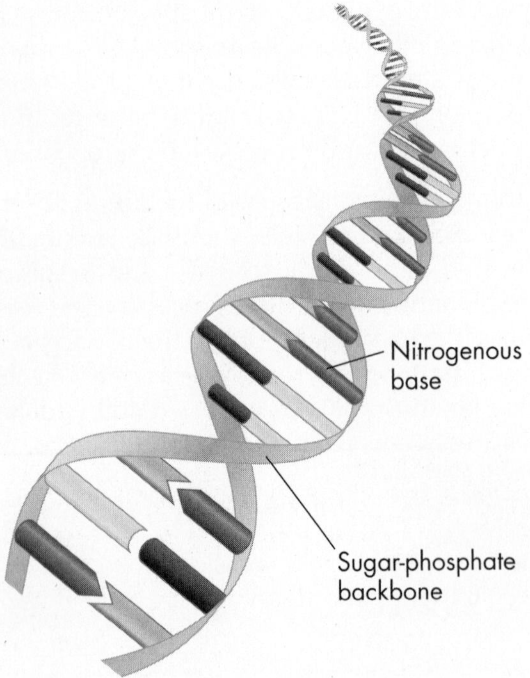

Many ideas and explanations that are currently known about the natural and physical worlds are a result of the use of physical, mathematical, and conceptual models. A *model* is a representation of an object or event. Physical models are replicas of an actual item. Mathematical models, such as equations, represent ideas of processes. A conceptual model is a system of ideas such as a scientific theory.

A model may be used because a process or idea is too large (such as models of human population growth) or too small to be studied directly, or because it is too dangerous (human viral transmission) or too expensive to be studied directly. It is important to note that models never represent a process or idea perfectly, and will change as more knowledge is gained through additional scientific research. As models become more sophisticated, they can more accurately predict the system they are concerned with.

TEKS End-of-Course Assessment Review

1. Define Which of the following questions is not a scientific question?

A What caused dinosaurs to become extinct?

B How is hydrochloric acid produced and contained in the stomach?

C How are proteins in the stomach different from proteins in the liver?

D Was Isaac Newton the greatest scientist that ever lived?

2. Define The circuitry for computers was invented after scientists learned how electrons flow through certain materials, such as silicon. Computer circuitry is an example of

F a prediction.

G a limitation of science.

H technology.

J a model.

3. Evaluate Your friend is arguing that synthetic internal organs for human transplant can never be developed; the technology needed to make them is too expensive and too complicated. Knowing what you know about science, how would you respond to your friend?

4. Identify Describe an area of study that is not science. Write 3 to 5 sentences describing why the area you chose is not science and how it could be changed to qualify as science.

Hypotheses

TEKS 2B

Know that hypotheses are tentative and testable statements that must be capable of being supported or not supported by observational evidence. Hypotheses of durable explanatory power which have been tested over a wide variety of conditions are incorporated into theories.

Vocabulary
hypothesis

What is a hypothesis?

Suppose you have two radish plants. Both are about the same size and appear equally healthy, and both are in pots that contain the same amount and type of soil. You place one radish plant by a sunny window and the other plant in a dark closet. After several days, you observe that the radish plant in the dark has become shriveled and its leaves have turned yellow. The radish plant in the sunlight remains healthy. Your explanation of this observation is that radish plants depend on sunlight to remain healthy.

In this example, you developed a tentative explanation, or scientific hypothesis, for the differences you observed between a plant kept in darkness and a plant exposed to sunlight. A scientific **hypothesis** is a tentative statement or explanation for an observation in nature. Scientific hypotheses are capable of being tested and supported or not supported through further observation and experimentation.

Why must a hypothesis be testable?

Typically, once a scientific hypothesis is stated, the next step is to develop an experiment or conduct observational research to identify evidence that either supports or does not support the hypothesis. This is because a hypothesis has no meaning unless there is observational evidence or data that supports it.

For example, the scientific hypothesis, *"Plants need sunlight to thrive and be healthy"* has no meaning without an experiment or data to support it. Therefore, a scientific hypothesis must be testable. Then, information and evidence gathered can be analyzed to draw conclusions about the hypothesis. In some cases, a hypothesis will be supported by the evidence that accumulates. In other cases it will not be supported.

Study Tip

The root words contained in *hypothesis* tell you the meaning of the word. *Hypo-* means "under," and *thesis* means "proposition." In a way, a hypothesis is an underlying proposition for an experiment or observation.

What if a hypothesis is supported?

Suppose you were to design a scientific experiment to test the effect of sunlight on the growth of plants. If you found that your experiment supported your hypothesis, would you be finished? Not quite. The experiment should be repeated several times to confirm the results and to ensure that no errors have been made.

In addition, a hypothesis should be tested over a variety of conditions to confirm that all variables have been considered that might alter the results. For example, in the radish experiment, another explanation for the difference in radish plants could be the temperature of the closet versus the temperature in the sun. In the best scientific tradition, it is also important to have others repeat the experiment separately to confirm the results. It is always possible that a single investigator may accidentally introduce some error or some bias into the results. The more investigators who replicate the results, the less likely it will be that any bias will be involved.

Hypotheses related to a given topic that have undergone significant testing by multiple scientists under a variety of conditions can be said to have durable explanatory power—that is, they have stood up to multiple tests by many scientists. If hypotheses have been consistently supported through multiple tests, they are incorporated into theories concerning their given topic. At that point, additional research and tests are devised in attempt to make sure the revised theory is still supported under all conditions.

What if a hypothesis is not supported?

On the other hand, suppose your experiment did not support the hypothesis. Would your experiment then be a failure? No; a scientific experiment is never a failure, as it leads to information and knowledge you did not previously have. But if it is not supported, the original hypothesis itself is not very useful for making predictions or understanding observations, so it is typically modified, or in some cases, discarded. If the hypothesis is modified, a new cycle of experimentation can begin. You can see the cycle of hypothesis development in **Figure 1**.

Figure 1
Development of a Hypothesis

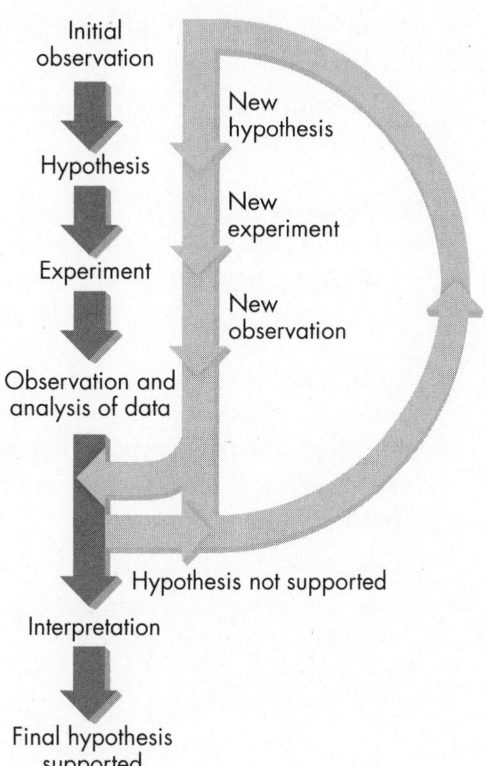

Why is a hypothesis only a tentative explanation?

It is important to note that hypotheses are only tentative explanations and are not proven facts, regardless of how many experiments and observations support the hypothesis. This is because as new data and evidence become available, a hypothesis may need to be revised or even rejected altogether. As such, a hypothesis can never be proven true or accepted as absolute truth. It can only be supported through further observation, evidence, and experimentation.

TEKS End-of-Course Assessment Review

1. **Infer** Which of the following would be a logical next step if a scientist's repeated experiments did not support his hypothesis?
   - **A** Alter the experimental results so that the hypothesis would be supported.
   - **B** Incorporate the scientific hypothesis into a theory.
   - **C** Modify the hypothesis and conduct a new experiment.
   - **D** Continue repeating the experiment until the hypothesis is supported.

2. **Identify** Why can a scientific hypothesis never be proven true?
   - **F** A scientific hypothesis is unreliable.
   - **G** Supporting evidence is difficult to identify.
   - **H** New evidence might become available that contradicts a scientific hypothesis.
   - **J** It is impossible to design an experiment that can directly test a scientific hypothesis.

3. **Form a Hypothesis** Suppose you were to plant iceberg lettuce seeds in your garden. Only a few of the seeds germinate, however. Form a hypothesis explaining why most of the seeds failed to germinate. Then explain why your statement is a hypothesis.

4. **Evaluate** Suppose you were to design several experiments to test your hypothesis in Question 3. None of your experiments supported your hypothesis, however. Was your hypothesis formation and experimentation a failure? Explain. Then, describe what steps you should take next.

Scientific Theories

TEKS 2C

Know scientific theories are based on natural and physical phenomena and are capable of being tested by multiple independent researchers. Unlike hypotheses, scientific theories are well-established and highly-reliable explanations, but they may be subject to change as new areas of science and new technologies are developed.

Vocabulary
scientific theory

What does it mean that scientific theories are considered well-established and highly-reliable explanations?

A scientific theory is different from the word *theory* as commonly used. If you say that "I have a theory as to why the basketball team lost that game," you mean that you suspect that you know the reason; you have a guess. But that is very different from a scientific theory.

A **scientific theory** is a well-established, highly-reliable explanation of a natural or physical phenomenon. Being established and reliable means that a theory has been repeatedly and consistently upheld by numerous, extensive scientific investigations conducted by many independent researchers.

A theory is powerful because it can be used to predict a wide variety of future events. A theory also explains how or why an event or process occurs. For example, the cell theory explains how cells are the basic unit of every living thing. This explanation can be applied to any organism under a wide variety of circumstances. For example, no organism has been found yet that is not made up of cells.

A good example of a biological theory is the germ theory of disease, which explains that communicable diseases are spread by microorganisms. The explanation is applied to help stop the spread of diseases. So far, no experiments have shown that communicable diseases are spread by any other means—that is, this theory is a well-established and highly-reliable explanation of how diseases spread.

Why must a theory be capable of being tested by multiple independent researchers?

Anyone could propose an explanation for events in nature. A scientific theory, however, has been tested by multiple independent researchers, meaning many scientists working separately from one another. This is important because individual researchers can make errors, introduce investigator bias, or use faulty methods. When a large number of independent researchers conduct investigations, the results are much more likely to be accurate.

Study Tip

To remember the power of a theory, think of the letters WEHR, which stand for **W**ell **E**stablished, **H**ighly **R**eliable.

How are theories subject to change as new areas of science and new technologies are developed?

Although theories are thoroughly tested and evaluated, they can be changed if further scientific study supports a better explanation for the phenomenon being investigated. A theory is the most useful and powerful explanation of the data available at the current time. Strictly speaking, a theory is neither accurate nor inaccurate.

All theories are subject to change. If new evidence is identified that is inconsistent with an existing theory, the theory might be revised or rejected. For example, doctors used to think diseases such as cholera and plague were spread by "bad air." This theory of disease was called "miasma theory." The theory seemed plausible because diseases were epidemic in places that smelled bad. Of course, we now have the germ theory of disease, and we understand that diseases spread easily because of microorganisms. Microorganisms thrive in filthy waterways and other examples of poor sanitation—which coincidentally, made air smell bad. But, as silly as miasma theory sounds now, it did pinpoint that disease was prevalent in areas of poor sanitation, so it did offer the first step on the path to an explanation of disease.

What is the relationship between a scientific theory and a scientific law?

A common misconception is that when enough evidence is gathered, a scientific theory can become a law. In fact, scientific laws and theories are very different.

Both laws and theories are supported by large bodies of evidence gathered by multiple independent researchers. However, a theory explains a phenomenon, while a law does not offer an explanation. For example, the law of conservation of energy states that energy can be changed from one form to another, but it is neither created nor destroyed. This law is well supported by the results of many experiments. But because it does not explain how energy is conserved, it is a law instead of a theory.

Figure 1

Common Misconceptions About Theories	
Misconceptions	**Facts**
A theory is a fact.	A theory can never be proven true. New technology, discoveries, and information can lead to its modification or rejection.
A theory is a guess.	In everyday language, *theory* refers to a guess or a suspicion. However, a *scientific* theory is an explanation that is both reliable and well-supported.
Over time, a theory can become a law.	A scientific theory cannot become a scientific law. A theory explains events, while a law does not.

TEKS End-of-Course Assessment Review

1. **Identify** What best defines a scientific theory?
   - **A** a well-established, highly-reliable explanation of a natural event
   - **B** a preliminary guess or idea about an event in nature
   - **C** a true statement about an event in nature
   - **D** a well-established principle that does not include an explanation

2. **Explain** When would an established scientific theory most likely be revised or replaced?
   - **F** when one scientist argues against the theory
   - **G** when public opinion amasses against the theory
   - **H** when new evidence is gathered that does not support the theory
   - **J** when the theory is promoted to a law

3. **Evaluate** Suppose you were to hear that a talented biology student in another class had just discovered a new theory of biology. Evaluate that claim based on three characteristics of a scientific theory.

4. **Describe** If scientific theories cannot be proven true, why are they so powerful and useful?

5. **Evaluate** Your friend is describing the concept of homeostasis. He states that even if he went outside in December in Minnesota wearing only a bathing suit, his body would continue to work to maintain a consistent and stable internal environment. Most likely, does the friend's description of homeostasis involve a hypothesis, a theory, or a law? Explain.

Scientific Hypotheses and Scientific Theories

TEKS 2D

Distinguish between scientific hypotheses and scientific theories.

What is a scientific hypothesis?

A scientific hypothesis is a proposed explanation for observations or an answer to a scientific question for which you can gather objective data that support or refute it. To create a hypothesis, a scientist asks a question about how or why a specific event occurs (or does not occur) and constructs a statement that explains the phenomenon. This statement, if testable, can be the hypothesis for an investigation.

Hypotheses are proposals. They are starting points for specific, controlled research projects. Scientists must test hypotheses. When possible, scientists test hypotheses by setting up experiments that involve independent variables, factors that change during an experiment, to determine if they affect the outcome. When a scientist changes an independent variable, he or she records any changes in the outcome, the dependent variable. Once the experiment is complete, the resulting data can be examined to determine if they support the hypothesis. If the hypothesis is not supported, the scientist must construct a new hypothesis, and the process begins again.

For example, suppose a researcher observed that gardens near pine trees seem to have a higher vegetable yield. He forms the following hypothesis: Adding pine needles to soil increases the nutrients that garden plants need to produce fruit. The researcher could test this hypothesis by devising and performing an experiment. One experiment might involve two test groups of seeds from the same batch of plants. The plots the seeds were planted in would receive identical amounts of water, sun, and insect exposure and would be kept at the same temperatures. The only difference would be that the researcher would add pine needles to one plot and not the other. At set intervals, he would note the vegetable yield and record the data. If the plants from the plot with pine needles had a higher vegetable yield, the evidence would support the hypothesis.

Study Tip

The prefix *hypo-* means "beneath" or "less than." You can think of a hypothesis as a less powerful statement than a theory.

How can you distinguish between scientific hypotheses and scientific theories?

In everyday conversation, the word *theory* generally means "suspicion." You might say, "I have a theory as to why you got a C on the biology test." But in science the word *theory* has a different meaning. A scientific theory is a well-supported explanation for observations made in many situations.

So theories are much broader than hypotheses. Most hypotheses refer to a specific situation or case, but a theory provides an explanation for a broad range of observations.

In biology, scientists might test hypotheses concerning the physical properties of a human skin cell, the effect temperature changes have on wildlife in a specific ecosystem, or how quickly a virus spreads in a given population. In contrast, the theories of biology explain the structure, function, growth, and reproduction of living organisms. For example, a theory might explain that all living things are made of cells (the cell theory). In the flowchart in **Figure 1**, you can compare the roles that hypotheses and theories play in scientific methodology.

Figure 1
Scientific Methodology

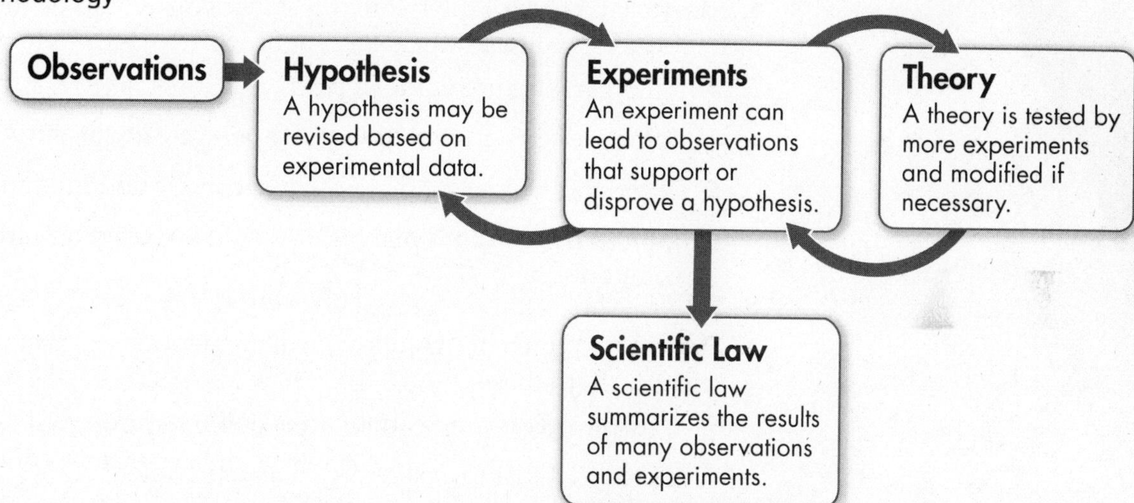

How do scientific theories develop?

One of the most important theories in biology is the cell theory, which states that all living organisms are composed of cells and that cells arise from other cells. Today, this theory is universally accepted. Scientists have explained the structure of cells and identified how cells reproduce and share genetic information with their daughter cells. With the aid of very powerful microscopes, scientists now can photograph and manipulate individual strands of DNA within cells.

Yet like many other theories, the cell theory developed gradually over time. The origin of the theory can be traced to Robert Hooke, a scientist who, in 1665, looked at slices of cork under a crude microscope. He saw tiny pores within the cork and noted they looked like the bare rooms monks lived in. This is why he called them "cells." But Hooke didn't know cells' structure or function. It wasn't until the mid-1800s that scientists Theodor Schwann, Matthias Schleiden, and Rudolf Virchow developed what we now consider to be the basis of cell theory: that cells are the fundamental units of life, that all living organisms are made of one or more cells, and that all cells arise from pre-existing cells. So it can be seen that it can take many years and many experiments throughout those years before a theory develops.

Technology is often essential in the development of a new theory or the revision of an existing theory. For example, in the 1960s, scientists used the electron microscope to observe that the mitochondria found in eukaryotic cells' cytoplasm have their own DNA. This discovery has given scientists greater insight into the human genome and that many traits are passed from generation to generation. Further discoveries of cell structure and function have also depended on new technology, well-constructed experiments, and logical reasoning.

TEKS End-of-Course Assessment Review

1. **Identify** Which of the following statements would be the most useful hypothesis for a scientific experiment?

   A All organisms are made of cells.

   B Tomato plants grow tallest at temperatures between 20°C and 30°C.

   C A vertebrate is an animal with a backbone and internal skeleton.

   D If life exists on other planets, it would be based on carbon compounds.

2. **Evaluate** Which of the following statements is the best definition of a scientific hypothesis?

   F a suspicion or hunch about an event in nature

   G a proposal that can be tested in an experiment

   H an idea or explanation that most people agree with

   J a well-supported explanation for a broad set of observations

3. **Distinguish** Suppose you were to read about a scientific statement based on data from hundreds of years of research and observation that applies to a broad set of naturally occurring events. Would you consider it a hypothesis or a theory?

   A a hypothesis

   B a theory

   C both

   D neither

4. **Distinguish** Suppose your lab partner states that he has just come up with a theory that explains the results of your last investigation. What are three reasons you could give him that his explanation is a hypothesis and not a theory?

Planning and Implementing Investigations

TEKS 2E

Plan and implement descriptive, comparative, and experimental investigations, including asking questions, formulating testable hypotheses, and selecting equipment and technology.

Vocabulary
control
independent variable
dependent variable

What are descriptive, comparative, and experimental investigations?

Scientists rely on several methods of investigation. A descriptive investigation involves making observations and collecting data about a natural or human-made system, such as weather patterns, plant growth, or simple machines. The investigation begins with a question, but variables are not manipulated and comparisons are not made.

A comparative investigation is similar to a descriptive investigation but involves the comparison of data collected about different organisms, objects, features, or events or collected under different conditions. The result of a comparative investigation is a comparison of collected data.

In an experimental investigation, the scientist controls or manipulates variables in order to test a hypothesis. A hypothesis is a tentative explanation of an observation; it can be tested experimentally to determine whether the tentative explanation accurately explains the observation.

An experimental investigation involves several test groups. All the test groups are alike except for the condition of the independent variable. For example, in an experiment to show the effect of temperature on algae growth, each test group could be an aquarium filled with water at a different temperature. Other factors that might affect algae growth, such as water quality and light, are kept the same in all the test groups. One of the aquariums would be kept at room temperature. This aquarium is the **control**, which represents typical conditions. A control provides a comparison for the other test groups, thus allowing the effect of the independent variable to be determined. Thus, the hypothesis is a statement that relates an independent variable with a dependent variable. The **independent variable** is the variable that is deliberately changed in the experiment, while the **dependent variable** changes in response to changes the investigator makes in the independent variable.

How can you plan and implement descriptive, comparative, and experimental investigations?

All types of science investigations begin with observations. Observations lead to questions. For example, you might observe that most of the plants in a garden are growing well, but that the tomatoes are growing poorly. For example, you could ask: Why are the tomatoes growing poorly?

Study Tip

Remember that the three types of investigations progress in complexity. All three types involve observation and asking questions; comparative and experimental investigations involve comparisons; and experimental investigations involve test groups and manipulating variables.

Are insects or other pests feeding on the tomato plants? Are the plants receiving the proper amounts of water, sunlight, or fertilizer?

To help answer these questions, you could plan and implement a descriptive investigation. You could observe the garden every day and record your observations of the growth of tomato plants, the weather conditions, and the presence of insects. Or you could choose a comparative investigation, in which you would compare the tomato plants in different gardens, or compare the tomato plants with other plants in the garden.

To plan an experimental investigation, your first step would be to form a testable hypothesis. An example of a testable hypothesis is, "Compared to green pepper plants, tomato plants produce a smaller harvest with the same amount of water." This hypothesis is testable because you can control the amount of water that the garden plants receive. The type of plant is the independent variable, and the mass of the season's harvest is the dependent variable.

To implement the experiment, divide the planted area into four sections. Each section would include the same quantity of identical tomato plants or identical pepper plants. The tomato and pepper plants would need to be equally mature. You would treat each section identically—give them the same amount of water, the same amount of sunshine, and the same amount of fertilizer. At the end of the growing season, add up the total mass of the harvest of each type of plant. If the mass of the pepper harvest exceeded the mass of the tomato harvest, then the results supported the hypothesis.

How can you select equipment and technology for an investigation?

An investigative procedure needs the appropriate equipment and technology to be conducted properly and accurately. Laboratory equipment must meet standards for both safety and accuracy. Some equipment and technology helps in taking measurements. An electronic balance, for example, can measure mass quickly and accurately. A graduated cylinder provides quick and accurate measurements for the volume of liquids. This equipment is also reliable, meaning repeated measurements of the same subject will yield very similar results. In the biology lab, remember to use only the scientific equipment that your teacher provides.

As you plan a scientific investigation, make a list of all the equipment and technology you will need. You may need to revise your list to use only the equipment available to you, and to use this equipment efficiently. For example, instead of using three volumetric flasks to measure the same volume of a liquid, you could use the same flask three times.

Computers and graphing calculators can help you store and analyze data. If your investigation will generate a large amount of numerical data, consider entering the data directly into a computer or graphing calculator. You may wish to enter sample data before the experiment to make sure that you understand the software.

 •

TEKS End-of-Course Assessment Review

1. **Identify** Which of these would you use to measure 0.2 milliliter?
   - A a pipette
   - B a beaker
   - C a measuring spoon
   - D a graduated cylinder

2. **Explain** Why is it important to use clear wording and clearly stated outcomes in a hypothesis?
   - F Hypotheses need to be explained clearly because they are scientific theories.
   - G Hypotheses have to be clear to explain natural phenomena to other scientists.
   - H Hypotheses have to be clearly expressed so that one can determine if an experiment confirms or refutes them.
   - J Since hypotheses may become part of a scientific theory, it is important to write them well.

3. **Evaluate** Which of these hypotheses would be most easily tested?
   - A If plants are overwatered, they die.
   - B If the weather is cold, people get sick.
   - C If 2 g of acetic acid are added to a mold colony in a 100-mL-diameter Petri dish, the mold colony will be reduced by 15 percent.
   - D Every plant cell has a cell wall, while every animal cell lacks a cell wall.

4. **Evaluate** Every morning in June from 6:00 to 8:00 A.M., a biologist records the number of bird species she sees in the same 1-square-kilometer plot of land. Is this a descriptive study, a comparative study, or an experimental study? Explain.

5. **Plan** Formulate a hypothesis and design an experimental investigation to determine how the amount of available sunlight affects the size of peppers growing on a plant. Determine your independent and dependent variables and what kind of equipment you will need.

Collecting and Organizing Data

TEKS 2F

Collect and organize qualitative and quantitative data and make measurements with accuracy and precision using tools such as calculators, spreadsheet software, data-collecting probes, computers, standard laboratory glassware, microscopes, various prepared slides, stereoscopes, metric rulers, electronic balances, gel electrophoresis apparatuses, micropipettors, hand lenses, Celsius thermometers, hot plates, lab notebooks or journals, timing devices, cameras, Petri dishes, lab incubators, dissection equipment, meter sticks, and models, diagrams, or samples of biological specimens or structures.

Vocabulary
qualitative data
quantitative data
accuracy
precision

How do scientists collect and organize qualitative and quantitative data?

Scientists might collect a huge amount of data during an investigation or experiment. These data include observations that they make with the aid of tools such as meter sticks, microscopes, cameras, and computers, as well as observations made with their senses.

Qualitative data are observations that don't include precise measurements. For example, in an investigation of the trees in a forest, the qualitative data could include descriptions of a tree's appearance and the texture of its bark or leaves. Qualitative data may also involve comparisons. An observation that a tree is taller or shorter than surrounding trees, or that its bark is darker or lighter, is also an example of qualitative data.

Quantitative data involves measurements of a specific property. Quantitative data about a tree could include measurements of the tree's height, age, and number of leaves. In many cases, measuring tools or instruments are essential for gathering quantitative data. Scientists use standard units of length, mass, volume, and other quantities, and their tools and instruments are calibrated to these units. Qualitative data can be statistically analyzed. For example, the average height of trees in a forest can be calculated by measuring the height of the trees.

Scientists often organize quantitative data in graphs, and data of all types in charts and tables. These methods help show patterns or trends in the data that might otherwise be difficult to observe. **Figure 1** describes several types of graphs.

Figure 1

Type of Graph	Purpose
Line graph	Shows the relationship between two variables, such as time and air temperature, or time and the height of a plant
Bar graph	Compares related data, such as the heights of several trees, or the ages of family members
Circle graph	Shows the parts of a whole, such as the percentages of elements in the human body

What kinds of tools can be used to collect and analyze data?

Various tools and technology can be used to collect and analyze scientific data. Computer-linked probes, spreadsheets, and graphing calculators are three examples of tools and technology used during scientific investigations.

Computer-linked probes are tools used to collect data during investigations. These devices transmit information directly to a computer or calculator. For example, a pH probe measures the pH of a solution and records and displays the information on a calculator or computer. A temperature probe can be used in place of a standard thermometer because it measures temperature and relays the information to a computer or calculator.

Graphing calculators generate graphs based on information that is input by hand or through a computer-linked probe. This type of calculator is a useful tool for analyzing trends in data.

Spreadsheets are computer programs used to record and manipulate data. A spreadsheet appears as rows and columns of cells. Each cell is simply a box into which a number can be entered. The cells in a spreadsheet can be linked by mathematical formulas. For example, a particular cell might contain the sum of the numbers in two other cells. Spreadsheets are useful for predicting how a change in one piece of data will affect other data.

What are accuracy and precision?

Scientists try to obtain quantitative data that are both accurate and precise. The **accuracy** of a measurement identifies how close that measurement is to an accepted or true value. If the actual mass of a soil sample is 5.13 g, then an accurate measurement of the mass of the sample should be close to this value.

Study Tip

When trying to remember the difference between accuracy and precision, keep in mind that an *a*ccurate measurement is close to the *a*ccepted or *a*ctual measurement.

Precision refers to how much a series of measurements varies. The more precise a series of measurements, the closer they are to one another. If an electronic balance consistently reports a mass of 5.13 g for the same soil sample, then the balance is very precise. If the balance sometimes reports a mass that is a little less or greater than 5.13 g, then it is less precise. If the balance consistently reports a mass of 20.52 g for the same soil sample, then it is very precise, but not very accurate.

To make accurate and precise measurements, scientists rely on tools and instruments that have been built specifically for scientific use. For example, to measure the volume of a liquid, scientists use laboratory glassware, such as graduated cylinders and volumetric flasks. These tools are more accurate than the measuring cups used for cooking. To measure a span of time, a stopwatch is more accurate and precise than a typical clock.

In science, data must be both accurate and precise in order to be useful. Carefully making measurements with high-quality measuring tools improves accuracy and precision of measurements. Repeating each measurement several times allows the precision of the measurements to be evaluated.

TEKS End-of-Course Assessment Review

1. **Evaluate** A student measured the mass of a soil sample several times. The measurements she recorded were 25.2 g, 35.1 g, 20.3 g, and 19.9 g. The actual mass of the sample is 30 g. Which statement best describes this student's results?
   - **A** both accurate and precise
   - **B** accurate but not precise
   - **C** precise but not accurate
   - **D** None of these

2. **Identify** A scientist investigates the effect of fertilizer on the growth of tomato plants. Which of the following are qualitative data that the scientists could obtain?
   - **F** the pH value of the soil at the beginning of the investigation
   - **G** the height in centimeters of the plants at the end of the investigation
   - **H** the intensity of the color of the tomatoes that grow on each plant
   - **J** the air temperature in degrees Celsius throughout the investigation

3. **Apply** A scientist is investigating a population of ladybugs. Which data from the investigation would best be displayed in a circle graph?
   - **A** the changing size of the ladybug population over time
   - **B** observations of the ladybugs' feeding habits and diet
   - **C** the fractions of ladybugs that have 2, 4, 8, or 10 spots on their bodies
   - **D** the numbers of ladybugs observed one morning at five different locations

4. **Describe** In a garden, you notice that the leaves of the sunflowers are covered with a white, moldy film. You suspect that microorganisms, such as fungi, are infecting the plants. Which tools or equipment would help you confirm your suspicion and, if possible, identify the microorganisms? Identify at least three tools or pieces of equipment and describe how they would be useful.

Data Analysis, Inferences, and Predictions

TEKS 2G

Analyze, evaluate, make inferences, and predict trends from data.

Vocabulary
inference

How do scientists analyze and evaluate data?

Scientists might collect a huge amount of data during an investigation or experiment. Scientists analyze and evaluate numerical data with concepts and formulas from statistics, the branch of mathematics that deals with numerical data.

Some useful concepts in statistics are the mean, median, and mode. The *mean* is the average value of a set of numbers. To calculate the mean, find the sum of all the values in the set and divide by the number of values. The *median* is the value that is in the middle when the values are arranged from lowest to highest. For an even number of values, the median is the average of the two values in the middle. The *mode* is the value that occurs most frequently.

How do scientists use data to make inferences and predict trends?

An **inference** is a logical interpretation based on prior knowledge and experiences. For example, look at **Figure 1**. Of the 12 plotted data points, three fall outside of the normal pattern. These points often indicate an error in the experimental procedure or design, or an error in measurements or calculations. Yet the data show a trend that can be used to make inferences. For example, although a pH of 4.5 was not measured, it can be inferred that the enzyme activity would be about 70 percent.

Figure 1

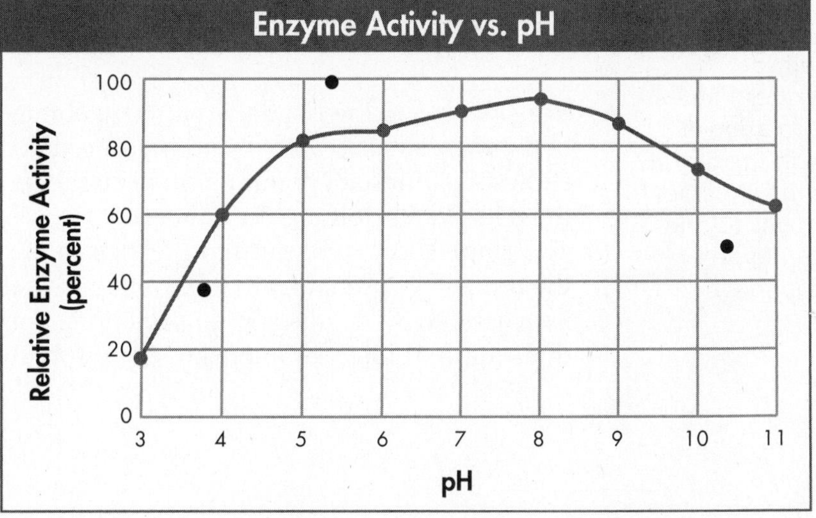

Graphing is a helpful way to predict trends in data. Trends in data graphs may be linear, meaning the data points fall on a straight line, or they may fall on a curved line. Sometimes a graph shows no clear trend in data. **Figure 2** shows several types of graphs that can be used to make predictions.

Figure 2
Various Types of Graphs

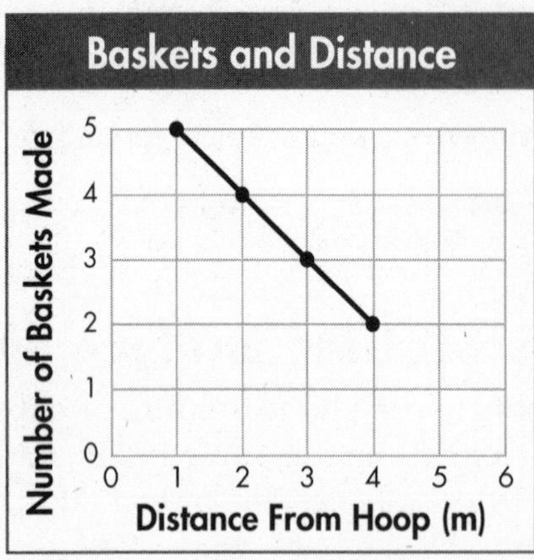

This graph shows a linear trend. Fewer baskets are made as the player moves farther from the hoop.

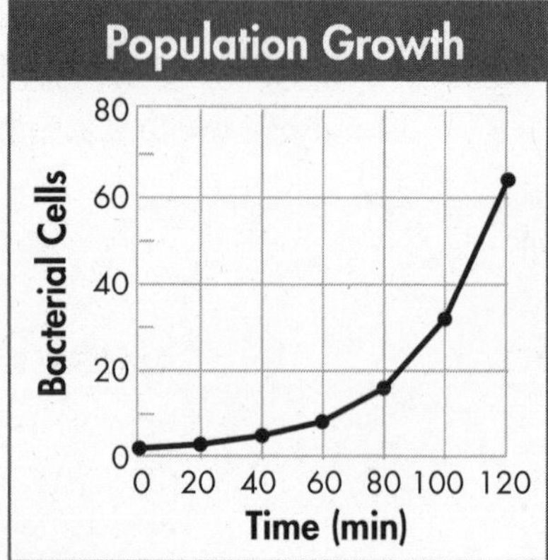

The rising curve in this graph shows exponential growth. Every twenty minutes, the population of bacteria becomes twice as large.

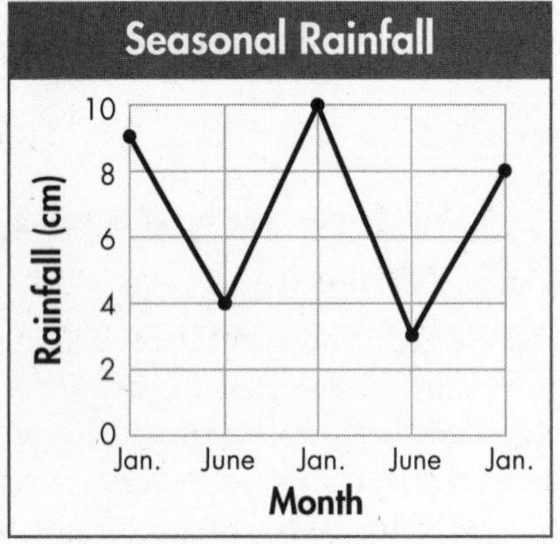

This graph shows a cyclical trend in data. Rainfall amount changes in the same way from year to year.

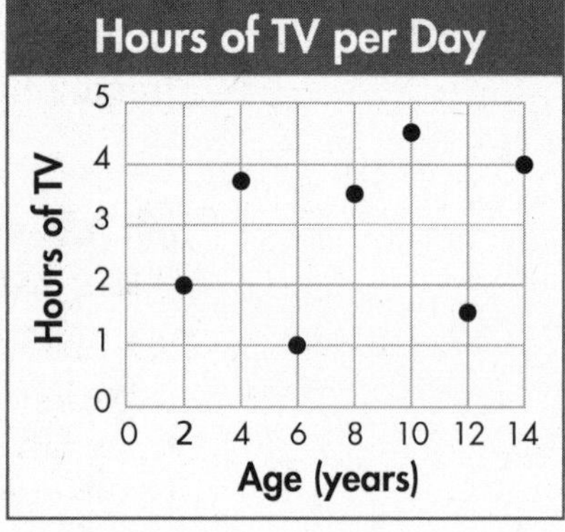

These data points show no trend. The data are not useful for making predictions.

Study Tip

When reading graphs, ask yourself the following questions: What information is contained in the graph? What are the variables? What happens to one variable as the other variable changes?

Consider the following data that were obtained from an investigation on herbivores, such as zebras, and their predators, such as lions. **Figure 3** shows the four data points as small circles. It also shows a line that connects the data points. Joining the data points by a line shows the "best-fit." The graph shows a linear trend related to the size of herbivore herds and the number of predators that hunt them. As the herd size of herbivores increases, so do the number of predators. You can use the line to predict that a herd of 1200 herbivores will support about 20 predators.

Figure 3

Herbivore Herd Size	Number of Predators
500	7.8
1000	16.6
1500	26.0
2000	33.7

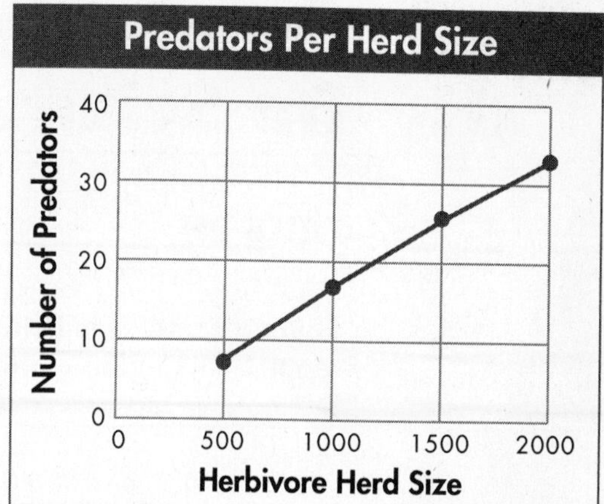

TEKS End-of-Course Assessment Review

1. Evaluate A biologist is studying the average daily temperature in 12 tropical habitats. She reports that the mean temperature point is 32.5°C. What can be concluded from this information?

A If any habitat recorded a temperature greater than 32.5°C, then at least one habitat must record a temperature less than 32.5°C.

B All 12 tropical habitats had daily temperatures of 32.5°C.

C None of the 12 tropical habitats had daily temperatures of 32.5°C.

D A temperature of 32.5°C is the most common temperature point among the 12 habitats.

2. Analyze A researcher is studying the effect of a new medication on cancer in rats. In seven of eight rats, the cancerous tumors shrank by 30 to 32 percent. But in one of the eight rats, the tumor shrank by 65 percent. How should the researcher analyze this data?

F calculate the average tumor reduction using data from all eight animals

G exclude the 65 percent data point from her report

H study the details of the trial with the outlier result and look for possible errors in the procedure, measurements, and calculations

J conclude that on rare occasions, tumors will shrink by 65 percent

3. Make Graphs Plot points that would represent the following data: For 10 plants, air temperature is not related to rate of photosynthesis. Is there a best-fit line? Explain.

Communicate Conclusions Based On Scientific Data

TEKS 2H

Communicate valid conclusions supported by the data through methods such as lab reports, labeled drawings, graphic organizers, journals, summaries, oral reports, and technology-based reports.

How do scientists communicate conclusions from their investigations?

Scientists use many different methods to communicate valid conclusions of their research. These methods include lab reports, labeled drawings, graphic organizers, journals, summaries, oral reports, and technology-based reports. Each method has benefits and drawbacks, and scientists may use a combination of several methods to present their conclusions.

Lab Reports Scientists use lab reports to communicate the procedure and results of an experiment. A lab report includes all the information that another scientist would need to repeat the experiment. It includes the hypothesis, list of materials and equipment, important background information, procedure, observations, and conclusions. It may also include graphs, graphic organizers, or other representations of data.

Labeled Drawings Labeled drawings may help communicate the procedure, observations, or conclusions of an experiment. These drawings help explain findings that may be difficult to communicate with only words. A drawing might show information such as the arrangement of laboratory equipment, the spatial arrangement of microbes in a petri dish, or an organism's anatomical structure.

Graphic Organizers In many cases, graphic organizers are more useful than paragraphs of text for presenting a conclusion or the data that support a conclusion. Examples of graphic organizers are shown in **Figure 1**.

Figure 1
A Flowchart and Venn Diagram

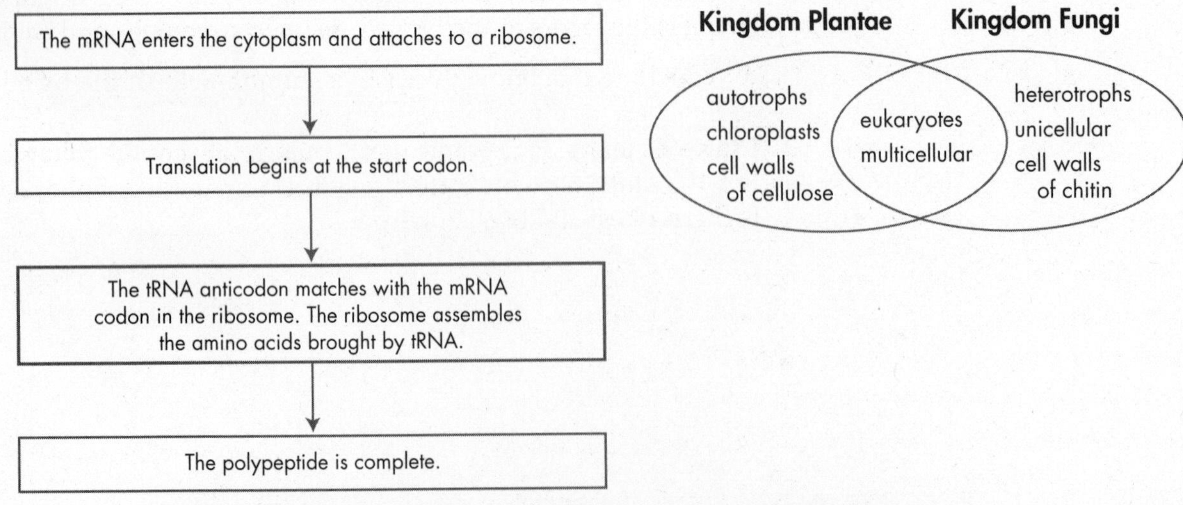

Study Tip

Review the lab reports you have recently produced. Note the different ways you communicated results based on the type of experiment or investigation you performed.

Scientists might choose a chart or table to present a set of related data. The data in a table may include both numeric measurements and observations described in words. A flowchart is useful to describe the steps of a process, especially when the steps can occur in several orders. A Venn diagram can show how two related observations or conclusions are similar to and different from one another.

Journals Science journals allow scientists to communicate their conclusions to the scientific community. When scientists have completed an investigation, they may present their conclusions as part of an article or report. Then they submit the article or report for publication in a journal that is appropriate to their field.

Peer review is a process in which scientists carefully review the work of other scientists. Before an article or report is published in a science journal, it undergoes peer review by independent scientists. The article is published only if the reviewers are convinced that the findings are genuine.

When scientific reports are published, they become available for other scientists to read, evaluate, and test. These reports enable the scientific community to keep informed about the work of other scientists and research groups.

Summaries A summary is a brief restatement of the purpose, procedure, and findings of an experiment. Scientists use summaries to communicate with the general public, their employers or the people providing their funding, and other scientists. In science journals, summaries are called *abstracts*. They are typically located at the beginning of an article and are designed to give the reader a general idea of what the article is about.

Oral Reports In an oral report, the scientist speaks directly to an audience about the results of an investigation. Oral reports may be very formal and follow the format of a journal article. Or an oral report could be more conversational. Many scientists use visual aids to accompany their presentations, such as projections from computers.

An oral report allows the presenter to interact with the audience. The audience may ask questions about the conclusions drawn from the experiment. Oral reports are especially useful for venues that showcase multiple experiments, such as science conferences or school science fairs.

Technology-Based Reports With a technology-based report, scientists can use computers and other types of technology to communicate conclusions. By using appropriate software, scientists can illustrate their conclusions with diagrams, animations, photographs, and narration or other audio components.

End-of-Course Assessment Review

1. **Identify** Which section of a journal article introduces the purpose of the article?
   - **A** procedure
   - **B** conclusion
   - **C** abstract
   - **D** data tables and graphs

2. **Analyze** What is an advantage of an oral report compared to other methods of communicating scientific conclusions?
   - **F** The scientist can communicate directly with an audience and respond to their questions and ideas.
   - **G** The scientist can precisely describe the hypothesis, procedure, and data obtained from an investigation.
   - **H** The scientist can present graphs and labeled diagrams to show trends in the data.
   - **J** The scientist can have conclusions accepted without rigorous peer review.

3. **Explain** Scientists may submit reports of their investigations to science journals for publication. How do science journals ensure that the reports are accurate?
   - **A** Science journals publish only reports of experiments conducted in laboratories.
   - **B** Science journals accept only reports from leading, famous scientists.
   - **C** Independent scientists review and evaluate the reports, and only approved reports are published.
   - **D** Science journals publish reports after they are published in magazines or newspapers.

4. **Evaluate** Which would be best represented by a flowchart?
   - **F** the pathway of chemical reactions that the body uses to break apart sugars
   - **G** the atmospheric pressure when an experiment was conducted
   - **H** a comparison of a plant cell and an animal cell
   - **J** the percent by mass of each element in the human body

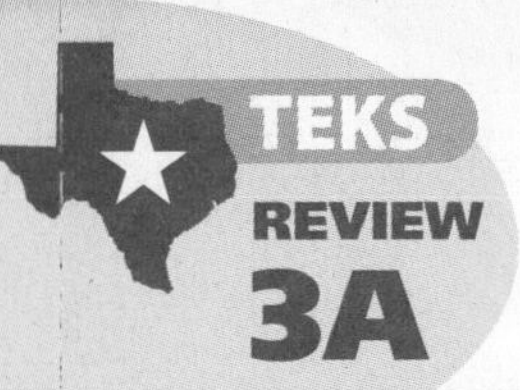

Analyzing, Evaluating, and Critiquing Scientific Explanations

TEKS 3A

In all fields of science, analyze, evaluate, and critique scientific explanations by using empirical evidence, logical reasoning, and experimental and observational testing, including examining all sides of scientific evidence of those scientific explanations, so as to encourage critical thinking by the student.

How can empirical evidence be used to analyze, evaluate, and critique scientific explanations?

When you *analyze* a scientific explanation, you determine what claim is being made and the evidence that is being used to support the claim. Often this evidence is in the form of empirical evidence, which is data based on observation or experience—that is, scientific experiments. *Evaluating* an explanation involves determining whether it is valid or useful. Part of the evaluation process is to review the evidence that supports the explanation.

Empirical evidence needs to be analyzed and evaluated carefully, and it may or may not agree with other types of evidence. For example, consider a laboratory experiment in which scientists test the effect of soil pH on the growth of soybeans. The empirical evidence from the experiment suggests that soybeans grow best at a pH of 6.5. However, a group of farmers report that their soybeans grow poorly at this pH.

How can this difference be explained? Does this mean that the scientists are incorrect, or that the experiment was badly designed? No, this is not necessarily the case. The conditions that were used in the laboratory experiment may have differed from those in the farmers' fields. The empirical evidence from the experiment is not incorrect. Rather, more data are needed to construct a logical explanation.

In their next experiment, the scientists compare how soybeans grow in different types of soil, while keeping pH constant. To evaluate how well the soybeans grow, they measure the concentration of manganese (Mn) in the leaves. Manganese is a mineral that plants need in small amounts and that scientists can use to measure overall plant health. **Figure 1** shows how manganese concentration in leaves varies according to the type of soil the plants are growing in.

Figure 1

Soil Type	pH	Mn in Leaves (ppm)
Clay-rich soil	6.5	210
Sandy soil	6.5	25

With this added empirical evidence, the scientists can construct a more useful explanation for why the soybeans in the farmers' fields did not grow well: The soybeans growing in the farmers' fields, which contained sandy soil, grew poorly because there was not enough manganese available in the soil for plant uptake; the manganese concentration in the plants grown in sandy soil was too deficient to support proper growth.

As with all scientific studies, this study is subject to critique. When you *critique* a scientific explanation, you identify specific problems with the scientific investigation or with the claims that the scientist is making based on the data. In this example, a useful critique is that the first study was not incorrect, but it was incomplete—more evidence was necessary to construct an explanation.

Study Tip

Remember that a scientific explanation should explain more than merely a single set of observations from an experiment. A useful explanation should be able to predict future events.

How can logical reasoning be used to evaluate scientific explanations?

In science, logical reasoning involves drawing valid conclusions or formulating ideas based on empirical evidence. As part of the experiment on soybean growth, the researchers measured the amount of manganese dissolved in the soil at different pH values. They found that the amount of soluble manganese in soil decreases as pH increases. From this evidence, is it logical to conclude that soil pH can change the amount of soluble manganese available in the soil? Yes. Is it logical to conclude that lower soil pH will increase soybean growth? No, not from this evidence alone.

How can experimental and observational testing be used to evaluate scientific explanations?

Experimental testing involves testing the effect of a variable while keeping other factors the same between the groups you are testing. In observational testing, variables are not directly tested. Instead, situations or models are directly observed and the observations are recorded as evidence.

Both types of testing can provide useful evidence for different scientific explanations. In the example of soybean growth, the experimental testing in the laboratory suggested a relationship among soil pH, soil manganese concentration, and the health of soybeans. The observational testing in the farmers' fields helped show that soil pH alone did not explain the health of soybeans.

How can all sides of scientific evidence be analyzed?

Sometimes, two sets of evidence may seem to disagree with or contradict each other. In the example of soybean growth, the ideal soil pH measured in the laboratory experiment disagreed with the results observed in the farmers' fields. Part of the scientist's job is to make sense of all sides of scientific evidence. In this example, evidence from additional experiments helped formulate a useful explanation.

In some cases, different scientists explain the same set of evidence in different ways. This is especially true when many variables could affect an outcome. For example, the health of soybeans could be affected by different plowing or planting techniques, quality of the seeds, trace minerals in the soil, and the weather. A scientist might cite any or all of these factors to explain poor soybean growth.

When scientists propose many explanations for the same observation, how can we decide which explanation is best? It is always important to evaluate how evidence was obtained and whether the evidence is reliable. Evidence gathered from a properly run scientific investigation—one that applies scientific methods to obtain precise and accurate data—is more likely to be reliable than information from untrained observers. Yet even scientists are subject to biases and personal opinions that may affect the results, which must be taken into consideration.

Ultimately, however, the power of a scientific explanation depends on its ability to predict future events. If a scientist claims that low manganese levels in the soil are the cause of poorly growing soybeans, then increasing these levels should improve the soybean crop.

TEKS End-of-Course Assessment Review

1. Analyze Which of the following describes empirical evidence?

A data from surveys and questionnaires

B Opinions from leading scientists

C measurements and observations from science experiments

D All of the above

2. Evaluate Which statement best explains why scientists often propose different explanations for the same event in nature?

F Many variables may affect an event, and not all variables are easy to test in laboratory experiments.

G Scientists often obtain different results from the same laboratory experiment.

H Scientists often ignore data that disagree with the data they obtain.

J Events in nature occur randomly and cannot be explained by the methods of science.

3. Critique A brand of laundry detergent is marketed with the slogan "Keeps your red clothes red and your white clothes white—even in the same wash!" What does this slogan suggest? How could you scientifically evaluate and critique the accuracy of the slogan?

Communicating and Applying Scientific Information

TEKS 3B

Communicate and apply scientific information extracted from various sources such as current events, news reports, published journal articles, and marketing materials.

Why is scientific communication important?

Whenever you talk on the phone, text someone, or listen to your teacher at school, you are communicating. Communicating is the process of sharing ideas and information with other people. The way scientists communicate with each other and with the public has changed over the centuries. In earlier centuries, scientists exchanged ideas through letters. They also formed societies to discuss the latest work of their members. When societies began to publish journals, scientists used the journals to publish the results of their research and to keep up with new discoveries.

Today, the Internet has become both a means of communication and a major source of information. One advantage of the Internet is that anyone with a computer can access the information. One disadvantage is that anyone can post information to the Internet without first having that information reviewed. To judge the reliability of information you find there, you have to consider the source. This same advice applies to articles in journals, magazines, newspapers, or the news you hear about on radio or television. If a media outlet has a reporter who specializes in science, the chances are better that a report will be more scientifically accurate.

How can you evaluate scientific information from various sources?

In science, you often need to do research to learn more about a particular topic and communicate your findings. Therefore, you need relevant, reliable information. Information qualifies as reliable if it comes from a person or organization that is reputable in a particular field and is not biased. Generally, universities, museums, and government agencies are good sources of reliable information. Personal blogs and politically motivated news reports are not reliable sources of information.

Study Tip

News reports, science journals, and marketing publications present scientific information in different ways and for different purposes. Remember these differences when you evaluate the scientific information you read or hear.

Current Events and News Sources News and entertainment media often report scientific discoveries. Sometimes reports are based on articles in scientific journals or interviews with scientists. In other cases, the reports are based on statements from companies, the government, or universities.

People use science-based stories in the news to help them make decisions. By applying the information they learn, people might decide to try a new medicine, to purchase a new product, to revise safety practices at work or home, or to change their diet or exercise habits.

Not all reports of science news present unbiased scientific information. Sometimes, information is deliberately misrepresented, or mixed up, to present a certain point of view. When you hear science news, consider the following questions:

- Does the news report directly quote the scientific publication? Or does it summarize the publication?
- Could the news medium or reporter have biases that could affect the way the information is being presented?
- Does the report include conclusions or comments from more than one scientist? (Remember that scientists may draw different conclusions from the same data.)

Basically, you need to ask yourself "Am I hearing a scientist's words, or the version of the scientist's words someone else wants me to hear?"

Marketing Materials Marketing materials include commercials, advertisements, brochures, posters, and product packaging. A wide variety of products are marketed with scientific information or with claims based on scientific information.

Laws dictate that companies cannot make false claims or invent scientific data to support a claim. For example, in 2010, some companies selling products that contained omega-3 fatty acids claimed that the products would help children develop healthy brain and vision functions. Scientific data did not support these claims. The Federal Trade Commission requested that the companies stop making these claims.

Yet even when marketing claims contain accurate scientific information, they can still be misleading. Consider this marketing logo on a box of toothpaste:

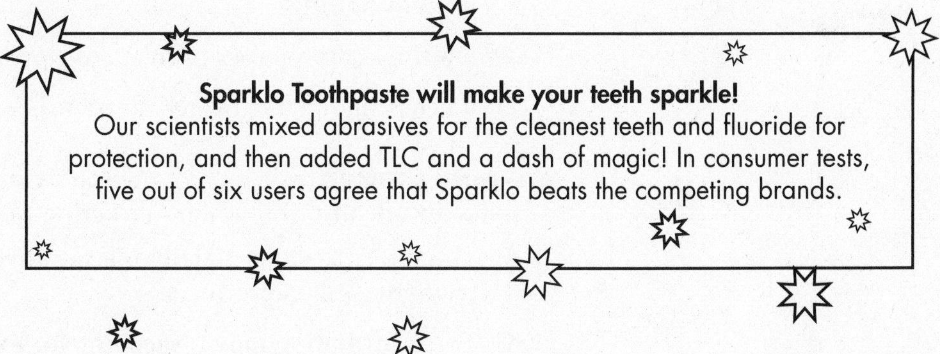

Sparklo Toothpaste will make your teeth sparkle!
Our scientists mixed abrasives for the cleanest teeth and fluoride for protection, and then added TLC and a dash of magic! In consumer tests, five out of six users agree that Sparklo beats the competing brands.

Like other marketing materials, these claims present both scientific information, such as the chemicals in the toothpaste, and nonscientific information, such as the claim about "TLC and a dash of magic." The information about the tests is presented as scientific data, but it could be misleading. Were the tests completely unbiased? How many tests were conducted? In what categories were the brands evaluated? How was "competing" defined? Before communicating or applying scientific information from marketing materials, you always need to ask yourself such questions.

Scientific Journals Scientists publish the results of their investigations in scientific journals. Typically, the reports are very detailed and technical, and they are intended for other scientists. Journal articles communicate much more information than stories in media that are meant for the general public. Journal articles are also subject to peer reviews, during which other scientists in the same field evaluate them. Peer reviews help ensure that journal articles present accurate, reliable information.

To approach a journal article, begin by reading the abstract, which is a summary of the article. It briefly describes the purpose of the investigation, the methods, and the conclusion. You can use the abstract to decide if the journal article will be useful to you. Other sections of the journal article describe the investigation in more detail.

You can apply scientific information from journal articles in many ways. The information might help you develop a hypothesis or procedure for a new investigation. The information might help you better understand a topic in your scientific studies. Or it might raise questions or help you understand issues in your daily life.

TEKS End-of-Course Assessment Review

1. **Evaluate** On an infomercial, the presenter is selling a new fertilizer. According to the presenter, scientific data show that the fertilizer doubles the speed of plant growth. Which activity would best help you evaluate the presenter's claim?

   A reading marketing materials for the new fertilizer

   B reading the journal article in which scientists report their plant growth findings

   C reading a newspaper or magazine article about the fertilizer

   D discussing the fertilizer with friends who have gardens

2. **Apply Concepts** Which of the following statements best describes the scientific information in marketing materials?

   F The information is usually inaccurate because the company is trying to sell its products.

   G The information may be accurate or inaccurate because no laws insist on accuracy.

   H The information is accurate but is often invented.

   J The information is accurate but sometimes misleading.

3. **Apply Concepts** How do people apply the scientific information that they learn from newspapers, magazines, and other sources? Why should people carefully evaluate this information?

Drawing Inferences From Promotional Materials

TEKS 3C

Draw inferences based on data related to promotional materials for products and services.

What sorts of data do you find in promotional materials?

Companies publish a variety of materials to help promote the products they offer. They hope that the data in these promotional materials will lead you to buy their products. Promotional materials take many forms, including advertisements, Web sites, and packaging. You encounter promotional materials everywhere: at home, on the highway, at shopping malls, even at school.

In many cases, promotional materials make scientific claims which are based on evidence from scientific investigations. Many companies are required to publish this evidence on the packaging of their products. Food companies, for example, must publish specific information for a food product on nutrition labels. Drug companies must publish the chemicals contained in the drugs, drug-safety data, and other information.

How can you draw inferences based on data related to promotional materials for products?

An inference is a logical interpretation based on prior knowledge and experience. For example, by observing the trees in your neighborhood, you might draw inferences about the shapes of trees and the maximum height that trees can grow. By observing patterns in the weather, you could draw inferences about the conditions that cause rain or snow to fall.

For many reasons, consumers should be wary of advertisers' claims. For example, consider these advertising claims for Milan Ice Water, a fictitious brand of bottled water:

- Milan Ice Water is the most environmentally responsible consumer product in the world.
- Our bottles are made of 75 percent recycled plastic.
- Milan Ice Water is the Healthy, Eco-Friendly Choice.

How can you evaluate these claims? One way is to decide whether they can be supported by data, and then to analyze that data. The first and third claims, even if they have merit, are not scientifically testable because they are too vague. When a company makes claims that are impossible to evaluate, you might choose to discount the claims altogether.

The second claim contains data, so you could evaluate it. You would need to gather more information, however. First, can you verify that their bottles contain 75 percent recycled plastic—will they supply those data to consumers? Second, what is the typical recycled plastic content in plastic water bottles—are Milan's bottles really more "eco-friendly" than others? Even if their bottles are made of 75 percent recycled plastic, additional information might reveal it as unremarkable. (Other companies' bottles may be made of 95 percent plastic.)

How can you draw inferences based on data related to promotional materials for services?

Suppose that one morning you wake up and find your sugar bowl is full of ants. You remember that a flyer has come in your mail from Pest-Be-Gone, a local pest control service. In that flyer is the table in **Figure 1**, which the company is using to show the frequency with which it gets repeat business from its customers. For *most* businesses, this is a positive statistic.

Figure 1

Pest-Be-Gone's Faithful Customers			
Company	Customers Returned in One Year	Customers Returned in Two Years	Customers Returned in Five Years
Pest-Be-Gone	75%	50%	5%
No Mo' Bugs	10%	20%	50%
Bugging Out	15%	20%	40%

But remember this is a pest-control business. Some of Pest-Be-Gone's repeat business might be from pleased customers who wanted it to remove other pests. But if that is the case, why does business drop off drastically after two years? Could it be the company never removed the original pests entirely, and after repeated calls over two years, most customers called someone else? The data certainly support that inference.

And why does the customer-return rate for the other two pest-control businesses show the opposite pattern? The data support the inferences that those companies removed the original pests, made a favorable impression, and were hired back for increasing amounts of additional work. Despite Pest-Be-Gone's favorable impression of itself, you should think twice before hiring the company.

Study Tip

Remember that a promotional claim can be accurate yet still be misleading. When evaluating a claim, decide whether or not data can support it. Then evaluate the reliability of the data.

Why is drawing inferences from promotional materials a useful skill?

Companies publish promotional materials to encourage you to buy their products and services. Laws regulate the claims that a company may make, but not the way that people interpret those claims. A company may or may not provide you with all the data you need to properly evaluate its products or services. And as with the Pest-Be-Gone data in the earlier example, you must always ask yourself if the data actually show what the company is telling you they show.

By drawing the proper inferences from promotional materials, you can make wise purchasing decisions. Your choices can help you save money, stay fit and healthy, and buy the quality of products and services that you demand and expect.

End-of-Course Assessment Review

1. **Infer** An airline promotes itself with the slogan, "Best care in the air for a low, low fare." What inference about the airline, if any, can be reasonably drawn from the slogan?

   A The airline offers the widest seats or most legroom.

   B The airline offers the most nutritious meals and snacks.

   C The airline offers the best care per dollar of passenger fare, as calculated with a precise mathematical formula.

   D No reasonable inference is possible.

2. **Infer** Which of the following types of data would best help you evaluate a DVD delivery service?

   F a table showing average delivery times

   G a table showing movies available for streaming

   H a list of upcoming releases

   J reviews on a competitor's Web site

3. **Identify** Which of these claims or slogans could best be evaluated by analyzing scientific data?

   A "Super Bran Cereal has 25 percent more nutritional value than the leading brand."

   B "More than 60 percent of students improve their grades by one letter after two months in our tutoring program."

   C "Our bottled water contains more hydrogen than the competitor's brand."

   D "The best brand of milk for your body."

4. **Discuss** Why do you think many promotional claims are accurate but can be misleading?

The Impact of Research on Society and the Environment

TEKS 3D

Evaluate the impact of scientific research on society and the environment.

What is scientific research?

Scientific research involves investigation and experimentation. Scientists may have many goals for their research. They may want to discover a pattern or trend in nature, provide evidence in support of an idea or theory, or develop a new technology or product.

Biologists, specifically, conduct research on the structure, function, and life cycles of organisms and the relationships between organisms and their environment. Biologists also examine and research existing and extinct organisms in order to classify them. In addition, biologists culture tissue from people who are ill to identify the pathogens causing the disease.

Biologists also spend time in the field. They might research ways to improve the yields of farm crops, or to help protect endangered animals in the wild. Sometimes biologists work closely with experts in other branches of science. For example, a biologist may help a chemist discover new drugs or medicines from plants.

Scientific research has had major effects on society and the environment. Only 150 years ago, the most efficient forms of transportation were animal-drawn wagons and wind-powered boats. Most people lived on small farms and grew all their own food. Diseases such as smallpox and tuberculosis killed thousands every year. Scientific research has changed life dramatically in 150 years, and it continues to do so.

What is the impact of research on society?

Scientific research can lead to many changes for a society. Sometimes these changes develop in ways that no one could predict.

In the 1860s, for example, billiards players were looking for a new material for billiard balls. Balls made of wood or clay worked poorly. Ivory worked well but was very expensive. In response to this challenge, researchers began experimenting with materials. American inventor John Wesley Hyatt developed celluloid, one of the first materials that we now call plastics. Celluloid proved very useful for making billiard balls and other products, including early motion picture films. (Motion pictures themselves have had a powerful effect on human society.)

Today, plastics are used to make a huge number and variety of products. Thin, flexible plastics are used in food wrap; while tough, sturdy plastics are used to make containers and furniture. Perhaps most importantly, plastics are used to make sterile, disposable medical equipment that greatly reduces the transmission of infections between patients. In the 1800s, not many people would have predicted the wide use of plastics today.

New research and the technology that results from it also change the work life of a society. New jobs arise and existing jobs become unnecessary. For example, one hundred years ago, workers in the northern United States cut ice from frozen lakes and stored it in warehouses to keep food cool in the summer. The invention of the refrigerator made these jobs unnecessary.

Today, computers and the Internet are changing the way many people work. Work that once needed to be performed in a central office building can now be performed almost anywhere. While computers are replacing jobs such as telephone operator and reservations agent, they are creating new jobs such as computer programmer and Web site designer. Computers also make factories more automated and efficient, which lowers the cost of products.

What is the impact of research on the environment?

Scientific research has helped identify environmental problems. It also has helped solve or improve many of these problems. But research that solves some problems can cause other problems.

For example, researchers in the early 20th century developed DDT, a pesticide that kills the mosquitoes that transmit malaria to humans. DDT was commonly used from the 1940s through the 1960s. In the 1950s and 1960s, scientist Rachel Carson researched the effects of DDT on the environment. Carson's results showed that DDT was collecting in the bodies of eagles, hawks, and other birds of prey. Because of the accumulation of DDT, the birds were producing eggs with thin, fragile shells, reducing hatching rates and causing a drop in bird populations. She published the results of her research in *Silent Spring* in 1962, one of the most influential books on the environment ever written. Carson's work led to the ban of DDT in the United States and many other nations. Since then, the populations of eagles and other birds of prey have recovered. The research of others has led to regulations on other toxic substances, including lead, mercury, and asbestos.

Study Tip

Remember that scientists study a wide variety of topics in the natural and physical world. Their research affects everyone's life.

The invention of plastics has greatly improved human life, but it has also affected the environment. Most plastics are *nonbiodegradable*, meaning that natural processes break them apart very slowly, if at all. Because plastic is so widely used, the amount of plastic waste keeps increasing, as you see in **Figure 1** (on the following page). More and more space is needed for landfills to store discarded plastic. Researchers continue to study effective ways to recover plastic from consumer waste and to recycle, and responsible manufacturers continue to reduce the amount of plastic in their products and packaging.

Figure 1

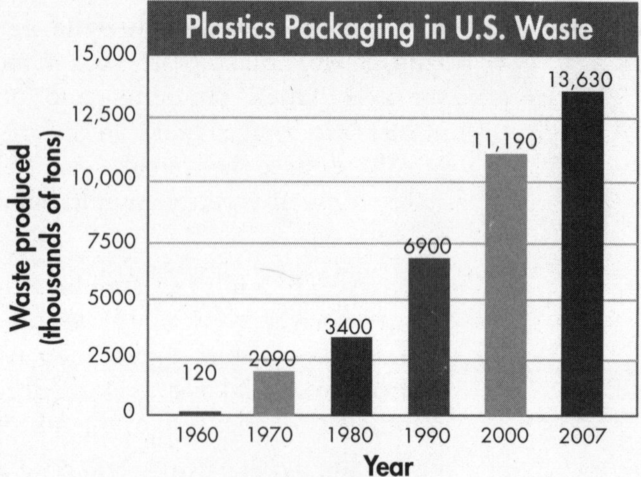

TEKS End-of-Course Assessment Review

1. **Evaluate** A biologist could best help achieve which of the following research goals?
   - **A** identifying the insects that are ruining a corn crop
   - **B** processing corn husks into diesel fuel
   - **C** explaining the rise of the Andes Mountains
   - **D** designing the most useful shape for a parachute

2. **Infer** What do the history of both plastics and DDT demonstrate about the results of scientific research?
   - **F** Research results can cause unexpected changes to society and the environment.
   - **G** With enough time, scientists always achieve the goals of a research project.
   - **H** Research results may have unintended effects, but those effects can be remedied.
   - **J** Research results cause changes to society that last 50 years at the longest.

3. **Evaluate** Write a short paragraph in response to this statement: "Scientific research can result in both benefits and drawbacks." Include a specific example in your answer (other than DDT or plastics).

Biological Models and Their Limitations

TEKS 3E

Evaluate models according to their limitations in representing biological objects or events.

What are the limitations of models that are used in biology?

Biologists use a wide variety of models to help them study and analyze objects and events. A model may be a physical model, such as a plastic model of the human body. Or a model may be an explanation of events in nature. For example, biologists use the model of ecological succession to explain the stages of natural land development.

All models have limitations. A model may accurately represent some characteristics of an object or an event, but distort or oversimplify other characteristics. **Figure 1** describes several examples of biological models and their limitations.

Figure 1

Limitations of Biological Models		
Model	**Usefulness**	**Limitations**
A labeled drawing of a typical animal cell Nucleus Mitochondrion Golgi apparatus	Identifies the structures of a cell Shows the relative sizes and locations of cell structures	Presents a flat image of a three-dimensional object Actual cells are more varied and complex than the model shows
Diagram of a food chain or web	Identifies feeding relationships among organisms in an ecosystem	Excludes many organisms that live in the ecosystem
Three-dimensional plastic model of the organs of the human body	Shows the relative sizes, shapes, and positions of organs	Simplifies or does not show the internal structures of organs Does not show variations in organs among individuals
Ecological succession	Demonstrates the stages in which plant and animal life colonize new or barren land	Stages of succession and colonizers may vary based on climate factors.
Computer models, such as climate	Allow scientists to manipulate variables and make predictions.	Limited by current knowledge and available data.

> **Study Tip**
>
> Remember the letters "PSK," which stand for purpose, scale, and knowledge. To evaluate the limitations of a model, you should identify its purpose and scale and apply your knowledge of biology.

How can you evaluate the limitations of a model?

Models are useful when you cannot directly access or measure what you would like to study, or you want to illustrate a particular structure or concept. Throughout your study of biology, you will encounter models of biological objects or events. You also may want to make your own models to communicate information that you gathered or the results of a laboratory investigation.

By properly evaluating the limitations of models, you can use models to learn and communicate information accurately. Following are some guidelines to help you evaluate the limitations of a model.

1. Identify the purpose of the model. Some models, such as the diagram of the cell, are intended to show the structures or the relative location of objects. Other models, such as the diagram of a food web, are intended to show relationships or processes.

Models in the form of a diagram or illustration are often accompanied by a title, a caption, or labels. Each provides clues to the model's purpose. To evaluate sophisticated or elaborate models, such as computer simulations, carefully follow any instructions for using the model.

2. Identify the scale of the model. Many models are useful because they represent very large or very small objects in a size that is easier to observe and study. The diagram of a cell is an example of a model much larger than the object it represents, while a backpack-sized model of an elephant is much smaller than a real elephant. The scale of the model identifies how much larger or smaller it is compared to the actual object.

The scale determines the amount of detail that the model can represent. A diagram of the cell that shows the nucleus and other cell structures would still be too small to show molecules, such as DNA and proteins. A small model of an elephant can show the shape of its head, trunk, and legs, but not the fine details of its skin.

3. Apply your knowledge of biology. Every model simplifies or excludes details about the object or event it represents. Applying your knowledge of biology will help you identify these details. For example, examine the diagram of the food chain shown in Figure 1. Food chains are usually a very simple representation of one particular feeding relationship in one particular food web in one particular ecosystem. One food chain can't give you a lot of information about an ecosystem, but it does give you some general information about one particular feeding relationship.

TEKS End-of-Course Assessment Review

1. **Evaluate** You are observing a lily flower and identifying its parts. To record your observations, you draw a labeled diagram of the lily on a sheet of paper. Which is the most significant limitation of the diagram as a useful model?

   A the scale of the diagram

   B the colors used in the diagram

   C the two-dimensional nature of the diagram

   D the size of the diagram

2. **Evaluate** Biology students can use computer simulations to study the organ systems of the human body. Which detail about the digestive system is a computer simulation least likely to represent accurately?

   F the location of the system in the body

   G the pathway of food through the system

   H the action of enzymes

   J the relative sizes of the organs

3. **Evaluate** Draw a model of an object or event in biology, such as a plant, an animal, or an interaction between plants and animals. Discuss the limitations of that type of model.

The History of Biology and Contributions of Scientists

TEKS 3F

Research and describe the history of biology and contributions of scientists.

What is the history of biology?

The history of biology includes events from early prehistory to the modern age. For thousands of years humans relied on their knowledge of plants and animals to survive. About 10,000 years ago, people began cultivating wheat, rye, and other grains. At about the same time, people in Asia and Africa were domesticating wild animals into the first farm animals, including sheep, pigs, cows, and goats. Later, philosophers of ancient Greece began classifying plants and animals and investigating human anatomy.

Yet ancient people had a limited knowledge of biology. Although they recognized the differences between living and nonliving things, they could not explain the reasons for these differences. The development of biology as a science occurred during the Renaissance, a period in Europe that lasted from the late 14th to the 17th century. Scientists have continued developing the field of biology ever since.

What contributions have scientists added to biology over the ages?

As in all sciences, our current body of biology knowledge is built upon the work of many contributors. **Figure 1** lists only a few of these important scientists.

Figure 1

Milestones in the History of Biology	
Year	**Milestone**
1665	Hooke observed cork and devised the term "cells."
1859	Darwin published his theory of evolution.
1866	Mendel published the results of his experiments on inheritance.
1928	Fleming discovered penicillin.
1953	Watson and Crick described the structure of DNA.
1962	Rachel Carson published *Silent Spring*.

Study Tip

Make a three-column chart to organize the information in this lesson. Include the names of the scientists, their contributions, and the dates of their work.

Van Leeuwenhoek, Hooke, and Other Scientists Who Developed the Cell Theory In 1665, Robert Hooke observed a thin slice of cork under a simple microscope. He identified tiny compartments that he called *cells* because they reminded him of cells in a monastery. A few years later, Anton van Leeuwenhoek used a microscope to observe "animalcules," tiny single-celled organisms.

In the mid 1800s, the work of Theodor Schwann, Matthias Schleiden, and Rudolf Virchow led to the development of the cell theory. The cell theory states that all living things are made of cells, and that cells arise from pre-existing cells. Scientists still apply the cell theory to explain life processes and how living things differ from nonliving things.

Linnaeus and Taxonomy In the 1700s, Swedish botanist Carolus Linnaeus developed the science of taxonomy, which is the naming and classification of organisms. In the Linnaean system, all types of organisms are given a two-word Latin name, such as *Felis domesticus* for the house cat. The first part of the name refers to a group of related organisms called a genus, and the second part refers to a specific type of organism called a species. Linnaeus also organized species into broader groups based on their characteristics. With some modifications, the Linnaean system remains in use today.

Mendel and the Study of Inheritance In the mid 1800s, Gregor Mendel, an Austrian monk, conducted experiments on pea plants. He chose certain plants to cross, or mate. Then he planted their seeds and observed the traits of the new plants as they grew. On the basis of his observations, Mendel proposed that traits are controlled by specific factors that pass from parent to offspring. These factors are now called genes. Mendel's work now forms the basis of genetics, the science of how traits are inherited and expressed.

Darwin and the Theory of Evolution In the 1830s, Charles Darwin observed a wide variety of plants and animals during a voyage around the world. His observations provided evidence for his theory of evolution by natural selection, which he published in *The Origin of Species* in 1859. Due to natural selection, organisms that are better adapted to their environment are more likely to survive and pass their traits to offspring. Darwin's work provided a scientific explanation for the history of life on Earth.

Since Darwin's time, scientists have continued to develop evolutionary theory. For example, in 1966, Lynn Margulis proposed the endosymbiotic theory, which states that complex cells are the result of cooperation among early single-celled organisms.

Pasteur, Fleming, and Microbiology Some people once thought that disease-causing "germs" could arise from nonliving matter, an idea referred to as spontaneous generation. In 1864, the experiments of Louis Pasteur showed that this idea was false, meaning that germs, such as bacteria, could arise only from other germs. Pasteur is now recognized as the father of microbiology, the study of microscopic organisms.

In 1928, Alexander Fleming discovered penicillin, the first known antibiotic. An antibiotic is a chemical that can kill bacteria. Many types of antibiotics are now in wide use. Prior to the discovery of antibiotics, deaths from bacterial diseases were very common. Antibiotics have saved a countless number of lives.

Watson, Crick, Franklin, and the Study of DNA By 1952, scientists had confirmed that deoxyribonucleic acid, or DNA, is the molecule that contains genetic information. However, the structure of DNA remained a mystery. The next year, James Watson and Francis Crick studied X-ray photographs of DNA taken by another scientist, Rosalind Franklin. Using these photographs as evidence, Watson and Crick proposed the double-helix model of DNA. A double helix is like a twisted ladder. In the years that followed, scientists discovered a lot about how DNA controls cell activities.

Carson and Ecology For many years, a chemical called DDT was used to kill mosquitoes and other insect pests. Then in 1962, Rachel Carson published *Silent Spring,* a book that described how DDT was collecting in the bodies of eagles and other birds. DDT weakened the birds' eggshells, and the bird populations were decreasing. Eventually the use of DDT was banned in some countries and limited in others. Carson's work helped launch the science of ecology, the study of how living things interact with one another and the environment.

TEKS End-of-Course Assessment Review

1. **Sequence** Which contribution is the most recent?
   - **A** Hooke's observation of cork cells
   - **B** Fleming's discovery of penicillin
   - **C** Pasteur's proof against spontaneous generation
   - **D** Mendel's experiments on pea plants

2. **Apply** The work of Rachel Carson is most similar to which of these topics that scientists research today?
   - **F** the increased resistance of bacteria to an antibiotic over time
   - **G** the mechanisms that regulate gene expression in bacterial cells
   - **H** the classification of a newly discovered species of plant.
   - **J** the accumulation of mercury in fish, due to mercury released from coal-fired power plants

3. **Research** In your opinion, what is the most significant discovery in the history of biology? Conduct research to help you form an answer.

Prokaryotic and Eukaryotic Cells

TEKS 4A

Compare and contrast prokaryotic and eukaryotic cells.

Vocabulary
nucleus
eukaryotic cell
prokaryotic cell

According to the cell theory, all living organisms are made up of cells that are surrounded by a membrane and contain genetic material. All cells can be classified into two broad categories based on whether they contain a nucleus. A **nucleus** is a membrane-enclosed structure that contains the cell's genetic material in the form of DNA. From the nucleus, DNA controls many of the cell's activities. **Eukaryotic cells** contain nuclei. **Prokaryotic cells** do not contain nuclei.

What are prokaryotes?

Prokaryotes are single-celled organisms that are generally small and simple. The DNA in prokaryotes is not bound within a nucleus but is found free-floating in the cytoplasm. Some prokaryotes contain internal membranes, but the membranes are generally less complicated than those found in eukaryotes. Despite their simplicity, prokaryotes carry out all the activities of living things. They grow, reproduce, and respond to the environment. Some prokaryotes can move by gliding along surfaces or swimming through liquids.

Prokaryotes are classified into two domains, or groups—Bacteria and Archaea. Bacteria, the larger of the two domains, are microorganisms that have many roles. Some bacteria cause illness. Other bacteria help us to digest our food. The metabolic activities of bacteria also provide us with many foods, such as yogurt. And, still other bacteria recycle nutrients in ecosystems by breaking down the remains of animals and plants.

Bacteria are usually surrounded by a cell wall that protects the cell from injury and gives the cell its shape. The cell walls of bacteria contain *peptidoglycan*—a compound of sugar and amino acids that surrounds the cell membrane. Some prokaryotes have a long whiplike appendage called a *flagellum*, which they use for movement. Prokaryotes also may have bristlelike appendages called *pili*, which can be used to anchor the bacterium to a surface or to other bacteria.

Archaea are similar to bacteria in both size and form but they also differ in several ways. The walls of Archaea lack peptidoglycan. In addition, their membranes contain different lipids. Archaea are far less common than Bacteria, and they often inhabit the most extreme of habitats, such as geysers that are close to boiling.

What are eukaryotes?

Eukaryotes—organisms that consist of eukaryotic cells—are amazingly diverse. Most living things you are familiar with are eukaryotes. Eukaryotes may be unicellular or multicellular. Eukaryotic cells are generally larger and more complex than prokaryotic cells. Most eukaryotic cells contain dozens of structures and internal membranes. Many eukaryotes have specialized cells, that have different functions than other types of cells. The most complex eukaryotes have specialized tissues, organs, and organ systems. Fungi, plants, animals, and the group often referred to as protists are all eukaryotes.

Cell biologists divide the eukaryotic cell into two major parts: the nucleus and the cytoplasm. The nucleus contains the genetic material and is separated from the rest of the cell. The cytoplasm is outside the nucleus and contains specialized structures called *organelles*. Following are descriptions of some organelles found in eukaryotic cells.

- Ribosomes receive coded instructions from the nucleus for making proteins; they are also found in prokaryotes.
- The endoplasmic reticulum is an internal membrane system where lipids, proteins, and other materials are assembled.
- The Golgi apparatus packages proteins for storage in the cell or for secretion outside the cell.
- Mitochondria convert the chemical energy stored in food into compounds that are easier for the cell to use.
- Chloroplasts in plant cells capture the energy from sunlight and convert it into chemical energy during photosynthesis.
- Lysosomes are small organelles filled with enzymes that break down lipids, carbohydrates, and proteins.
- Vacuoles are saclike structures that store materials such as water, salts, proteins, and carbohydrates.

Study Tip

Comparing and contrasting two sets of data is easy to do using graphic organizers. A compare-and-contrast table is one way to easily show similarities and differences. A Venn diagram also easily shows similarities and differences.

How do prokaryotic and eukaryotic cells compare and contrast?

Prokaryotic and eukaryotic cells are alike in that they both use DNA as genetic material, contain ribosomes, and have cell membranes. Both types of cells grow in size and maintain homeostasis.

They differ in that prokaryotic cells are less complex and smaller than eukaryotic cells. Eukaryotic cells contain a nucleus and other membrane-bound organelles, but prokaryotic cells do not contain a nucleus or other membrane-bound organelles. Although both types of cells divide, prokaryotic cells divide by binary fission and eukaryotic cells divide by mitosis. **Figure 1** compares and contrasts several characteristics of prokaryotic and eukaryotic cells.

Prokaryotes vs. Eukaryotes		
Characteristic	**Prokaryotes**	**Eukaryotes**
Cell size	Small	Usually ten or more times larger than prokaryotes
Number of cells	Unicellular	Some unicellular; many multicellular
Contain DNA as genetic material	Yes	Yes
Contain ribosomes	Yes	Yes
Contain a nucleus	No, DNA floats freely in cell	Yes, DNA within nucleus
Contain membrane-bound organelles	No	Yes
Cell division	Binary fission (simple cell division)	Mitosis
Cell structures	Contain cell walls	Fungi, plants, and many protists have cell walls; animals do not have cell walls.
Domains	Bacteria, Archaea	Eukarya
Kingdoms	Eubacteria, Archaebacteria	Protista, Fungi, Plantae, Animalia

Figure 1

End-of-Course Assessment Review

1. Draw Conclusions A scientist observes a cell that is surrounded by a cell wall and that lacks a nucleus and membrane-bound organelles. What can the scientist conclude about the cell?

A The cell is prokaryotic.

B The cell is eukaryotic, and a member of kingdom Plantae.

C The cell is eukaryotic, and a member of kingdom Fungi.

D The cell is part of a multicellular organism.

2. Explain Which characteristic describes all eukaryotes but no prokaryotes?

F presence of a nucleus in cells

G presence of a cell wall

H multicellular organization

J genetic information stored in DNA

3. Explain The simplicity of prokaryotic cells prevents them from

A growing and reproducing.

B responding to their environment.

C forming specialized tissues and organs.

D moving through their environment.

4. Compare and Contrast Describe three similarities and three differences between prokaryotic cells and eukaryotic cells.

Cellular Processes

TEKS 4B

★ READINESS ★

Investigate and explain cellular processes, including homeostasis, energy conversions, transport of molecules, and synthesis of new molecules.

Vocabulary
homeostasis
passive transport
diffusion
facilitated diffusion
active transport
ribosome
endoplasmic reticulum
Golgi apparatus

Why are cellular processes important?

Recall that cells are the basic units of life. To stay alive, unicellular organisms and the individual cells of multicellular organisms need to have the ability to perform specific processes. Many of these processes involve maintaining homeostasis, converting energy from one form to another, transporting molecules, and synthesizing new molecules.

What is homeostasis?

A cell can survive and function only within specific ranges of temperature, pH, water content, and other conditions. **Homeostasis** is the relatively constant internal physical and chemical conditions that organisms maintain. In the human body, homeostasis depends on organ systems working together to meet the needs of cells. The circulatory system supplies cells with water, oxygen, and nutrients, and it carries away their wastes. Messages from the nervous and endocrine systems control cell activities and allow cells to respond to changes in the body's environment.

What energy conversions take place within a cell?

According to the first law of thermodynamics, energy cannot be created nor destroyed. But energy can change from one form to another. Cells convert energy from one form to another as they carry out life processes.

For example, plant cells convert light energy into chemical energy when they make glucose during photosynthesis. In both plant and animal cells, the chemical energy stored in glucose is used to make compounds for growth and reproduction. The muscle cells of animals convert chemical energy into the energy of motion. Cells in fireflies convert chemical energy into light energy.

According to the second law of thermodynamics, whenever energy changes form, some of it is lost as heat. Inside the human body, the heat released by chemical reactions maintains a body temperature of about 37.0°C (98.6°F).

Study Tip

The main difference between passive and active transport is whether energy is needed or not. A task that requires "active" work requires energy.

Figure 1
Passive and
Active Transport

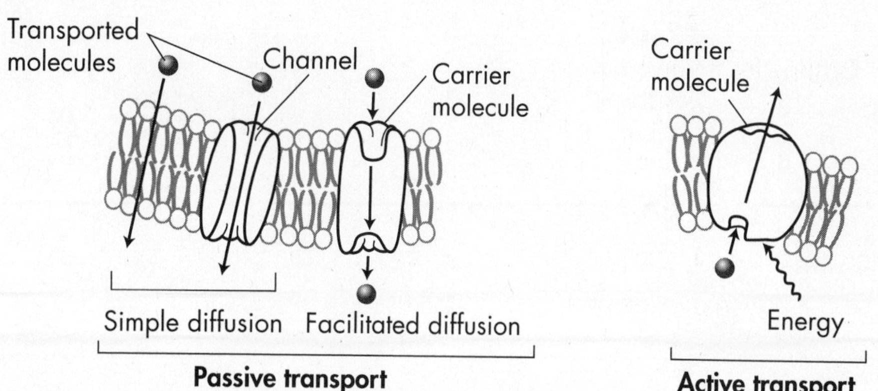

How are molecules transported by cells?

To survive, all cells must transport substances across the cell membrane, which is the barrier between a cell and its surroundings. Substances pass through cell membranes by passive transport, active transport, and bulk transport.

- **Passive transport** is the diffusion of a substance across the cell membrane without the use of energy. **Diffusion** occurs when a substance, such as oxygen or carbon dioxide, moves from an area of higher concentration to an area of lower concentration until equilibrium is reached.

  Another type of passive transport is **facilitated diffusion**, which involves proteins that span the cell membrane. These proteins increase the rate of diffusion of certain molecules. For example, *osmosis* is the facilitated diffusion of water across the cell membrane. Water moves through channels in cell membranes called aquaporins. Without aquaporins, water would diffuse across a cell membrane much more slowly.
- **Active transport** occurs when energy is used to move a substance across a cell membrane. In active transport, substances are moved from regions of low concentration to regions of high concentration—the opposite way that they would move by diffusion. In many cells, protein pumps perform active transport as they transport sodium, potassium, and calcium ions across cell membranes.
- Bulk transport is the movement of large molecules with the use of vesicles. A *vesicle* is a tiny sac formed by the cell membrane. Vesicles may carry molecules into the cell (*endocytosis*) or out of the cell (*exocytosis*). Bulk transport also requires energy from the cell.

How do cells synthesize molecules?

Cells synthesize a wide variety of complex molecules including proteins, lipids, and carbohydrates. A large majority of the molecules that cells make are proteins, which have a variety of functions. Some proteins have structural roles in the cell. Others are *enzymes*, which increase the rate at which chemical reactions occur. Three organelles in particular are involved in synthesizing molecules: ribosomes, the endoplasmic reticulum, and the Golgi apparatus. The organelles are shown in **Figure 2.**

Figure 2
Organelles Involved in Synthesis

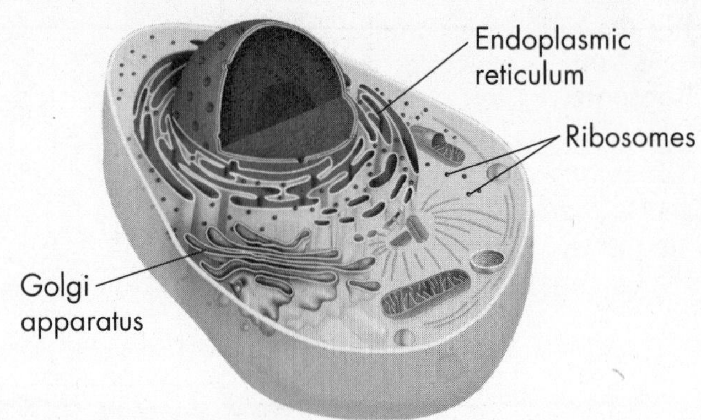

- **Ribosomes** are small particles of RNA and protein found throughout the cytoplasm in all cells. Ribosomes follow instructions to make proteins from DNA in the nucleus.
- The **endoplasmic reticulum (ER)** is a membrane system in eukaryotic cells where lipids, some proteins, and other molecules are assembled. There are two types of ER—smooth and rough. Smooth ER contains enzymes that are important in the synthesis of lipids. In some cells, especially liver cells, smooth ER enzymes detoxify harmful chemicals. Rough ER has ribosomes attached to its surface. Proteins that are assembled in these ribosomes enter the ER where they are modified. They leave the rough ER in vesicles that transport the proteins to the Golgi apparatus.
- The **Golgi apparatus** is a stack of membranous sacs. Here, products made in the ER are modified, stored, and prepared to be sent to destinations inside or outside of the cell.

TEKS End-of-Course Assessment Review

1. Explain If a particle enters a cell by active transport, then the particle is

A needed for synthesizing a large molecule.

B more concentrated outside the cell than inside it.

C more concentrated inside the cell than outside it.

D being moved without the use of energy.

2. Analyze Which energy conversion take place in some plant cells, but never in animal cells?

F chemical energy to light energy

G chemical energy to the energy of motion

H the energy of motion to sound energy

J light energy to chemical energy

3. Organize Use a flowchart to show the steps of protein synthesis, starting with ribosomes.

Viruses

TEKS 4C

READINESS

Compare the structures of viruses to cells, describe viral reproduction, and describe the role of viruses in causing diseases such as human immunodeficiency virus (HIV) and influenza.

Vocabulary
virus
capsid
lytic cycle
lysogenic cycle
retrovirus

How do viruses compare to cells?

A **virus** is a nonliving particle made up of proteins, nucleic acids, and sometimes lipids. Viruses can reproduce only by infecting living cells. A virus consists of a core of DNA or RNA surrounded by a protein coat, called a **capsid.**

Unlike a cell, a virus lacks structures to take in food, break apart food for energy, or synthesize molecules. Because viruses are noncellular and cannot perform most functions of life, scientists classify viruses as nonliving particles. However, viruses are able to perform one life function—reproduction—with the aid of a host organism. Host organisms can be eukaryotes or prokaryotes. Viruses that use prokaryotes as host cells are called bacteriophages or phages. You can see a comparison of viruses and cells in **Figure 1**.

Figure 1

Viruses and Cells

Characteristic	Virus	Cell
Structure	DNA or RNA in capsid, some with envelope	Cell membrane, cytoplasm; eukaryotes also contain nucleus and many organelles
Reproduction	Only within a host cell	Independent cell division, either asexually or sexually
Genetic Code	DNA or RNA	DNA
Growth and Development	No	Yes; in multicellular organisms, cells increase in number and differentiate
Obtain and Use Energy	No	Yes
Response to Environment	No	Yes
Change Over Time	Yes	Yes

Phage

Eukaryotic cell

How do viruses reproduce?

Viruses reproduce by taking over the host cell. The process begins when a virus attaches to the outside of a cell. The virus then injects its genetic material into the cell. After the viral genetic material enters a host cell, one of two processes may occur.

Study Tip

The adjective *lytic* and the prefix *lyso-* both come from the Greek word *lyein*, meaning "to loosen, or break up."

In the **lytic cycle**, the host cell starts making messenger RNA from the viral DNA. The messenger RNA takes over the host cell. Copies of viral DNA and the viral protein coats are made and assembled into new viruses. Then, the host cell bursts and the new viruses infect other cells.

In a **lysogenic cycle,** the virus does not reproduce immediately after infecting the host cell. Instead, the viral DNA is inserted into the DNA of the host cell. The viral DNA may stay within the host DNA for quite some time. However, eventually it may become active, remove itself from the host DNA, and begin a lytic cycle that produces new viruses.

Many viruses contain RNA as their genetic material. Some RNA viruses are called retroviruses. **Retroviruses** produce a DNA copy of their RNA genes when they infect a cell. AIDS is a disease caused by a retrovirus.

How does the human immunodeficiency virus (HIV) cause disease?

One of the most harmful viruses is the human immunodeficiency virus (HIV). It causes a deadly disease called acquired immunodeficiency syndrome, or AIDS. The progress of AIDS can be managed, but the disease itself has no cure. Since the 1980s, when it was first identified, AIDS has killed millions of people throughout the world.

HIV infects and destroys immune system cells called helper T cells. Helper T cells play a key role in keeping the body free from disease. When HIV attacks a helper T cell, it binds to the cell membrane and enters the cell. Once the virus is inside the cell, it uses the cell's structures to make new viruses. Then the virus destroys the cell. The new viruses are released into the bloodstream. They travel throughout the blood, infecting and destroying other helper T cells.

As an HIV infection progresses, more helper T cells are destroyed. Doctors determine the number of helper T cells in the blood of people with HIV infections to monitor how far their infections have progressed. The fewer helper T cells in the blood, the more advanced the infection.

As the immune system becomes increasingly compromised by HIV, the body becomes more susceptible to diseases that seldom show up in people with a healthy immune system. Such diseases are called opportunistic diseases. When a person with HIV develops one or more opportunistic diseases, the person is considered to have AIDS. Opportunistic diseases—not HIV—are generally the cause of death in people with AIDS.

At present, there is no cure for AIDS. Unfortunately, HIV mutates and evolves very rapidly. For this reason, the virus has been able to evolve into many different strains that are resistant to virtually all drugs used against them. Because HIV evolves so rapidly, no one has developed a vaccine that offers protection for any length of time. Researchers continue to study HIV and search for a vaccine against it.

How does the influenza virus cause illness?

Influenza, also known as the flu, is another RNA virus. The influenza virus infects the respiratory tract of humans (as well as other animals). The death of infected cells and a person's immune system response causes inflammation. This inflammation leads to the sore throat and mucus secretions that are early symptoms of the flu.

In most people, the infection causes mild to severe illness, including fever, cough, headache, and a general feeling of tiredness. Most people have symptoms for one to two weeks. However, compared with other viral respiratory diseases, influenza can cause a more severe illness.

There are two main types of influenza virus: Types A and B. These viruses are responsible for seasonal flu epidemics each year. However, similar to HIV, the influenza virus constantly evolves and changes. The Centers for Disease Control and Prevention (CDC) recommends getting a flu vaccine every year because the vaccine is altered every year in response to the evolving viruses.

TEKS End-of-Course Assessment Review

1. Compare How are viruses and cells alike?

- **A** Both contain genetic material.
- **B** Both contain structures for making proteins.
- **C** Both are able to break apart food for energy.
- **D** Both can be organized into complex organisms.

2. Describe After a virus infects a cell, which cell activity is directly involved in viral reproduction?

- **F** taking in food
- **G** dividing to produce daughter cells
- **H** making proteins
- **J** breaking apart food for energy

3. Explain What is one reason that an HIV infection is so serious?

- **A** DNA is the genetic material of HIV.
- **B** HIV can be passed through casual contact.
- **C** HIV injects genetic material directly into cells.
- **D** HIV infects cells of the immune system.

4. Compare and Contrast How are the influenza virus and HIV similar? How are they different?

The Cell Cycle

TEKS 5A

★ READINESS ★

Describe the stages of the cell cycle, including deoxyribonucleic acid (DNA) replication and mitosis, and the importance of the cell cycle to the growth of organisms.

Vocabulary
cell cycle
binary fission
interphase
mitosis
cytokinesis
sister chromatid

What is the cell cycle?

All cells come from existing cells. The **cell cycle** is the stages of growth and reproduction for a cell. Both prokaryotic and eukaryotic cells have cell cycles that can be thought of as the life cycle of a cell.

Prokaryotic cell division is called **binary fission**, a type of asexual reproduction that results in two genetically identical cells. The prokaryotic cell cycle involves cellular growth, the replication of DNA, and the formation of fibers that cause the cell membrane to indent and divide.

A multicellular organism grows because its cells produce more cells. As shown in **Figure 1,** the cell cycle of eukaryotic cells has four phases. Three of the phases—G_1, S, and G_2—are grouped together and called **interphase.** During G_1, or first gap, phase, the cell grows larger and makes proteins and organelles. Next is the S, or synthesis, phase, during which DNA replication occurs. During G_2, or second gap, phase, more growth and protein synthesis occurs and the cell prepares to divide.

The M phase, sometimes called the mitotic phase, is the shortest of the phases. The M phase includes two processes: mitosis and cytokinesis. **Mitosis** is the division of the nucleus. **Cytokinesis** is the division of the cytoplasm.

Figure 1
The Cell Cycle

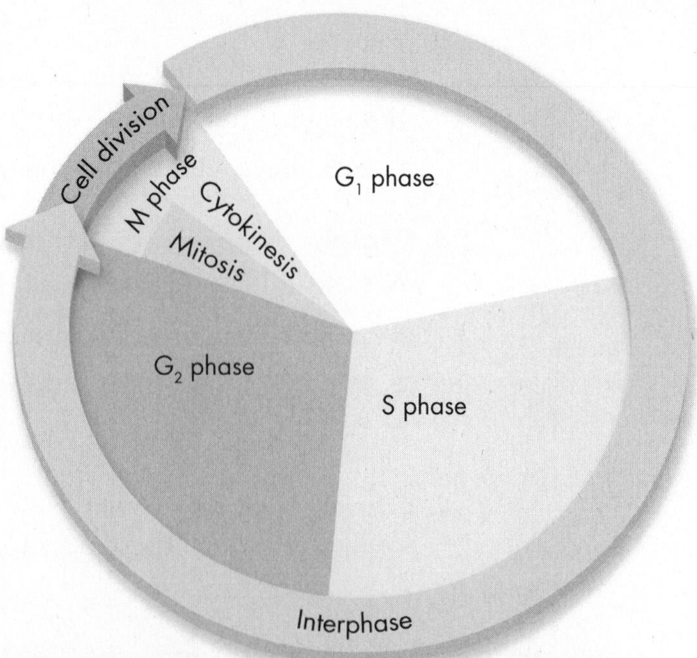

Study Tip

To remember the stages of mitosis, think of the acronym PMAT. The letters stand for prophase, metaphase, anaphase, and telophase.

How is DNA replicated?

First, during the S phase, DNA separates into two strands. Each strand serves as a template for a new DNA molecule. An enzyme called DNA polymerase joins nucleotides and "proofreads" the new DNA molecule. DNA replication results in two new molecules of DNA, each with an original strand and a new strand. Once replication is complete, a cell contains two strands of each chromosome called **sister chromatids**. The two sister chromatids are connected near their center by a structure called a *centromere*.

What occurs during mitosis and cytokinesis?

Refer to **Figure 2** as you read about each stage of mitosis. The product of mitosis is two daughter cells, each with identical genetic information as the parent cell.

Prophase The nuclear envelope breaks apart, and the chromosomes enlarge and thicken. In the cytoplasm, small tubules gather into a spindle, an apparatus that binds to and separates chromosomes.

Metaphase In this phase, the spindle attaches to the chromosomes and moves them into a line across the center of the cell.

Anaphase This is the shortest phase of mitosis. As the spindle contracts, the sister chromatids separate and are pulled to opposite sides of the cell.

Telophase The nuclear envelope reforms, the chromosomes shrink, and the spindle breaks apart.

During late telophase, one cell divides into two cells during cytokinesis. In animal cells, the cell membrane is drawn inward until it pinches off and two cells form. In plant cells, the cell membrane does not pull inward. Instead, a cell plate forms between the divided nuclei. The cell plate develops into two cell membranes. Then a cell wall forms between the two new membranes.

Figure 2
Mitosis and Cytokinesis

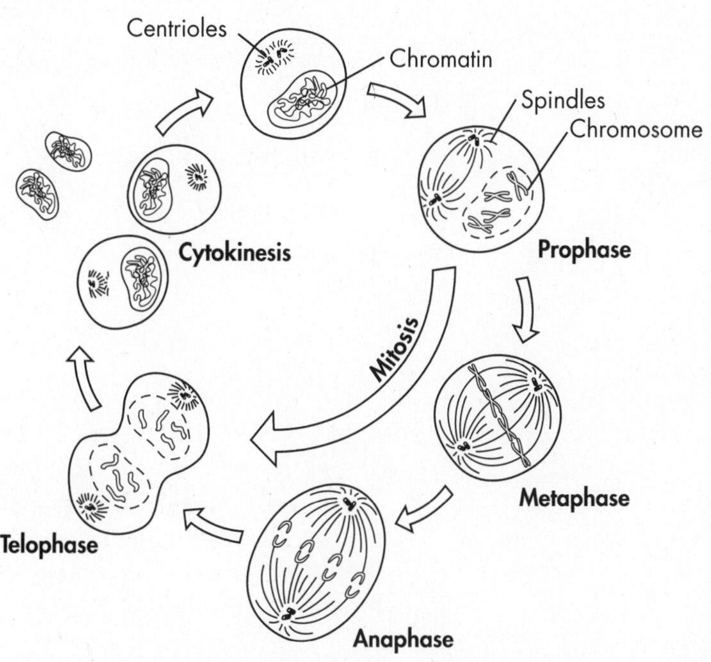

Why is the cell cycle important for the growth of organisms?

The cell cycle allows multicellular organisms to grow, and when necessary, to grow very quickly. The division of a single cell produces 2 cells. The two cells divide to produce 4 cells, which divide to produce 8 cells, and so on. With this type of pattern, called *exponential growth,* the first cell of a new organism can give rise to millions, billions, or trillions of cells in a few weeks or months.

The cell cycle also ensures that all cells of the organism have the same chromosomes and the same DNA. This is important because DNA contains genetic information that applies throughout the body of the organism, as well as to different stages of the organism's life.

TEKS End-of-Course Assessment Review

1. **Explain** Why is the S phase of the cell cycle essential for cell division?
   - **A** The S phase allows the cell to grow to the proper size for mitosis to be successful.
   - **B** The S phase produces two chromatids per chromosome.
   - **C** The S phase doubles the number of chromosomes per cell.
   - **D** The S phase halves the number of chromosomes per cell.

2. **Interpret** The cell of a fruit fly has 4 chromosomes. At the end of the mitotic (M) phase of the cell cycle, what best describes the chromosome content of a fruit fly cell?
   - **F** 4 chromosomes, each containing 2 chromatids
   - **G** 4 chromosomes, each containing 1 chromatid
   - **H** 2 chromosomes, each containing 2 chromatids
   - **J** 8 chromosomes, each containing 1 chromatid

3. **Identify** Which stage of mitosis is shown in the illustration?
   - **A** prophase
   - **B** metaphase
   - **C** anaphase
   - **D** telophase

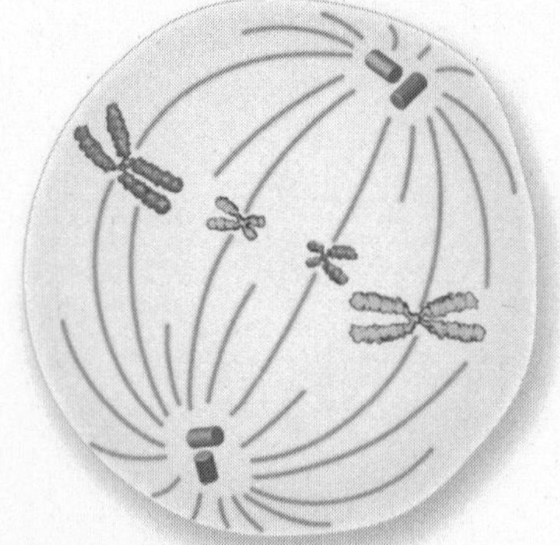

4. **Analyze** A multicellular organism contains many types of cells, such as the cells that make up muscles, bones, skin, and nerves. The cells look different and have very different functions. Do all of these cells have the same DNA? Explain.

Specialized Cells in Plants and Animals

TEKS 5B

Examine specialized cells, including roots, stems, and leaves of plants; and animal cells such as blood, muscle, and epithelium.

Vocabulary
companion cell
guard cell
platelet
epithelial cell

How are cells specialized?

In multicellular organisms, cells are specialized for particular functions. When examined under a microscope, the shape, structure, and components of a cell can provide clues about the cell's function. For example, human red blood cells are disk-shaped, which allows them to fit through microscopic blood vessels. Cells that produce and secrete a large quantity of proteins contain more endoplasmic reticulum than cells that do not.

What types of specialized cells make up roots, stems, and leaves?

Roots, stems, and leaves contain three types of tissues: dermal, ground, and vascular. These three tissues contain specialized cells that may differ from plant part to plant part.

Figure 1
Root Structures

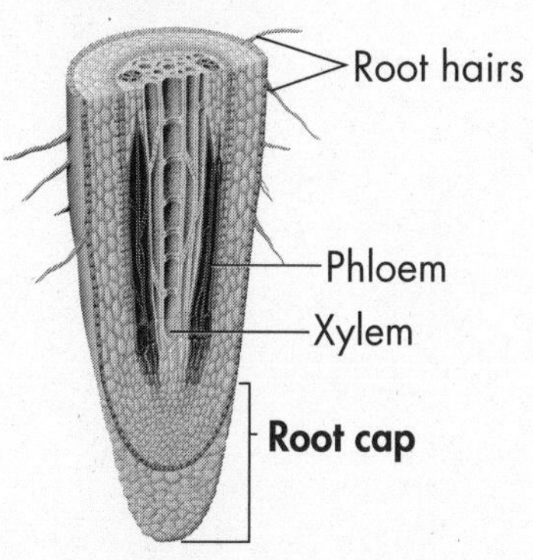

Dermal Tissue This type of tissue lines the outside of a plant with a layer of epidermal cells. In stems and leaves, epidermal cells secrete a waxy coating called cuticle, which protects the plant from injury and water loss. As shown in **Figure 1,** some root epidermal cells have projections called root hairs, which increase the surface area available for water absorption.

Ground Tissue Ground tissue consists of three types of specialized cells. Parenchyma cells have thin walls and large central vacuoles. In leaves, photosynthesis takes place in ground tissues. In roots, starch is stored in ground tissues. Collenchyma cells help support larger plants with strong, flexible cell walls. Sclerenchyma cells have thick, rigid cells walls that make ground tissue durable.

Vascular Tissue This tissue is the transport system in a plant. It consists of xylem (transports water) and phloem (transports sugars) as shown in **Figure 2** on the next page. Xylem contains tracheids and vessel elements. Tracheids are long, hollow cells with thick walls and openings between cells. Vessel elements, found in angiosperms, are stacked on top of each other. The cell walls between cells disintegrate, forming a tube. Tracheids and vessel elements are dead cells with no cytoplasm.

Phloem contains specialized cells called sieve tube elements and **companion cells** that support sieve tube elements. Sieve tube elements are arranged end to end. Holes in cell walls allow material to pass from cell to cell. Mature cells have no nuclei or cytoplasm and few organelles.

Study Tip

The letters *w* and *x* are adjacent in the alphabet, which can help you remember that *w*ater is carried in *x*ylem. The letters *ph* are pronounced the same as *f*, which can help you remember that food is carried in *ph*loem.

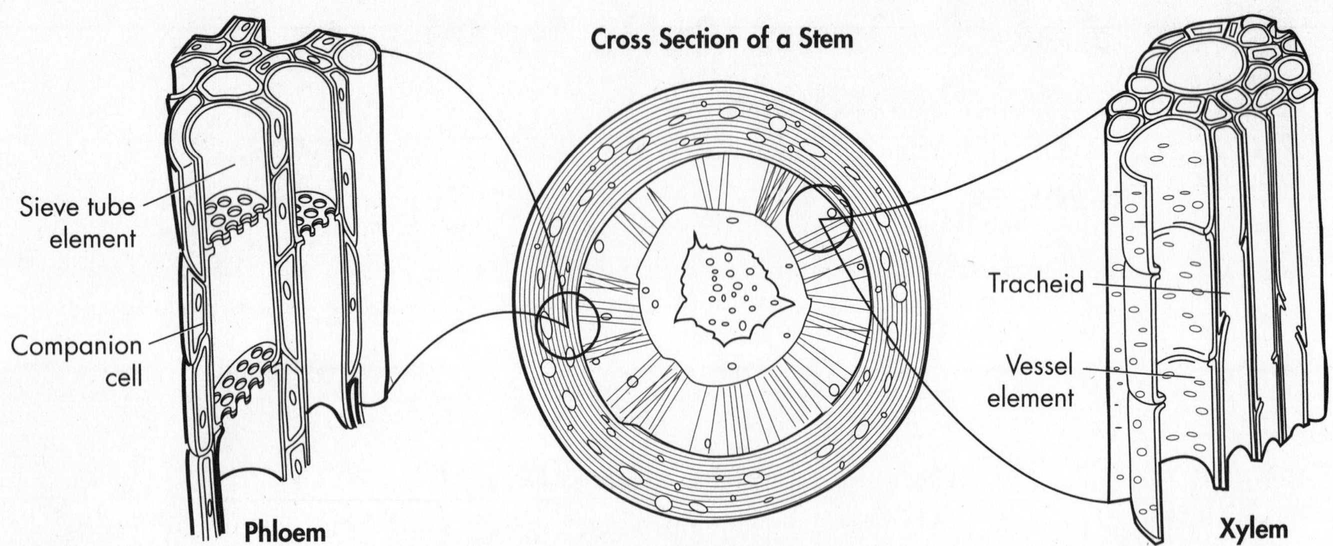

Figure 2
Vascular Tissue Cells

Other Specialized Plant Cells In addition to the cells already discussed, there are many other specialized plant cells.

- Cells found in root caps secrete a slippery substance that protects the growing root as it pushes through soil.
- Leaves have **guard cells,** which swell when water is abundant and shrink when water is scarce. As shown in **Figure 3,** when guard cells swell, they pull away from each other and open a pore in the leaf called a stoma (plural: stomata). When guard cells shrink, the stoma closes. Carbon dioxide, oxygen, and water vapor move in and out of a plant through stomata. By opening and closing stomata, guard cells help plants regulate water levels.

Figure 3
Guard Cells and Stomata

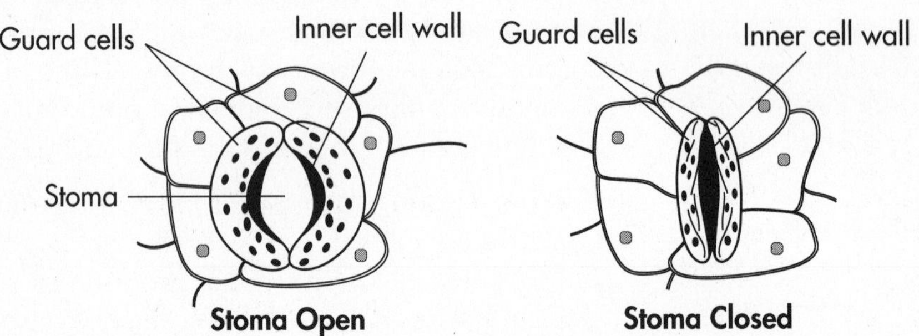

What are some specialized cells found in animals?

Animals rely on a huge variety of specialized cells. Some of these cells are muscle cells, blood cells, and epithelial cells.

Muscle Cells There are three main types of muscle cells, as shown in **Figure 4,** with differing characteristics one can see under a microscope.

- Skeletal muscles, which pull on bones when they contract, have cells that are striated (striped) and contain multiple nuclei.
- Cardiac muscle cells are found only in the heart. The cells are striated like skeletal muscle cells, but are smaller and usually only have one or two nuclei.

Figure 4 Muscle Cells

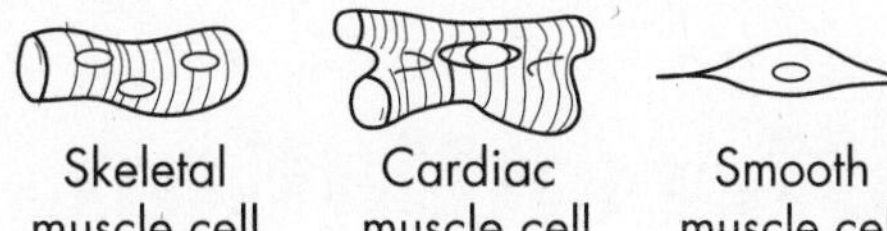

- Smooth muscle cells are found in organs such as the stomach and intestines. The name reflects the fact that they do not have striations.

Blood Cells A drop of blood viewed under a microscope will reveal three types of blood cells: red blood cells, white blood cells, and platelets.

- Red blood cells are red because they contain hemoglobin, an iron-containing protein that binds oxygen. Their centers are thin because they do not have nuclei.
- White blood cells, which are part of the immune system, are smaller and less abundant than red blood cells.
- **Platelets** are small fragments of certain bone marrow cells that cling to wounds and are part of the blood clotting process.

Figure 5
Examples of Epithelial Cells

Simple squamous

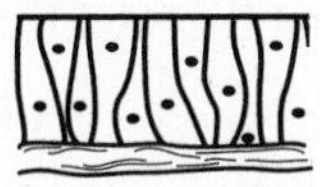

Pseudostratified

Epithelial Cells Animals have many types of **epithelial cells,** which line the outside of the body and organs. Their structure varies depending on their function. For example, simple squamous epithelial cells, which line blood vessels, are flat and platelike. The cells are not as tightly packed together as other types of epithelial cells, which allows gases and nutrients to diffuse between blood and body tissues. Pseudostratified columnar epithelial cells vary in height. Some of these cells that line the respiratory tract have cilia that sweep debris and mucus toward the top of the throat.

TEKS End-of-Course Assessment Review

1. **Identify** Smooth muscle cells are responsible for controlling the
   - **A** movement of food through the digestive tract.
   - **B** the flow of blood through the circulatory system.
   - **C** size of pupils in the eye.
   - **D** All of these

2. **Examine** You are examining a cross section of part of a plant under a microscope. Which observation would lead you to conclude that you are examining a root, rather than a leaf or a stem?
   - **F** the presence of xylem and phloem
   - **G** the presence of guard cells
   - **H** the shape of the cross section
   - **J** an abundance of parenchyma cells storing starch

3. **Apply Concepts** Suppose you just got a paper cut. Name as many specialized cells as you can that are or will become involved in the cut and its healing.

Cell Differentiation

TEKS 5C

Describe the roles of DNA, ribonucleic acid (RNA), and environmental factors in cell differentiation.

Vocabulary
cell differentiation
stem cell
RNA interference (RNAi)

What is cell differentiation?

A multicellular organism begins as a single cell. Through the processes of the cell cycle and mitosis, the cell divides into two daughter cells, which then divide repeatedly by mitosis. However, daughter cells are not necessarily identical to parent cells, especially during early stages of development. The process of **cell differentiation** produces specialized cells, which are cells that have characteristic structures that allow them to perform specific functions.

Cell differentiation occurs in **stem cells**, which are unspecialized cells that can differentiate into other types of cells. Stem cells may produce other stem cells or specialized cells, such as nerve, muscle, or blood cells. However, not all stem cells have the same differentiation potential.

- *Totipotent* cells can produce any cell in an organism and they can produce the cells of tissues surrounding an embryo. Organisms consist of these cells during the earliest stages of development **(Figure 1)**.
- *Pluripotent* cells form from totipotent cells. In an embryo (at this stage called a blastocyst), these cells develop into three layers, called *germ layers*: the ectoderm, endoderm, and mesoderm. Each germ layer gives rise to a specific set of tissues and organs in the developing embryo.

Figure 1
Stem Cells

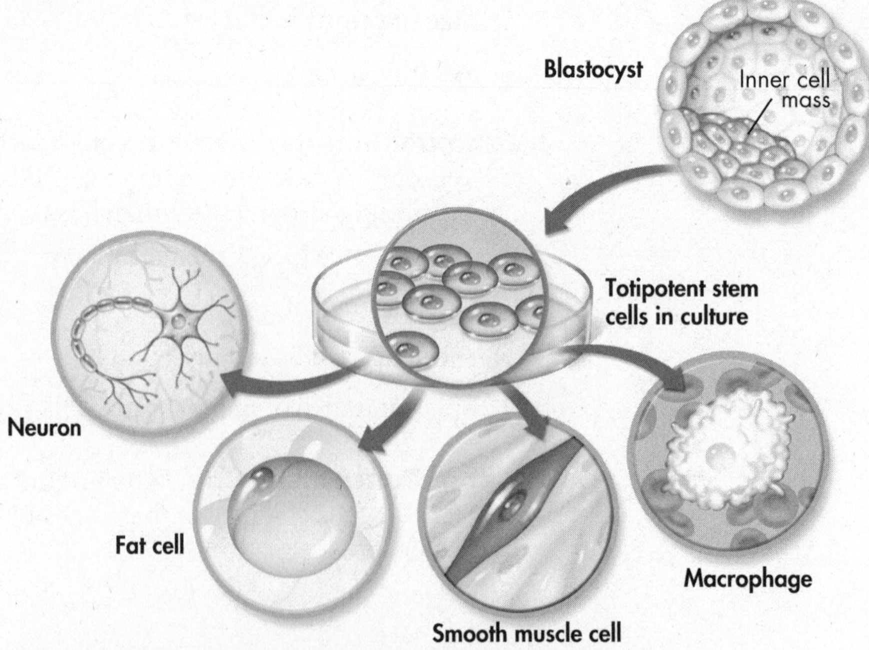

- *Multipotent* stem cells, which are found in the adult organism, can develop into only a few types of cells. Stem cells in bone marrow, for example, can develop into several types of blood cells, but not cells of other tissues.

Study Tip

Remember that all DNA is copied during replication, but only certain genes are transcribed and translated into proteins.

What are the roles of DNA and RNA in cell differentiation?

DNA is the genetic material that carries inherited information from parent to offspring. With only a few exceptions, all the cells in an organism have the same DNA in their nuclei. During a normal cell cycle, the cell's DNA is copied and passed to daughter cells. The process of copying DNA is called *DNA replication*.

If all cells of an organism have the same DNA, how is cell differentiation possible? In each cell, only certain *genes*, which are functional units of DNA, are actively decoded into proteins. The other genes are present in the cell, but they are dormant (not active).

The information in a gene is decoded in a two-step process that involves ribonucleic acid (RNA), a nucleic acid similar to DNA. First, in a process called *transcription*, the gene is used as a model, or template, to make a strand of messenger RNA (mRNA). Then, in a process called *translation*, the information in mRNA is decoded to make a protein. Proteins have many functions in cells. Some proteins act as structural components of cells. Others are enzymes that speed up chemical reactions in the cell.

Although the entire DNA molecule is copied during replication, only certain genes in a cell are transcribed and translated. The active transcription and translation of a gene, or *gene expression*, is regulated in several ways. For example, chemicals in cells called transcription factors influence which genes are transcribed and when they are transcribed. Transcription factors are involved in the differentiation of stem cells into many types of specific tissues from the time of embryonic development.

After a gene is transcribed, its translation may be prevented by a process called **RNA interference (RNAi).** RNAi involves small molecules of RNA (called microRNA) that bind to mRNA. Once mRNA is bound by the microRNA, the mRNA is cut into fragments and can no longer be translated into a protein. RNAi is receiving a lot of attention from researchers as a way to control gene expression in the laboratory.

What are the roles of environmental factors in cell differentiation?

Many factors in a cell's internal or external environment affect which genes are expressed. Gene expression, in turn, affects how a cell differentiates. Internal environmental factors include proteins and other molecules, such as hormones, that are made within the organism. External environmental factors such as temperature, oxygen, and available nutrients also affect gene expression. Pollution is another external factor that can influence gene expression. Some pollutants that enter the body can mimic chemical signals sent by cells. This may cause some genes to be expressed that normally wouldn't be expressed or vice versa.

Hormones are chemicals in plants and animals that are produced in one part of the organism and that affect another part of the organism—including, at times, its gene expression. Plant hormones trigger stems to grow toward the light, roots to grow toward water, and fruit to ripen. Hormones in humans have many effects on growth and development, as well as food digestion and preparing the body for activity or rest.

Climate factors often affect gene expression. In many plants, for example, the length of day or night triggers when leaves bud, flowers bloom, and leaves drop. In other plants, temperature changes affect these events.

TEKS End-of-Course Assessment Review

1. Explain Which of the following helps explain the different sets of proteins produced by a muscle cell and a nerve cell of the same animal?

A In each cell, RNA interference acts to stop the translation of different genes.

B In each cell, the DNA molecule contains different sets of genes.

C In each cell, the DNA molecule contains different arrangements of the same genes.

D Each cell produces different types of hormones.

2. Infer A scientist is studying changes in the cells of a fish embryo over time. Which observation of a group of cells would show that they had begun differentiating into muscle cells?

F the replication of DNA specific to muscle cells

G the presence of genes specific to muscle cells

H the presence of a cell protein specific to muscle cells

J the presence of totipotent stem cells

3. Draw Conclusions Every year in early October, the leaves of a tree change color. What is the most likely factor that triggers the changing color of leaves in this tree?

A changes to the DNA in the cells of the leaves

B changes to the RNA in totipotent stem cells of the tree

C decreasing hours of daylight

D decreasing moisture in the soil

4. Describe How can cell differentiation be affected by internal cell activities and external factors from the environment?

The Cell Cycle and Cancer

TEKS 5D

Recognize that disruptions of the cell cycle lead to diseases such as cancer.

Vocabulary
tumor
malignant
metastasis
cancer

What can happen when the cell cycle is disrupted?

The cell cycle is the process in which cells grow, replicate DNA, and divide to form daughter cells. During the embryonic stage of life, cells divide frequently to form the body of the organism. But later, the cell cycle is more tightly regulated and controlled. This control allows the body to maintain its size and keep tissues healthy. When old cells die, controlled cell division allows new cells to replace them. In certain instances, cell division can allow damaged organs or body parts to regenerate.

However, sometimes the control of the cell cycle is disrupted. Like other functions of cells, the cell cycle depends on DNA. When DNA is damaged or altered, it can undergo a mutation, which is a permanent change to the information it carries. In some cases, the mutation can cause an abnormal pattern of growth and division. The cell may divide quickly and repeatedly, and it may cease to fill a useful role in the body.

A mass of rapidly growing, abnormal cells is called a **tumor**. Some tumors are *benign*, or harmless, because their cells do not spread beyond the tumor. Benign tumors are noncancerous. Other tumors, called **malignant** or cancerous tumors, have cells that can spread to other areas of the body. Often malignant cells spread by entering the blood or lymph, another type of body fluid. The spread of malignant cells is called **metastasis**. **Figure 1** shows the development of a cancerous tumor.

Figure 1
Development of Cancer

❶ A cell begins to divide abnormally.

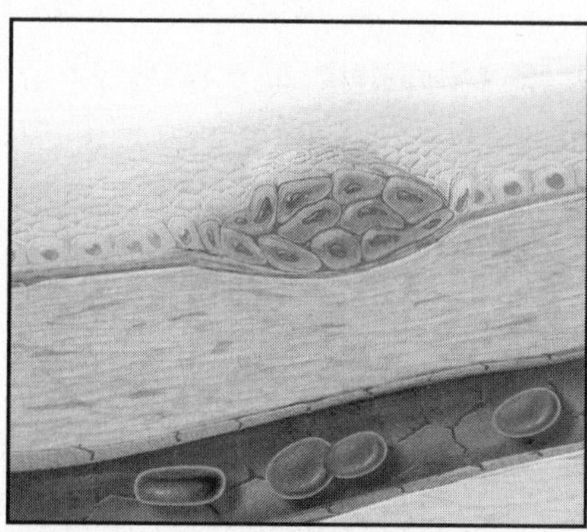

❷ The cancer cells produce a tumor, which begins to displace normal cells and tissues.

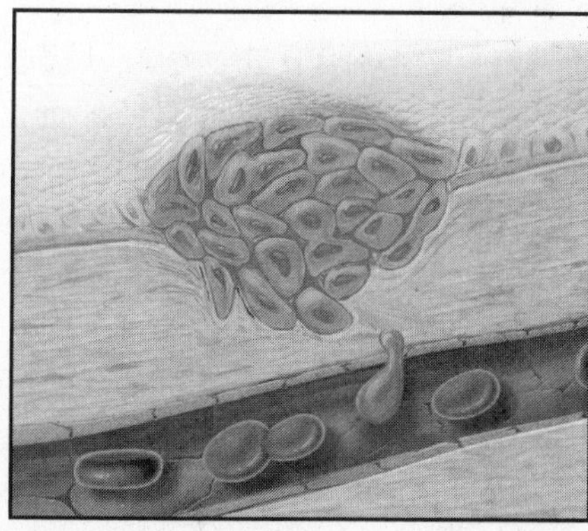

❸ Cancerous tumors are most dangerous when they metastasize, and their cells travel to other parts of the body and form new tumors.

What causes a disruption of the cell cycle that leads to cancer?

Cancer is a general name for a disruption in the cell cycle that eventually disturbs the proper functioning of a body. Cancer can occur in almost any organ including the skin, liver, lungs, brain, reproductive organs, and endocrine glands. Blood and lymph tissues can also become cancerous. It is not a single disease, but rather a group of diseases characterized by cells that grow abnormally and may spread to other parts of the body. **Figure 2** describes the five main types of cancers.

Figure 2

Five Major Types of Cancers		
Types	**Characteristics**	**Examples**
Carcinomas	Involve cells that cover external or internal body parts	Cancers of the lung, breast, and colon, and some skin cancers
Sarcomas	Involve cells in bones, muscles, fat, or connective tissue	Bone cancers; Kaposi's sarcoma
Lymphomas	Begin in lymph tissues or the immune system	Hodgkin's disease, non-Hodgkin's lymphoma
Leukemias	Begin in the bone marrow and spread through the blood; do not involve tumors	Many types of acute and chronic leukemia
Adenomas	Involve tumors in endocrine glands	Cancers of the thyroid, pancreas, and pituitary glands

Cancer can be caused by a variety of agents called *carcinogens*. Examples of carcinogens include certain chemicals in tobacco smoke, industrial chemicals such as benzene, asbestos, and high-energy radiation. Moderate or long-term exposure to the ultraviolet radiation in sunlight can promote the development of skin cancer.

Some viruses, called oncogenic viruses, can disrupt the cell cycle of cells they infect. HIV and some strains of HPV (human papilloma virus) are examples of oncogenic viruses.

Although cancer is not inherited, genes can affect a person's risk of developing certain types of cancer. Evidence suggests that cancers of the breast, colon, and ovaries have a genetic risk component.

How is cancer treated?

There are three main methods of treating cancer: chemotherapy, radiation, and surgery. In many cases, cancer patients receive combinations of all three methods. Treatment plans are based on how advanced the cancer is and where the tumor or tumors are located.

Chemotherapy In chemotherapy, chemicals are used to kill or slow the growth of cancer cells. These treatments take advantage of the fact that cancer cells divide more rapidly than normal cells. The chemicals may also affect normal cells that divide rapidly, such as the cells in hair follicles.

Study Tip

The word *benign* is related to the words *benefit* or *beneficial* from the Latin word for the adjective *well*. Although benign tumors are not beneficial, they are usually harmless.

Radiation Therapy A concentrated dose of high-energy radiation, such as X-rays or gamma rays, damages the DNA of cancer cells and kills them or prevents them from dividing. As with chemotherapy, though, the treatment may also damage normal cells. However, the normal cells can repair themselves, and the cancerous cells cannot.

Surgery In many cases, surgeons can remove a tumor from the body with minimal damage to tissues or organs. During surgery, physicians can also determine if the cancer has spread to other tissues.

Other Treatments Some patients may receive drugs that target cancer cells. The drugs interfere with molecules involved in the growth of tumors without harming normal cells. Other drug treatments may block the blood supply to tumors. Like normal body cells, tumor cells require oxygen and nutrients.

Most forms of cancer are easier to treat when they are detected early. Advanced stages of cancer, especially after tumors have metastasized, are much more difficult to treat successfully.

TEKS End-of-Course Assessment Review

1. **Compare** According to the text and **Figure 2**, what do all five of the major types of cancer have in common?
   - **A** All involve cells that cover internal or external body parts.
   - **B** All involve glands of the endocrine system.
   - **C** All involve malignant tumors.
   - **D** All involve disruptions to the cell cycle.

2. **Predict** Which example of cancer would most likely benefit from the surgical removal of a tumor?
   - **F** an early stage of leukemia (cancer of the blood)
   - **G** an advanced stage of lymphoma (cancer of the lymphatic system)
   - **H** an early stage of skin cancer, a type of carcinoma
   - **J** pancreatic cancer that has metastasized throughout the body

3. **Explain** Why is early detection of a malignant tumor often the key to successful treatment?

4. **Recognize** Usually when the DNA of a cell mutates to the point that the cell cannot function properly, the cell goes through a process called apoptosis, or programmed cell death. Why do you think that cancer cells do not undergo this process?

The Components of DNA

TEKS 6A

★ READINESS ★

Identify components of DNA, and describe how information for specifying the traits of an organism is carried in the DNA.

Vocabulary
chromosome
gene

What is DNA?

A nucleic acid, called deoxyribonucleic acid (DNA), is the genetic material that holds the blueprint for an organism's genetic makeup and life processes. DNA is coiled inside the nucleus of eukaryotic cells. One stage of the cell cycle includes DNA replication, which allows the information needed to carry on life processes to be passed to new cells. DNA is also passed from parent to offspring when an organism reproduces.

DNA is packaged into structures called **chromosomes**. Within chromosomes, DNA is organized in units called **genes** that are found in specific places on chromosomes. Genes hold the information for traits such as blood type, eye color, and the potential length of your fingers. If you were to compare a chromosome to an encyclopedia of an organism's makeup, then genes would be the entries in the encyclopedia.

What are the components of DNA?

DNA is a polymer, which means it consists of repeated units. The units in DNA are called *nucleotides*. As shown in **Figure 1,** nucleotides contain three parts: a phosphate group, a 5-carbon sugar called deoxyribose, and a nitrogenous base.

The phosphate and sugar units make up the "backbone" of the DNA molecule, and each single strand has identical versions of these units. However, one of four nitrogenous bases may make up a nucleotide: adenine (A), guanine (G), cytosine (C), or thymine (T).

Figure 1
Components of DNA

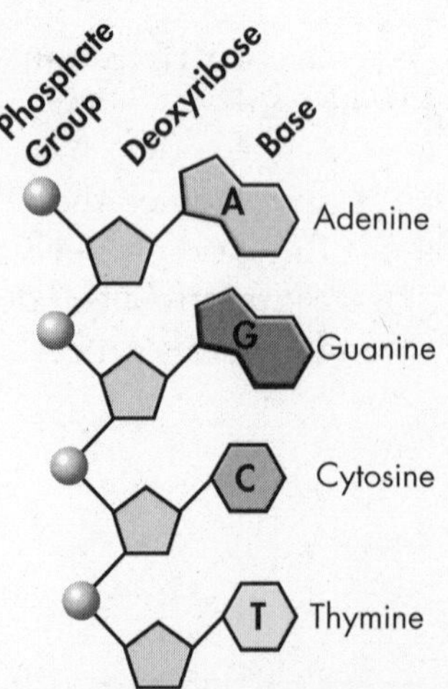

A DNA molecule is made of two nucleotide strands joined in a twisted ladder shape called a double helix. Each phosphate and sugar backbone is like one side of a ladder. The nitrogenous bases extend out from either side and meet in the middle like the rungs of a ladder (**Figure 2**).

Figure 2
Double Helix

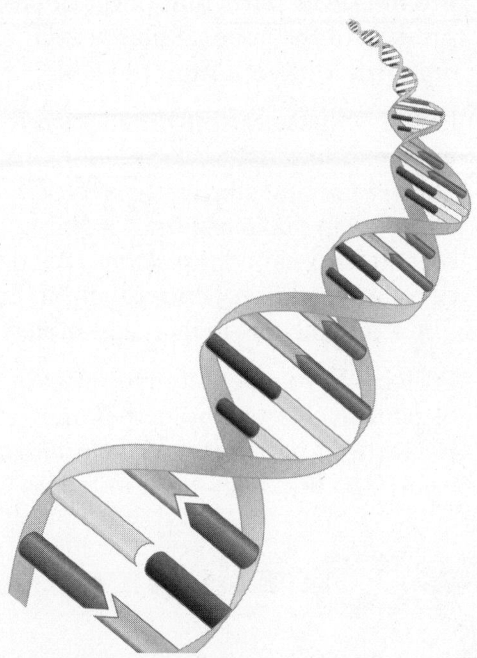

As shown in **Figure 3**, guanine binds with cytosine and adenine binds with thymine. Each of these pairs (G-C and A-T) is called a complementary base pair. The nitrogenous bases of the two strands are held together by hydrogen bonds. The bases can be in any order, and one gene may contain hundreds or thousands of nucleotides.

Figure 3
Base Pairing

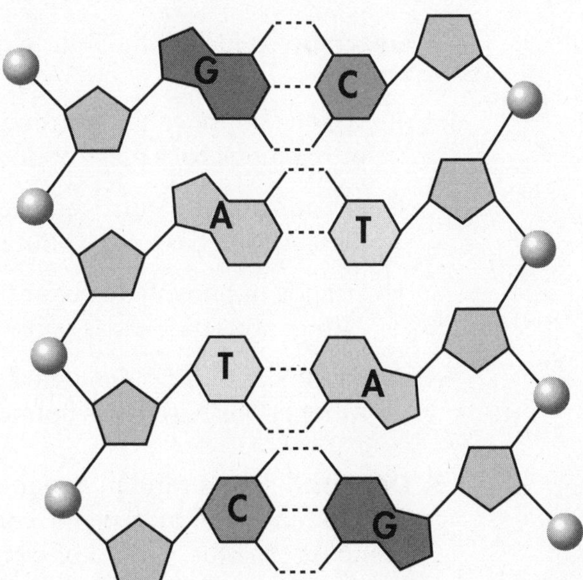

Study Tip

Compare a molecule of DNA to a zipper. The fabric strip of the zipper represents the sugar-phosphate backbone, while the teeth of the zipper are like the complementary base pairs that join together with hydrogen bonds.

How is information for specifying traits carried in DNA?

DNA contains genetic information in a sort of code, which is based on the order of the four nitrogenous bases: adenine, guanine, cytosine, and thymine. The particular order of bases within a gene determines the product of the gene. Differences in base order make the DNA of one organism different from the DNA of another organism.

For cells to use the information in DNA to make products, first the information must be decoded. DNA is decoded in a two-step process. During the first step, called *transcription,* a strand of DNA is used as a template to make a strand of RNA, a single-stranded nucleic acid. In the second step, called *translation,* the order of the nucleotides in RNA is decoded into a sequence of amino acids, the building blocks of proteins. The amino acids are then assembled into proteins.

Proteins have an endless number of roles in shaping the traits of organisms. For example, they may form structures in cells, act as catalysts in reactions (enzymes), transmit signals throughout the body (hormones), or help an organism fight invaders (antibodies).

End-of-Course Assessment Review

1. **Identify** Which of the following is a complementary base pair?
   - **A** guanine–thymine
   - **B** guanine–guanine
   - **C** adenine–cytosine
   - **D** guanine–cytosine

2. **Describe** Which of the following correctly describes the structure of DNA?
   - **F** strands of phosphate-nitrogen backbone, with complementary nitrogenous base pairs bound into a double helix
   - **G** strands of sugar-nitrogen backbone, with complementary deoxyribose base pairs bound into a double helix
   - **H** strands of phosphate-sugar backbone, with complementary nitrogenous base pairs bound into a double helix
   - **J** strands of phosphate-sugar backbone, with complementary nitrogenous base pairs bound into a single helix

3. **Describe** One strand in a segment of a gene has the base sequence TGCTTA. What would be the complementary sequence of nucleotides found on the other strand of DNA? Explain your answer.

6B The Genetic Code

TEKS 6B

Recognize that components that make up the genetic code are common to all organisms.

Vocabulary
codon

What is the genetic code?

DNA is the molecule that codes for the traits of organisms. It is made up of units called nucleotides. Members of the same species share certain common nucleotide sequences. Individuals within a species have slight variations within their DNA, which makes every individual unique. These differences in DNA account for the differences in body parts, structures, and other features of organisms. Generally, the more closely related two organisms are, the more alike their nucleotide sequences will be.

The way in which information is carried in DNA and translated to proteins seems to be common to all organisms. First, DNA is transcribed into a molecule of messenger RNA (mRNA). Then the mRNA is translated into a strand of amino acids that can be assembled into a protein. The genetic code is the matching of nucleotide sequences in DNA and RNA to the amino acids that will be used to make a protein.

What are the components of the genetic code?

DNA nucleotides contain three components—deoxyribose, one or more phosphate groups, and one of four nitrogenous bases. The four bases are adenine (A), guanine (G), cytosine (C), and thymine (T). You can think of DNA as a book made of very long words, and each word is made from four letters repeated in different combinations.

Proteins are made by the joining of amino acids into long chains called polypeptides. Each polypeptide contains a combination of any or all of the 20 different amino acids. The properties of proteins are determined by the order in which different amino acids are joined together to produce polypeptides. How is it possible that only four bases in DNA can code for 20 different amino acids? The answer is that the code relies on sequences of three nucleotides called **codons.** A codon consists of three consecutive bases that specify a single amino acid which is to be added to the polypeptide. There are also codons that start or stop the translation process.

During transcription, DNA is used as a blueprint to make mRNA. An important difference between RNA and DNA is the substitution of uracil (U) in RNA for thymine (T) in DNA. **Figure 1** on the next page, shows the triplet codons in mRNA and the amino acids that they code for.

Study Tip

Remember that a codon in DNA or RNA corresponds to one amino acid. You can tell that codons such as AUG and AUU are part of RNA, not DNA, because they include uracil (U).

Figure 1
The Genetic Code

First base	Second base: U	Second base: C	Second base: A	Second base: G	Third base
U	UUU, UUC — Phenylalanine UUA, UUG — Leucine	UCU, UCC, UCA, UCG — Serine	UAU, UAC — Tyrosine UAA Stop codon UAG Stop codon	UGU, UGC — Cysteine UGA Stop codon UUG Tryptophan	U C A G
C	CUU, CUC, CUA, CUG — Leucine	CCU, CCC, CCA, CCG — Proline	CAU, CAC — Histidine CAA, CAG — Glutamineine	CGU, CGC, CGA, CGG — Arginine	U C A G
A	AUU, AUC — Isoleucine AUA AUG Methionine start codon	ACU, ACC, ACA, ACG — Threonine	AAU, AAC — Asparagine AAA, AAG — Lysine	AGU, AGC — Serine AGA, AGG — Arginine	U C A G
G	GUU, UUC, GUA, GUG — Valine	ACU, ACC, ACA, ACG — Alanine	GAU, GAC — Aspartic acid GAA, GAG — Glutamic acid	GGU, GGC, GGA, GGG — Glycine	U C A G

In the genetic code table shown, the first base is down the left side of the table. The second base is listed across the top of the table, and the third base is listed down the right side. Notice that most amino acids are specified by more than one codon. Glycine, for example, is encoded by GGU, GGC, GGA, and GGG. The codon for methionine is AUG, which also acts as the start codon. Three codons—UAA, UAG, and UGA—are stop codons. They signal that formation of polypeptide strand is complete.

The components of the code are universal in that all known organisms have DNA, use codons with three nucleotides to code for amino acids, and use organelles such as ribosomes for protein synthesis. However, scientists have found a few exceptions to the universal nature of the genetic code. In a few organisms, a codon may code for a different amino acid than it does in most other organisms.

TEKS End-of-Course Assessment Review

1. **Calculate** A segment of a gene contains 27 nucleotides, none of which include stop or start codons. How many amino acids does this segment code for?
   - **A** 3 amino acids
   - **B** 9 amino acids
   - **C** 27 amino acids
   - **D** 81 amino acids

2. **Predict** A mutation of a gene occurs because of a change to one of the nucleotides in a sequence of DNA while the DNA is being copied. Which mutation would have the greatest effect on the protein that the gene codes for?
   - **F** the change of a codon from UCU to UCG
   - **G** the change of a codon from UAA to UAG
   - **H** the removal of one nucleotide near the beginning of the gene
   - **J** the addition of nucleotides after the stop codon

3. **Contrast** Which component of the genetic code differs between DNA and RNA?
   - **A** three nucleotides per codon
   - **B** the presence of adenine (A) in codons
   - **C** the presence of uracil (U) in codons
   - **D** the presence of amino acids in codons

4. **Evaluate** In the process of translation, a strand of mRNA is decoded into the amino acids of a protein. Why is it important that mRNA be translated in one direction only? Choose a specific codon to discuss as an example.

5. **Apply** A section of protein is made up of the following amino acids: arginine-serine-proline-proline-aspartic acid-glycine-alanine-glycine. Explain why it would be difficult to use Figure 1 to derive the mRNA sequence for this protein.

Transcription and Translation

TEKS 6C

Explain the purpose and process of transcription and translation using models of DNA and RNA.

Vocabulary

messenger RNA (mRNA)
ribosomal RNA (rRNA)
transfer RNA (tRNA)
transcription
translation
anticodon

What is RNA?

In a eukaryotic organism, each cell holds DNA in its nucleus. DNA contains all the instructions the organism needs to produce the proteins necessary for life. RNA (ribonucleic acid) is involved in translating DNA into a series of amino acids and assembling proteins.

The structure of RNA is similar to that of DNA, but with a few important differences. Both are composed of a long strand of nucleotides, each with a sugar-phosphate backbone and one of four nitrogenous bases. However, RNA is single-stranded whereas DNA is double-stranded. Another difference is that the sugar in RNA is ribose, while the sugar in DNA is deoxyribose. Finally, RNA contains the nucleotide uracil (U) instead of thymine (T).

There are three major types of RNA:

- **Messenger RNA (mRNA)** carries part of the genetic information of DNA from the nucleus to the ribosomes in the cytoplasm, where the information is translated into a protein.
- **Ribosomal RNA (rRNA)** is found in ribosomes, organelles where proteins are assembled from amino acids.
- **Transfer RNA (tRNA)** attaches to individual amino acids and transfers them to ribosomes.

All three types of RNA are involved in protein synthesis. Protein synthesis occurs in two major steps called transcription and translation.

What is the purpose and process of transcription?

In **transcription**, a gene located on the DNA serves as a template for the assembly of a molecule of RNA. Transcription begins when the enzyme RNA polymerase binds to a nucleotide sequence in a region near the gene. This region is called the *promoter.* At the promoter, RNA polymerase breaks hydrogen bonds between base pairs and separates the two strands of DNA **(Figure 1)**. It then moves down one strand of the DNA molecule and transcribes the nucleotide sequence, base by base, onto a complementary strand of RNA.

Figure 1
Transcription

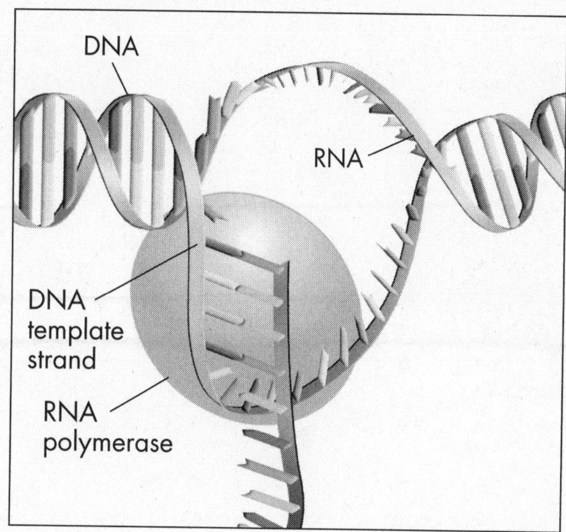

Once the strand of RNA is complete, it undergoes an editing process. Sections that do not code for amino acids to build proteins, called *introns*, are removed. The sections left, called *exons*, are joined together. This edited molecule of RNA is now a molecule of mRNA.

Next mRNA leaves the nucleus and enters the cytoplasm. There it binds with a ribosome. Ribosomes are small organelles found throughout the cytoplasm, which are made of ribosomal RNA (rRNA) and proteins. Every ribosome has a site to which mRNA binds.

What is the purpose and process of translation?

In the process of **translation**, the codons in mRNA are decoded into a series of amino acids that will make up a protein. A codon is a group of three nucleotides that specifies a particular amino acid. The decoding process involves molecules of transfer RNA (tRNA) that move through the cytoplasm. A tRNA molecule binds to both a specific amino acid and a codon of mRNA.

Study Tip

Think about the meanings of the words *transcription* and *translation*. To transcribe is to make a copy, and transcription is the process of copying the information in DNA into a molecule of mRNA. To translate is to change from one language to another. In translation, the coded information in mRNA is translated into a sequence of amino acids in a protein.

The structure of the tRNA molecule is important to its function. At one end of the molecule is a section that bonds to the amino acid. At the other end is an **anticodon**, which is a group of three nitrogenous bases that is complementary to an mRNA codon.

Translation begins when a ribosome attaches to a mRNA molecule. As each codon of the messenger RNA moves through the ribosome, the proper amino acid is brought into the ribosome by tRNA. The tRNA carries each amino acid to the ribosome according tho the coded message in messenger RNA. The ribosome joins together each amino acid. In this way the protein chain grows. When the ribosome reaches a stop codon, it falls away from the protein chain and the messenger RNA molecule. **Figure 2** on the next page illustrates the process of translation.

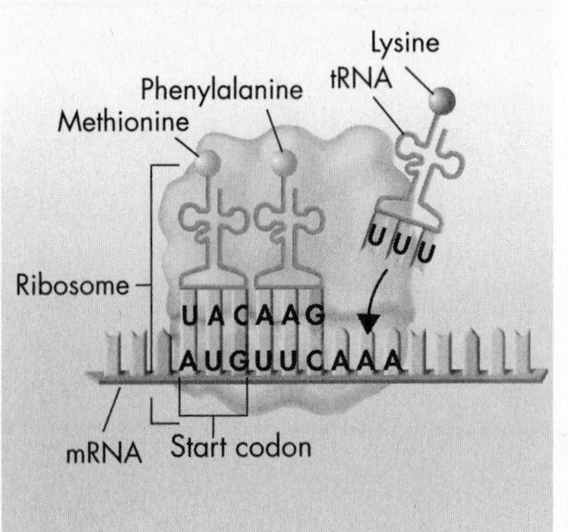

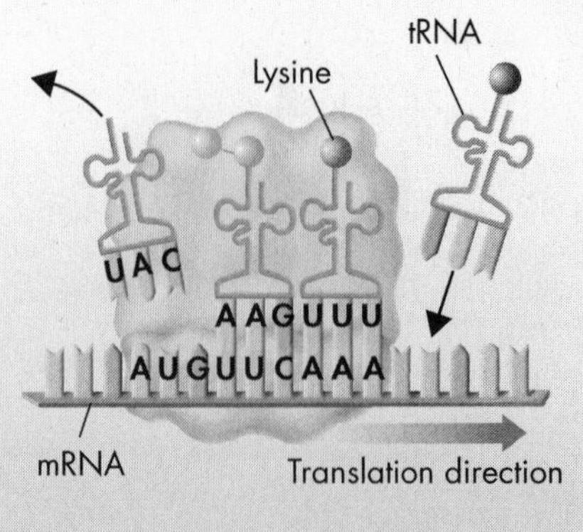

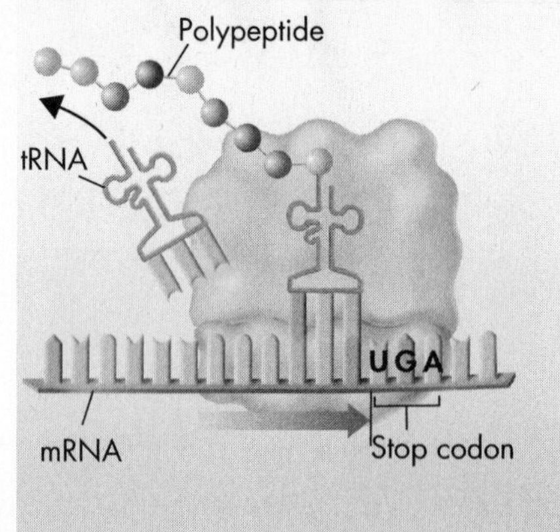

Figure 2
Translation

End-of-Course Assessment Review

1. **Identify** Which of the following is true of translation?
   - **A** It requires DNA and ribosomes.
   - **B** It takes place on ribosomes in the cytoplasm.
   - **C** It requires only ribosomal RNA (rRNA) and ribosomes.
   - **D** All the above

2. **Sequence** Which step of transcription occurs first?
   - **F** RNA polymerase slices a gene out of the DNA molecule.
   - **G** The two strands of DNA separate.
   - **H** RNA polymerase assembles nucleotides into RNA.
   - **J** RNA polymerase binds to a promoter.

3. **Compare and Contrast** Describe the similarities and differences in the structures of DNA and RNA.

4. **Explain** What is the purpose of translation and transcription?

5. **Use Models** Sketch a flow diagram beginning with a DNA molecule and indicating all of the major steps that occur during transcription and translation. Your diagram should end with a fully synthesized protein.

The Regulation of Gene Expression

TEKS 6D

Recognize that gene expression is a regulated process.

Vocabulary
gene expression
operon

What is gene expression?

During transcription, an active gene is transcribed into mRNA. Then during translation, mRNA is translated into a protein. All these steps—from the start of transcription to the assembly of a protein—are controlled and regulated by the processes of **gene expression**.

When cells divide during mitosis or binary fission, each daughter cell receives a complete copy of the organism's DNA. In multicellular organisms, cells have the same genetic information regardless of their location or function. If all cells have the same DNA, why does a muscle cell look and function so differently from a skin cell? Cells differ from one another and perform different tasks because of differences in gene expression. Some genes may be expressed in a muscle cell that are not expressed in a skin cell and vice versa. Also, different genes may be expressed in response to environmental factors or during different stages of an organism's life cycle.

Gene expression is also important in single-celled organisms. For example, different genes may be expressed at different times in response to changes in the environment.

How is gene expression regulated in prokaryotes?

Prokaryotic DNA contains **operons**, groups of genes that are regulated together. Operons are located next to two regulatory regions of DNA—a promoter and an operator. RNA polymerase binds to the promoter, which is a signal that shows RNA polymerase where to begin transcription. The operator is adjacent to the promoter and it controls the rate of transcription. A protein called a *repressor* can bind to the operator. If the repressor binds to the operator, then RNA polymerase cannot access the operon and transcription does not occur.

An example of an operon is the *lac* operon in the bacterium *E. coli*. This group of three genes must be turned on before the bacterium can use lactose as food. When lactose is not present in the bacterium's environment, the repressor binds to the operator. The protein blocks the movement of RNA polymerase along the DNA, and the operon is not transcribed into RNA. When lactose is present, however, the repressor binds to lactose instead of to the operator. Like a gate lifting across a road, the path of DNA is cleared for transcription to occur (see **Figure 1**).

Study Tip

To visualize the *lac* operon, draw a picture of a train stopped at a gate. Label the train "RNA polymerase," the gate "repressor," and the region of track under the gate "operator." The track represents the DNA that RNA polymerase transcribes.

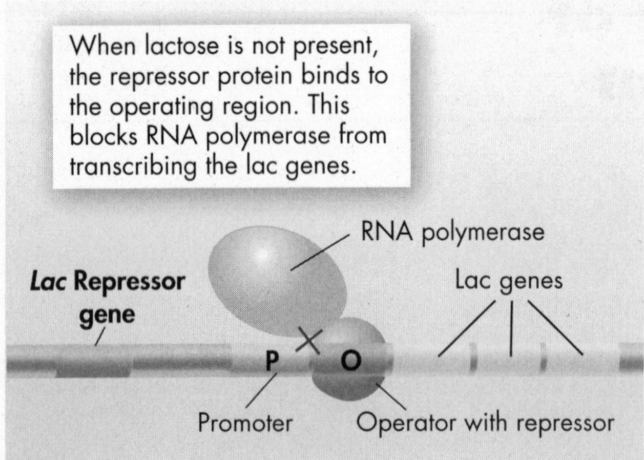

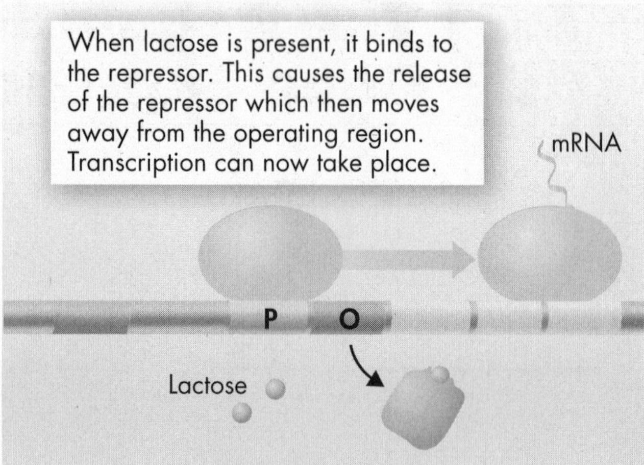

When lactose is present, it binds to the repressor. This causes the release of the repressor which then moves away from the operating region. Transcription can now take place.
mRNA
P
O
Lactose

Figure 1
Gene Expression in Prokaryotes

How is gene expression regulated in eukaryotes?

In eukaryotes, genes are rarely found in clusters that are activated by the same promoter. Many eukaryotic genes are preceded by a short region of DNA called the TATA box that positions RNA polymerase. Cells also regulate gene expression with DNA-binding proteins called *transcription factors* **(Figure 2).** There are many types of transcription factors. Each type of transcription factor affects gene expression in different ways. Some roles of transcription factors include opening tightly packed chromatin (which enhances transcription), attracting RNA polymerase, or blocking access to certain genes. In many cases a group of specific transcription factors must be present for RNA polymerase to attach to a binding site.

Figure 2
Gene Expression in Eukaryotes

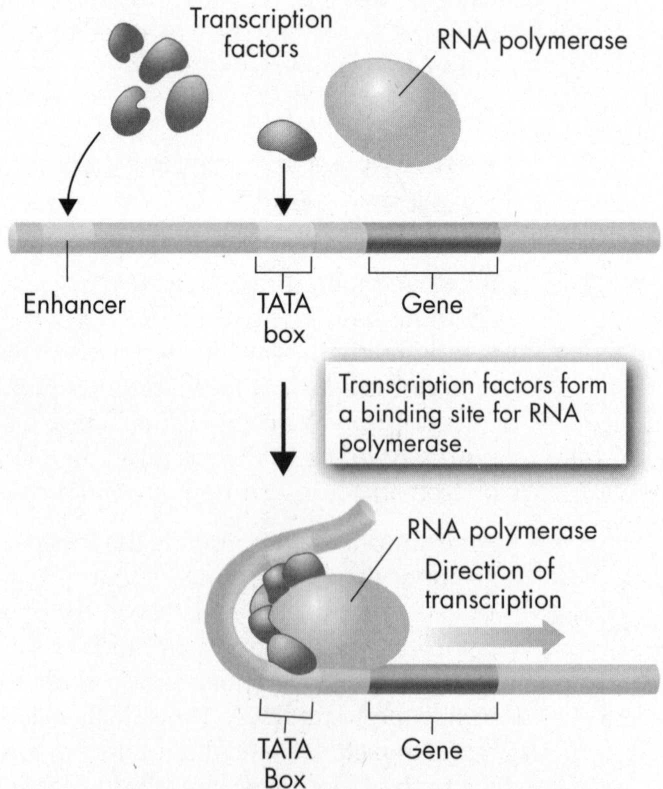

After transcription is finalized, other mechanisms could stop gene expression. For example, mRNA may be prevented from leaving the nucleus, or its stability could be affected. Without mRNA, translation cannot occur.

TEKS End-of-Course Assessment Review

1. Sequence Which event occurs first in a common process of gene expression in eukaryotes?

A A molecule of mRNA leaves the nucleus and enters the cytoplasm.

B RNA polymerase attaches to a gene and transcribes it.

C Transcription factors bind to DNA, forming a binding site for RNA polymerase.

D Transcription factors bind to mRNA, activating RNA polymerase.

2. Recognize When are the *lac* genes expressed?

F at all times

G at random, rare times

H when lactose is present in the environment

J when lactose is absent from the environment

3. Explain In a multicellular organism, why is it essential that gene expression is properly regulated in all cells?

4. Analyze What is the benefit of a regulating mechanism such as the *lac* operon?

Mutations

TEKS 6E

★ READINESS ★

Identify and illustrate changes in DNA and evaluate the significance of these changes.

Vocabulary
mutation
point mutation
frameshift mutation

What are mutations?

A **mutation** is a change to the structure or organization of DNA. A *gene mutation* involves a change to a single gene. A *chromosomal mutation* involves changes to the structure or organization of a chromosome.

Some mutations have little or no effect on an organism. Yet others can make a gene useless or harmful. For example, mutations that affect the cell cycle can lead to cancer. On rare occasions, a mutation can be beneficial. Beneficial mutations may alter the function of a protein in such a way that it makes an organism more fit to survive in its environment.

Mutations are most likely to occur during DNA replication prior to mitosis or meiosis. Some mutations occur due to environmental agents that damage DNA, such as radiation and some pollutants. Only mutations that occur during meiosis or in cells that undergo meiosis can be passed to offspring.

What are the effects of gene mutations?

A gene mutation that changes one base pair of a gene is called a **point mutation**. There are three types of point mutations: substitutions, insertions, and deletions.

Substitutions In a *substitution* mutation, one base pair in a gene is replaced with another base pair. A substitution mutation may be neutral if it does not change the protein that the gene codes for. For example, if a substitution mutation causes a codon to change from CUU to CUA, the finished protein will not be altered because both codons code for the amino acid leucine.

Other substitution mutations may be either beneficial or harmful, with a harmful effect the more common. These mutations do cause changes to proteins. For example, consider the substitution mutation shown in **Figure 1.** The mutation caused adenine to be placed in mRNA instead of guanine. The result is that the protein contains the amino acid histidine instead of arginine. A mutation such as this can have a significant effect on the health of an organism. For example, in one of the genes that codes for hemoglobin (a blood protein), the substitution of a thymine (T) for an adenine (A) causes a change to one amino acid. The altered hemoglobin is the cause of sickle cell disease.

Study Tip

To remember the types of point mutations and their effects, use sentences with three-lettered words as examples. A deletion mutation might change "The fat cat was old." to "Thf atc atw aso ld."

Figure 1
Substitution Mutation

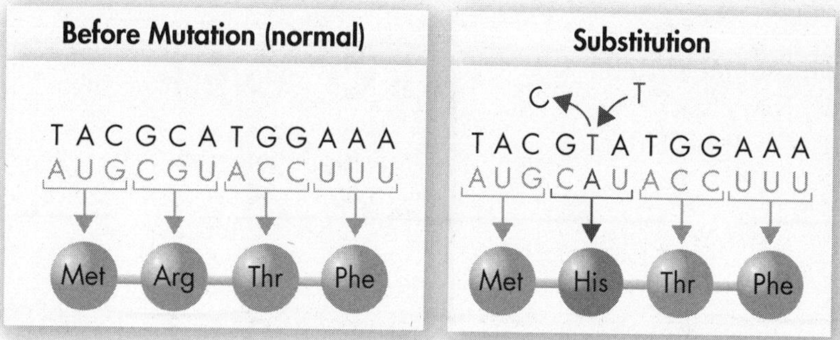

Insertions and Deletions In an *insertion* mutation, a base pair is added to the gene. In a *deletion* mutation, a base pair is removed from the gene. Insertion and deletion mutations usually have a drastic effect on the protein that the gene codes for. Consider the example shown in **Figure 2,** in which an additional uracil (U) becomes part of an mRNA molecule. Because codons are read in groups of three, all codons after the inserted uracil are translated differently. The result is a useless protein. Insertion and deletion mutations are also called **frameshift mutations** because they change the "reading frame" of codons.

Figure 2
Insertion Mutation

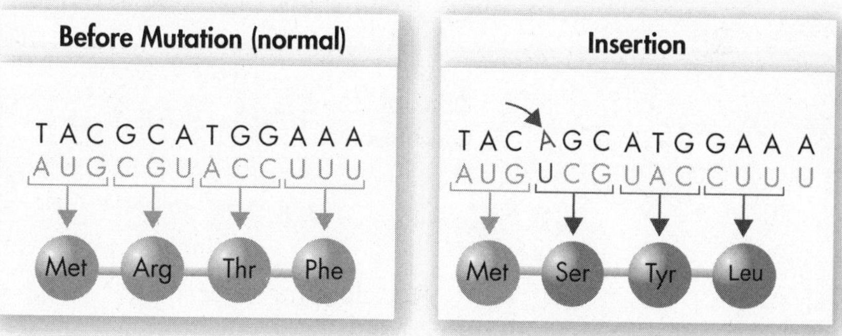

What are the effects of chromosomal mutations?

Chromosomal mutations may change the structure of chromosomes. A *deletion* is the removal of part of a chromosome, while a *duplication* is the addition of an extra copy of a section. Other chromosomal mutations change the positions of genes along one or more chromosomes. In an *inversion*, a set of genes reverses its position on a chromosome. In a *translocation*, sets of genes exchange positions on two nonhomologous chromosomes.

Much like gene mutations, chromosomal mutations can have a variety of effects. However, many chromosomal mutations are lethal to offspring that inherit them. A deletion may remove an essential set of genes from the genome. An inversion or translocation can disrupt proper gene expression, which often depends on the gene's position on the chromosome. **Figure 3** on the following page illustrates the four types of chromosomal mutations.

Figure 3
Chromosomal Mutations

Original Chromosome	
Original Chromosome: A B C D E F	Deletion: A C D E F
Original Chromosome: A B C D E F	Inversion: A E D C B F
Original Chromosome: A B C D E F	Translocation: A B C J K L D E F
Original Chromosome: A B C D E F	Duplication: A B B C D E F

TEKS End-of-Course Assessment Review

1. Identify Which type of mutation is shown in the illustration below?

Original Chromosome A B C D E F

Mutation

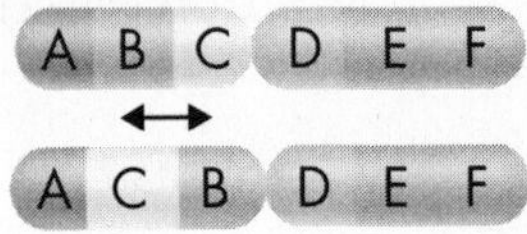

A deletion of a base pair

B duplication of part of a chromosome

C inversion of parts of a chromosome

D translocation of a base pair

2. Evaluate What factor most affects whether a mutation will be passed to offspring?

F the type of cell in which the mutation occurs

G whether the mutation is a gene mutation or chromosomal mutation

H whether or not the mutation is neutral

J the location of the mutation on the DNA molecule

3. Illustrate Compare the effects of the addition of one nucleotide, two nucleotides, and three nucleotides to a location in a gene. Include illustrations in your response.

Patterns of Inheritance

TEKS 6F

★ READINESS ★

Predict possible outcomes of various genetic combinations such as monohybrid crosses, dihybrid crosses, and non-Mendelian inheritance.

Vocabulary
allele
genotype
phenotype
heterozygous
homozygous
monohybrid cross
law of segregation
dihybrid cross
law of independent assortment

How do genetic combinations affect offspring?

In the mid 1800s, an Austrian monk named Gregor Mendel studied the inheritance of traits in pea plants. He proposed the idea that units he called factors control traits. Today Mendel's factors are called genes.

As Mendel proposed, a pea plant, like many organisms that reproduce sexually, has two versions of every gene. One copy is included in each of the two gametes (sperm and egg cells) that the plant receives from its parents. However, the two versions may not be identical. Different forms of a gene are called **alleles.** For example, the gene that controls the color of pea seeds has two alleles: yellow and green. A **genotype** is the genetic makeup of an organism. A **phenotype** is an organism's physical traits.

Mendel also concluded that when an organism has two different alleles for the same trait, only the dominant allele is expressed. This is called the *principle of dominance.* The allele that is not expressed is recessive. Mendel used capital letters to represent dominant alleles and lower case letters to represent recessive alleles. In pea plants, yellow seed color (*Y*) is dominant and green seed color (*y*) is recessive.

A genotype of two different alleles, such as *Yy*, is described as **heterozygous.** Organisms that are heterozygous for a trait are also called hybrids. A genotype with the same alleles, such as *YY* or *yy*, is **homozygous.** Seeds with both the heterozygous genotype (*Yy*) and the homozygous dominant genotype (*YY*) are yellow. Only homozygous recessive seeds (*yy*) are green.

Study Tip

The prefix *homo-* means "same", and *hetero-* means different. A homozygous genotype has two of the same alleles, while the heterozygous genotype has two different alleles.

How are genes inherited in a monohybrid cross?

A **monohybrid cross** is a cross of two organisms that are heterozygous for one trait. **Figure 1** on the next page shows how Punnett squares can help predict the outcome of a monohybrid cross. Each of the four possible outcomes is equally likely because of the **law of segregation**, which states that the two alleles segregate, or separate, during gamete formation. In this example, half of the gametes will contain the dominant (*Y*) allele and the other half will contain the recessive (*y*) allele.

Figure 1
Monohybrid Cross

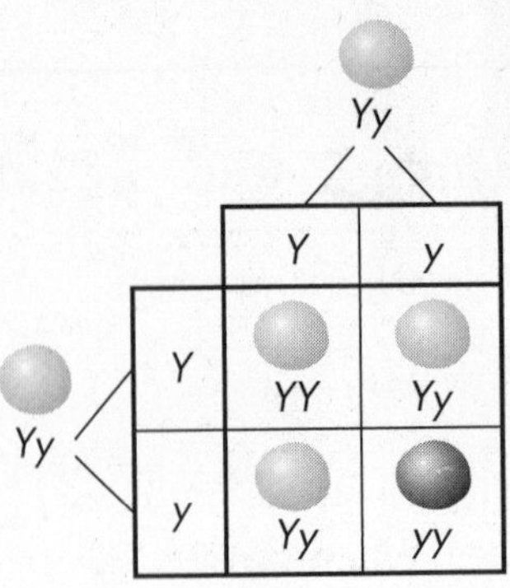

As the Punnett square shows, the genotypic ratio of the offspring is 1 *YY* : 2 *Yy* : 1 *yy*, or 1:2:1. It also shows the phenotypic ratio of 3 plants with yellow peas to 1 plant with green peas. This means that if 100 pea seeds are harvested after a monohybrid cross, it can be predicted that about 75 seeds will grow into plants with yellow peas and about 25 seeds will grow into plants with green peas.

How are genes inherited in a dihybrid cross?

A **dihybrid cross** is the cross of two organisms that are hybrids for two traits. Notice in **Figure 2** that there are 16 possible genotypes for the offspring, but only four phenotypes. The phenotypic ratio is 9:3:3:1.

The 16 genotypes are equally likely to occur because the way that one pair of genes separates does not influence how the other pair separates. The **law of independent assortment** states that the alleles for two traits, such as pea color and pea shape, segregate independently of one another. The law applies to many pairs of traits. However, some traits are linked, meaning their alleles do not segregate independently.

Figure 2
Dihybrid Cross

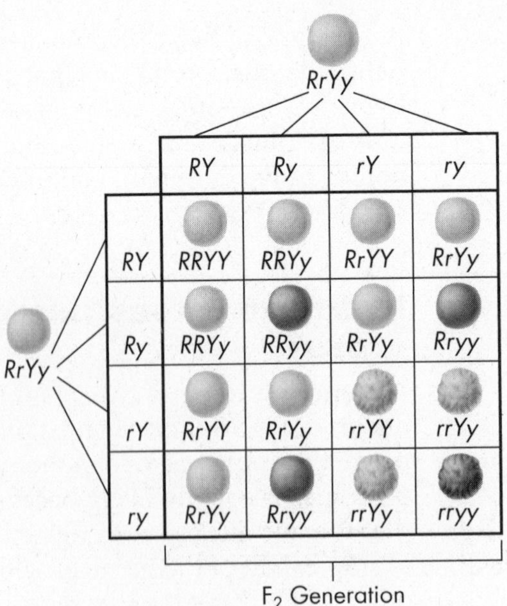

What are some other patterns of inheritance?

Many traits are expressed or inherited in ways that differ, at least partially, from Mendel's explanation. Here are some examples.

Incomplete Dominance Some alleles are only partially dominant over recessive alleles. In snapdragons, for example, the allele for red flowers (*R*) is partly dominant over the allele for white flowers (*r*). The heterozygous genotype (*Rr*) has pink flowers.

Codominance Sometimes two alleles are expressed in the heterozygous genotype. In chickens, the alleles for black feathers and white feathers are both expressed in the heterozygous genotype. These chickens have a mix of black feathers and white feathers.

Multiple Alleles Many genes have more than two alleles. Human blood type, for example, is affected by three alleles for the same gene. The alleles for type A and type B blood are codominant. The allele for type O blood is recessive to the alleles for type A and B.

Polygenic Traits Many traits are determined by multiple genes. Height and skin color in humans are examples of polygenic traits.

Maternal Inheritance Chloroplasts and mitochondria both contain genes that are passed from generation to generation only in egg cells. Your mitochondrial genes are the same genes found in your mother's mitochondria.

TEKS End-of-Course Assessment Review

1. **Identify** A cross of two pea plants produces 40 seeds. Among the plants grown from these seeds, 29 plants produce round peas (*R*) and 8 plants produce wrinkled peas (*r*). The remaining plants did not mature. What are the genotypes of the parent plants?

   A *RR* and *rr* **C** *Rr* and *Rr*

   B *Rr* and *rr* **D** *RR* and *Rr*

2. **Classify** In horses, hair color is determined by a single gene. In a hair pattern called roan, white hairs are evenly distributed with hairs of a darker color. This observation suggests which type of inheritance?

   F dihybrid cross

   G codominance

   H incomplete dominance

   J polygenic inheritance

3. **Predict** In a certain type of snail, brown shell color (*B*) is dominant over cream color (*b*). What is the predicted phenotypic ratio among the offspring from a monohybrid cross for shell color? Draw a Punnett square to help find the answer.

6G Meiosis and Sexual Reproduction

TEKS 6G

Recognize the significance of meiosis to sexual reproduction.

Vocabulary
sexual reproduction
meiosis
tetrad
crossing-over

How is meiosis significant to sexual reproduction?

In **sexual reproduction**, a sperm cell from an adult male and an egg cell from an adult female unite to form a fertilized egg, or zygote. The zygote then develops into an adult organism. Sperm cells and egg cells are called gametes. Gametes are haploid cells produced by the process of meiosis. During meiosis, a diploid cell divides twice, resulting in four haploid cells. Only gamete-producing cells undergo meiosis.

Haploid cells have just one chromosome of each type. They have half the number of chromosomes as other cells in the body called diploid cells. Diploid cells have a matching pair of chromosomes, one set that was inherited from the sperm cell and one set that was inherited from the egg cell. Two chromosomes of the same type are called homologous chromosomes.

Homologous chromosomes are pairs of chromosomes that have corresponding genes. Human body cells have 46 chromosomes, or 23 pairs of homologous chromosomes. A human receives 23 chromosomes from one parent and 23 chromosomes from the other parent. The diploid number for humans is 46, and the haploid number is 23.

Figure 1 Meiosis

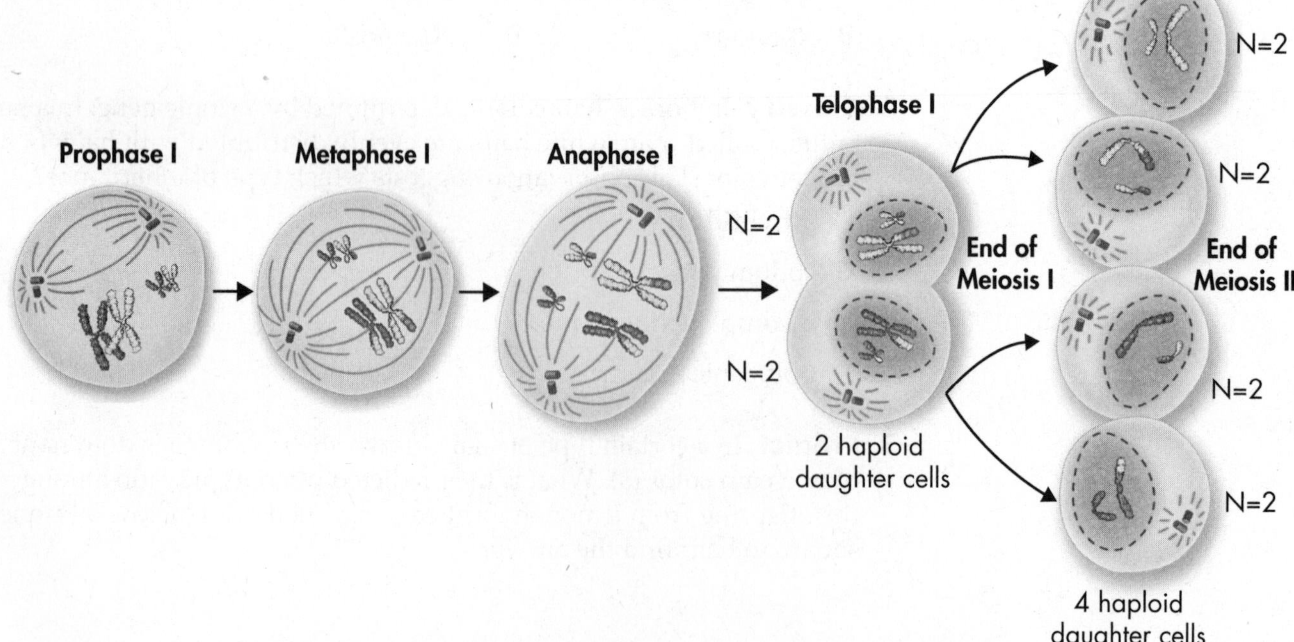

What are the stages of meiosis?

During meiosis, a cell undergoes two separate cell divisions, called meiosis I and meiosis II. The stages of meiosis are shown in **Figure 1.** In males, the divisions produce four sperm cells from the parent cell. In females, one egg cell and three polar bodies are produced. Only the egg cell is involved in reproduction. Following is a brief description of the stages of meiosis I and meiosis II.

Prophase I Each chromosome is made of two identical chromatids because of DNA replication that occurred during interphase. As with prophase in mitosis, chromosomes uncoil and the spindle apparatus forms.

Homologous chromosomes join together side-by-side. The pair of chromosomes is called a **tetrad**. At this point, **crossing-over** may occur, in which a section of one chromosome exchanges places with the complementary section on its homologous chromosome. Crossing-over is significant to sexual reproduction because it produces new combinations of alleles.

Figure 2
Crossing-Over

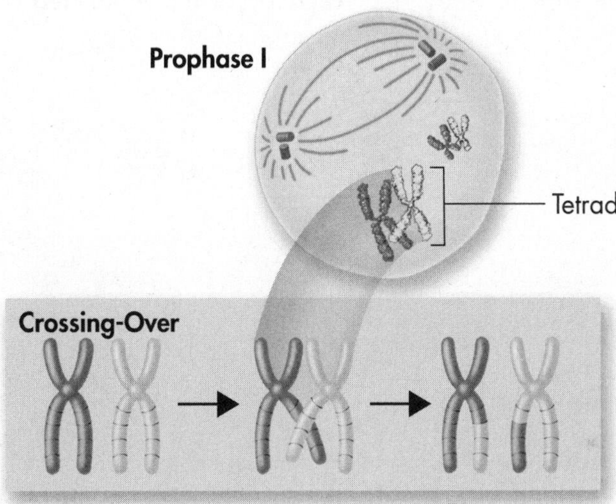

Metaphase I The tetrads align along the middle of the cell. Fibers of the spindle apparatus are joined to each tetrad and prepare to separate them. The orientation and order of each tetrad are independent of the other tetrads, which is called independent assortment. As a result, the gametes that form from meiosis contain a random combination of the haploid number of chromosomes. For example, by chance the 23 chromosomes in a haploid human an egg cell may contain 8 chromosomes inherited from the woman's mother and 15 chromosomes inherited from the woman's father.

Anaphase I The spindle apparatus separates the homologous chromosomes.

Telophase I and Cytokinesis A new nuclear membrane forms around each group of chromosomes. During cytokinesis, the cell divides into two daughter cells. This process forms two haploid cells, each with one chromosome from each homologous pair. However, each chromosome still consists of two chromatids that are separated during meiosis II.

Study Tip

Sketch a diagram of the phases of meiosis I and meiosis II. Use different colors to track the chromosomes.

Meiosis II In prophase II, the spindle apparatus forms and attaches to the chromosomes. In metaphase II, the chromosomes are aligned in the middle of the cell. In anaphase II, the chromosomes separate into individual chromatids. In telophase II and cytokinesis, the nuclei form and the cell divides. The end products are four haploid daughter cells with a variety of allele combinations that may be passed on to the next generation.

TEKS End-of-Course Assessment Review

1. Identify Which choice describes the illustration below?

A prophase I; replicated chromosomes pair with homologous chromosomes

B metaphase II; chromosomes line up in the center of the cell

C anaphase II; paired chromatids separate

D telophase I: separated chromosomes gather at either end of a cell

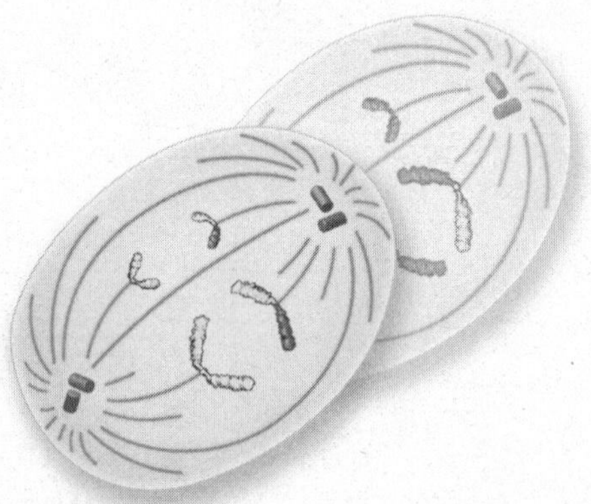

2. Analyze Typically genes found on the same chromosome are inherited together. This phenomenon is known as gene linkage. Which statement accurately describes the relationship between gene linkage and independent assortment?

F Genes do not assort independently, but chromosomes do.

G Chromosomes do not assort independently, but genes do.

H Both genes and chromosomes assort independently.

J Neither genes nor chromosomes assort independently.

3. Apply How is meiosis significant to sexual reproduction?

DNA Analysis

TEKS 6H

Describe how techniques such as DNA fingerprinting, genetic modifications, and chromosomal analysis are used to study the genomes of organisms.

Vocabulary
genome
chromosomal analysis
karyotype
DNA fingerprinting
genetic modification

What is a genome?

A **genome** is the set of genetic information that an organism carries in its DNA. Modern technology allows genomes to be studied more closely than ever before. In 2003, an international group of scientists completed the Human Genome Project, in which the group determined the sequence of nucleotides in all the genes of the human genome—about 3 billion base pairs. The results are helping scientists explain how genes control traits and identify the cause of particular genetic diseases.

How can chromosomal analysis be used to study a genome?

Chromosomal analysis is the detailed study of the chromosomes of a cell. It is an important starting point when one is studying the genome of a particular organism. It can also identify some genetic abnormalities and predict the likelihood of some diseases that have a genetic component.

A **karyotype** is a visual display of all the chromosomes in an organism's genome, arranged by decreasing size. To produce a karyotype, a researcher photographs chromosomes in a cell during mitosis and then arranges the photographs by size. Karyotypes can reveal genetic abnormalities in an individual, such as an extra chromosome or a chromosome that is missing a piece.

Figure 1 shows a human karyotype. Note that there are 23 pairs of homologous chromosomes—22 pairs of autosomes and one pair of sex chromosomes (in this case, XY).

Figure 1
Human Karyotype

1 2 3 4 5 6 7 8
9 10 11 12 13 14 15 16
17 18 19 20 21 22 X Y
23

How can DNA fingerprinting be used to study a genome?

DNA fingerprinting is a technique that compares specific sections of two or more DNA samples. The technique is used for a wide variety of purposes including forensics, studying the migration patterns of animals, and determining evolutionary relationships.

DNA fingerprinting can be particularly useful in determining if a particular person was at a crime scene. Every person's genome contains sections of repeated DNA sequences between genes. What varies from person to person is the number of times these sequences are repeated. When the sections are compared, the results can show, with a high degree of certainty, whether DNA samples came from the same person, from people who are closely related, or from people who are not related at all. One common method of DNA fingerprinting—gel electrophoresis—is shown in **Figure 2.**

1. Restriction enzymes are used to cut DNA samples into fragments.
2. The fragments are placed at one end of a gel, and an electric field is applied to them in a process called gel electrophoresis.
3. Because DNA is a negatively charged molecule, the fragments move toward the positive end. Shorter fragments move at a faster pace than longer fragments.
4. Radioactive probes are applied to the gel. The probes label the sections with highly variable regions. This produces a banding pattern that can be compared between the samples.

Figure 2
Producing a DNA Fingerprint

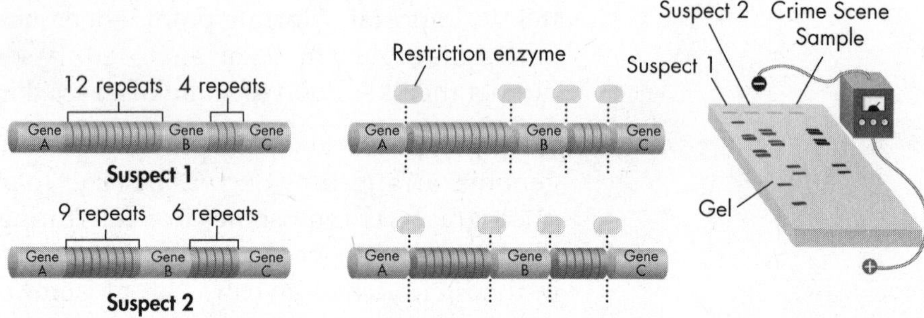

How can genetic modification be used to study a genome?

Genetic modification, which is also called genetic engineering, involves directly changing the genome of an organism. The process often involves the use of recombinant DNA (rDNA), in which a gene from one organism is introduced into the genome of another organism. In the new genome, the transferred gene produces the same protein as in the original genome. Genetic modification has given researchers ample opportunities to discover how particular genes function when isolated from their genome.

An organism that undergoes genetic modification is called a genetically modified organism, or GMO. Today, GMOs include many farm crops, such as corn, soybeans, and alfalfa. These plants received genes from other organisms that provide resistance to pests, drought, or other stresses.

 •

Study Tip

Recall that the same genetic code is used in all organisms. The common genetic code makes all of these DNA technologies possible, especially genetic modification.

In addition, many animals have undergone genetic modification, including mice used for laboratory experiments. Genetically modified salmon could be the first genetically modified animal to be approved for human consumption. The genetically modified salmon grow faster and larger than other salmon.

Another use of GMOs is the production of medicines, sometimes called *pharming*. In one example of pharming, a gene for the production of a useful substance, such as human insulin, is transferred to a strain of bacteria. The bacteria then produce insulin, which is collected and purified for human use.

GMOs are controversial. Some critics are concerned that introduced genes could spread to wild plants and animals and introduce undesired characteristics. Proponents argue that GM foods allow people to produce more food for the growing human population.

TEKS End-of-Course Assessment Review

1. **Apply Concepts** Nondisjunction is an error that occurs during meiosis when a gamete doesn't receive a copy of one chromosome. Which technique could be used to reveal this abnormality?
   - **A** karyotyping
   - **B** DNA fingerprinting
   - **C** genetic modification
   - **D** gel electrophoresis

2. **Infer** A type of GMO is a crop plant known as *Bt* corn. The corn contains a gene from a bacterium that makes the corn resistant to pests. The pest resistance is produced by
   - **F** bacteria.
   - **G** the natural proteins of the crop plant.
   - **H** the production of a single bacterial protein.
   - **J** the production of several bacterial proteins.

3. **Contrast** Describe the differences between DNA fingerprinting, chromosomal analysis, and genetic modification.

4. **Apply** How could DNA fingerprinting be used in a criminal investigation?

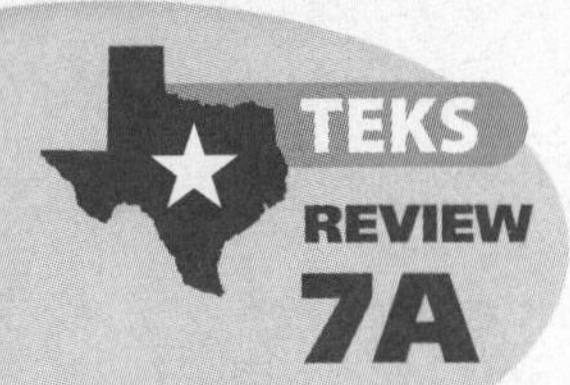

Evidence of Common Ancestry

TEKS 7A

★ READINESS ★

Analyze and evaluate how evidence of common ancestry among groups is provided by the fossil record, biogeography, and homologies, including anatomical, molecular, and developmental.

Vocabulary
fossil
biogeography
homologous structure
vestigial structure

What is common ancestry?

Common ancestry is the concept that a group of closely related species are all descended with some modifications from the same ancestor. Descent with modification is the idea that living species have descended—with changes due to adaptation and natural selection—from species that lived before them. Over many generations, adaptation can lead to successful species evolving into new species. As species change over time, they may exploit new or different niches or thrive in different habitats. For example, groups of ancient jawless fishes gave rise to the jawless fishes of today and to the ancestors of the incredible array of fishes with jaws.

Identifying common ancestry is important to piecing together the history of life on Earth. Scientists analyze a wide variety of evidence to determine groups of organisms that have recent common ancestors.

How does the fossil record provide evidence of common ancestry among groups?

Fossils are the preserved remains or traces of ancient organisms. When fossils are found in layers of sedimentary rock that can be dated, the history of a particular group can be studied through the examination of deeper and deeper rock layers. The fossil record can be used to evaluate how species have changed from their ancestors. For example, fossils of early jawless fishes have been found in sedimentary rock more than 560 million years old; fossils of sharks and rays have been found in rock 530 million years old; and fossils of fishes similar to modern bony fishes have been found in rock 160 million years old. These findings provide evidence about the order in which certain features evolved over time.

Intermediate forms found in the fossil record can provide evidence of relationships among living organisms and common ancestors that looked and lived quite differently. For example, intermediate form fossils of a mammal with reduced hindlimbs—related to both modern day whales and an ancient ancestor who lived on land—provide evidence that whales evolved from an ancient extinct terrestrial mammal.

On a greater scale, the fossil record enables biologists to hypothesize about how different groups are related to one another. Those hypotheses are summarized in the tree of life, which shows the lines of descent that link different groups of organisms **(Figure 1)**.

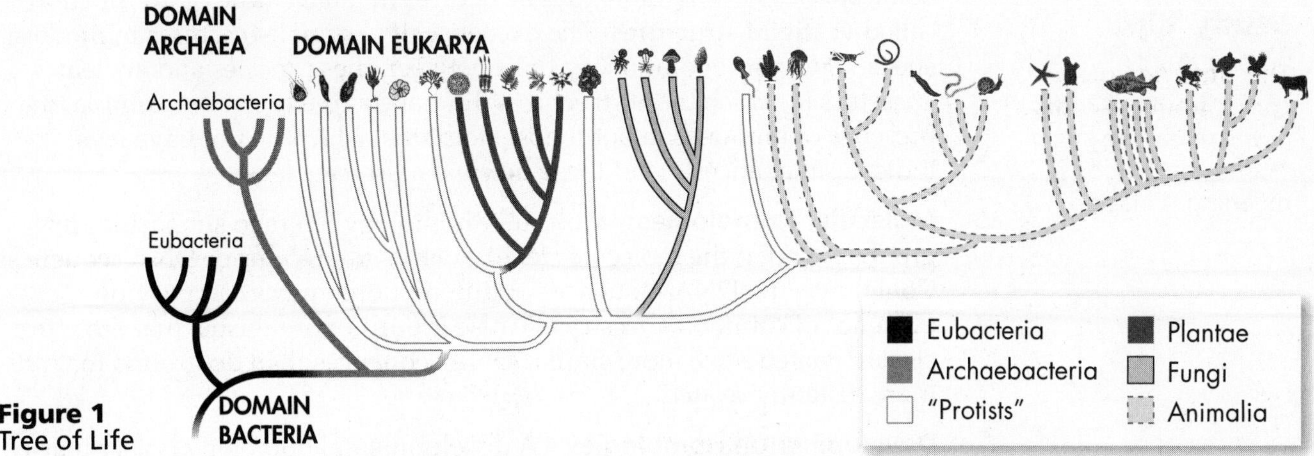

Figure 1
Tree of Life

How does biogeography provide evidence of common ancestry among groups?

Biogeography is the study of where species live now and where species and their ancestors lived in the past. Biogeography can provide clues to common ancestry in two ways. First, it can provide evidence as to how closely related species differentiated under different selection pressures. Darwin's finches, which are found only on the Galápagos Islands, exemplify how many species can evolve from the same ancestor through the process of geographical isolation. Geographical isolation occurs when members of a species are separated from each other and the separate populations experience different selection pressures.

Biogeography can also provide evidence as to how distantly related groups have evolved similar traits under similar selection pressures. For example, grazing animals, such as cattle, zebras, and llamas, evolved on temperate grasslands in different parts of the world. Their biogeography suggests that many of their similar traits, such as teeth for grinding grass and long legs, evolved long after they diverged from a common ancestor.

How do homologies provide evidence of common ancestry among groups of organisms?

Species with a common ancestor often share similar characteristics. This relationship is called a homology. Homologies between species can be used as evidence of common ancestry. Scientists often look at anatomical, molecular, and developmental homologies.

Anatomical Homologies Similar anatomical structures, such as limbs or organs, can also be evidence of common ancestry. For example, the forelimb bones of vertebrates that live on land all have some common structures. These common structures are evidence of a common ancestry dating back to fishes. Structures, such as forelimb bones, that show similarities between groups of organisms, are called **homologous structures**. The more similar the homologous structures, the more closely related the species. For example, the forelimbs of an alligator and a chicken are more similar in structure than those of an alligator and a horse. This is evidence that reptiles and birds have a more recent common ancestry than do reptiles and mammals.

Study Tip

The word *homology* comes from the roots *homo*, meaning "same," and *logos*, meaning "relation."

Some species have homologous structures that have little or no function, called **vestigial structures**. The existence of vestigial structures in modern species suggests evolutionary links between these species and ancient ancestors in which these structures did have a function. For example, the presence of hipbones in bottlenose dolphins, which do not have legs, indicates that ancestors of these dolphins did have legs.

Molecular Homologies Molecular homology refers to similarities in groups found at the molecular level, such as in proteins or DNA sequences. Comparing the DNA sequences of different organisms can provide evidence of common ancestry because groups of organisms that are more closely related have more similar DNA sequences than do groups that are more distantly related.

Developmental Homologies A developmental homology is a similarity in a stage of embryonic development. These similarities have been noted in vertebrates and even in plant embryos. If embryos of different groups have similar structures during the same stage of development, it is likely that the groups have a common ancestry.

TEKS End-of-Course Assessment Review

1. Analyze Why are homologous arm bones evidence for common ancestry among vertebrate groups?

- **A** because the common ancestor likely passed the traits for arm bones to its descendants
- **B** because the arm bones show how two closely related organisms can have different structures
- **C** because the arm bones show how ancient organisms were more complex than modern organisms
- **D** because the arm bones show that fossil record is true and accurate

2. Evaluate Scientists have observed many close similarities in the DNA sequences of whales and dolphins. This observation is evidence for which idea?

- **F** Whales are ancestors of modern dolphins.
- **G** Whales and dolphins both evolved from a relatively recent common ancestor.
- **H** Whales and dolphins are members of the same species.
- **J** Whales and dolphins can breed with one another to produce a new species.

3. Apply Concepts A scientist studies two organisms with many similar traits. He hypothesizes that they are closely related, although they lived in different areas of the world. But a comparison of their DNA sequences reveals that they are actually distantly related. How could biogeography explain these findings?

Evolution and the Fossil Record

TEKS 7B

Analyze and evaluate scientific explanations concerning any data of sudden appearance, stasis, and sequential nature of groups in the fossil record.

Vocabulary
index fossil
adaptive radiation
punctuated equilibrium
gradualism

What are the scientific explanations concerning data of the sequential nature of groups in the fossil record?

Most of the fossil record is distributed in layers of sedimentary rock. These rock layers accumulate over time. Deeper rock layers, and the fossils within them, are older than layers closer to the surface and the fossils within them. To draw conclusions about the evolution of a species or a group of species, scientists study fossils of their ancestors through sequential rock layers.

Scientists use index fossils to help them decipher the fossil record. **Index fossils** are fossils of species that are easily recognizable, that lived during a specific geologic time span, and that had a wide geographic range. These fossils help scientists date the age of rock layers and other fossils in different locations.

Figure 1
Index Fossils

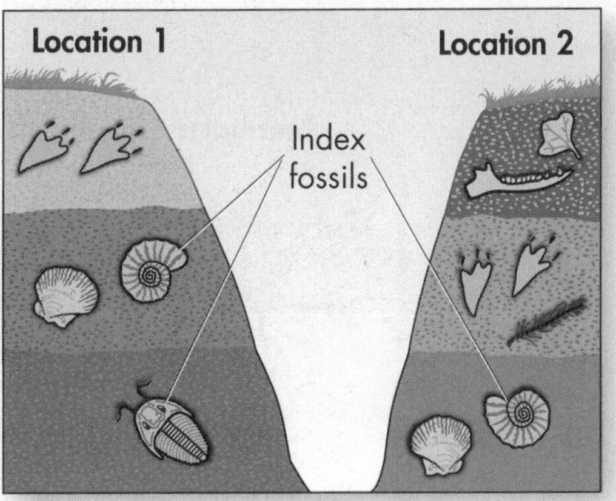

The process of adaptive radiation also explains the sequential nature of groups in the fossil record. In **adaptive radiation**, several diversely adapted species evolve from a common ancestor. Adaptive radiation typically occurs when a species is introduced to an unpopulated area, such as a recently formed volcanic island. Or it may occur when the environment changes suddenly and many species go extinct at once, opening niches for the survivors. Over time natural selection and other evolutionary mechanisms lead to the emergence of many new species. The mass extinction of 65 million years ago, during which all the dinosaurs died, allowed for the adaptive radiation of mammals.

What are the scientific explanations concerning data of sudden appearance in the fossil record?

Fossils that represent a new species may appear suddenly in the fossil record. (The term *suddenly* is relative and, in the case of fossil evidence, could mean hundreds of thousands of years.) To explain many of these species, scientists have inferred that their immediate ancestors are missing from the fossil record. The fossil record is incomplete for several reasons. Only a small fraction of organisms die in ways, or in places, that enable them to become fossilized. Natural geologic processes such as erosion and mountain building can change or reorder sedimentary rock layers. Where these processes occur, the fossil record may be confused or even destroyed.

Another explanation for the sudden appearance of species is a model of evolution called punctuated equilibrium. As shown in **Figure 2, punctuated equilibrium** describes a pattern of evolution in which long stable periods are interrupted by brief periods of more rapid change. In this model, the amount of genetic change increases rapidly and leaves little evidence of transitional forms in the fossil record. Punctuated equilibrium may occur when small populations become isolated from larger ones or after mass extinctions when surviving organisms fill new niches.

Another model of evolution is called gradualism. **Gradualism** is the evolution of a species by gradual accumulation of small genetic changes over long periods of time. Gradualism explains the appearance of new species as a slow and steady process taking millions of years. Both gradualism and punctuated equilibrium are accepted as valid models of evolution. Species may evolve by either of these processes, depending on the selection pressures to which they are subjected.

Figure 2
Punctuated Equilibrium and Gradualism

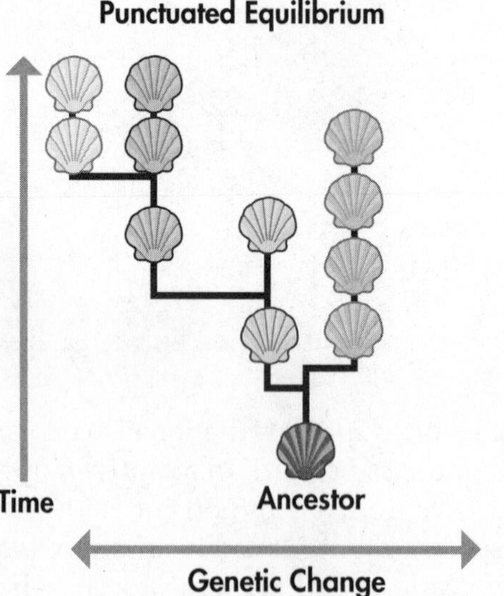

Punctuated equilibrium involves stable periods interrupted by rapid changes.

Gradualism

Time

Ancestor

Genetic Change

Gradualism involves a slow, steady change in a particular line of descent.

Study Tip

Remember that in *stasis*, things *stay* the same.

What are the scientific explanations concerning data of stasis in the fossil record?

Stasis occurs when the structure of a species in the fossil record does not change over a long period of time (though genetic changes may still be occurring). Horseshoe crabs are an example of organisms whose structure have stayed the same for a very long time. Stasis in the fossil record is linked to the evolutionary model of punctuated equilibrium. In this model, stasis in the fossil record is normal and might appear for long spans of time until it is suddenly broken by a period of dramatic change. These periods of rapid evolution show a large number of new species in the fossil record.

TEKS End-of-Course Assessment Review

1. Evaluate A scientist discovers a fossil of an ancient reptile. The reptile species appears suddenly in the fossil record. According to the evolutionary model of punctuated equilibrium, what is the most likely explanation for its sudden appearance?

A The fossil record concerning this species is complete.

B The species evolved relatively quickly from its immediate ancestor.

C The species evolved very slowly and gradually over millions of years.

D Fossils readily form in the region where the species lived.

2. Analyze How do scientists explain the incompleteness of the fossil record?

F Geological events such as erosion might confuse or even destroy parts of the fossil record.

G Evolution occurs only after a species has existed for millions of years, so many fossils have been lost.

H The fossil record contains only animals and no plants.

J Fossils are the remains of organisms that have recently died.

3. Explain Sixty-five million years ago, all dinosaurs and many other species went extinct. The adaptive radiation of mammals helps explain which observation of the fossil record after that mass extinction?

A a rapid increase in mammal diversity

B stasis among certain mammal species

C a gradual decrease in mammal diversity

D a rapid decrease in the size of mammals

4. Evaluate How do scientists use stasis in the fossil record as evidence for evolution of species?

5. Contrast Gradualism and punctuated equilibrium are two models that explain the appearance of new species in the fossil record. Describe how these models are different.

Natural Selection and Population Change

TEKS 7C

Analyze and evaluate how natural selection produces change in populations, not individuals.

Vocabulary
population
adaptation
fitness
natural selection
directional selection
stabilizing selection
disruptive selection

What is natural selection?

A **population** is a group of individuals of the same species who interbreed. Individuals in a population have varying traits. For example, some hawks may have sharper eyesight that allows them to capture more prey. A variation that makes an organism more successful in its environment is called an **adaptation.** Individuals with adaptations that help them survive and reproduce in their environment have high fitness. **Fitness** refers to an organism's ability to survive and reproduce in its environment.

Although individual variation is at the root of natural selection, populations evolve by natural selection. **Natural selection** is a process in which organisms with adaptations best suited to their environment leave more offspring than other organisms. Because these organisms produce more offspring, their genetic variations become more prevalent in a population and the population changes, or evolves.

In **Figure 1,** you can see the conditions under which natural selection occur. These snails have an inherited variation that affects their fitness. Snails with blunt shells are less likely to be eaten and are more likely to pass their genes to offspring than snails with pointed shells. Over time, snails with blunt shells will become more prevalent in the population.

Figure 1
Natural Selection

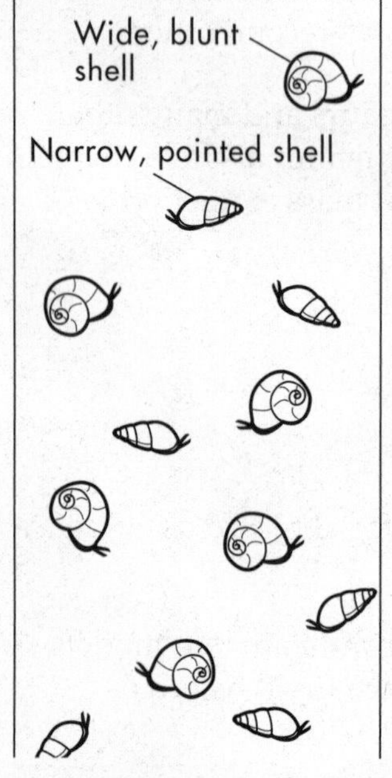

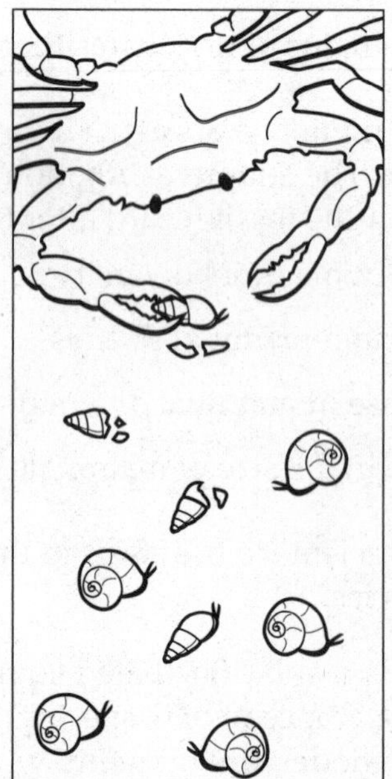
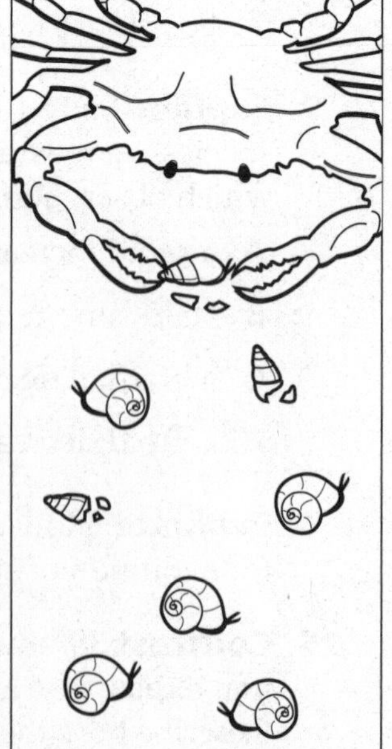
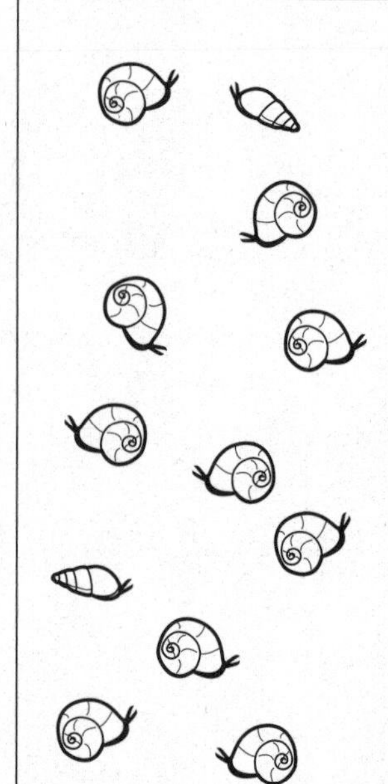

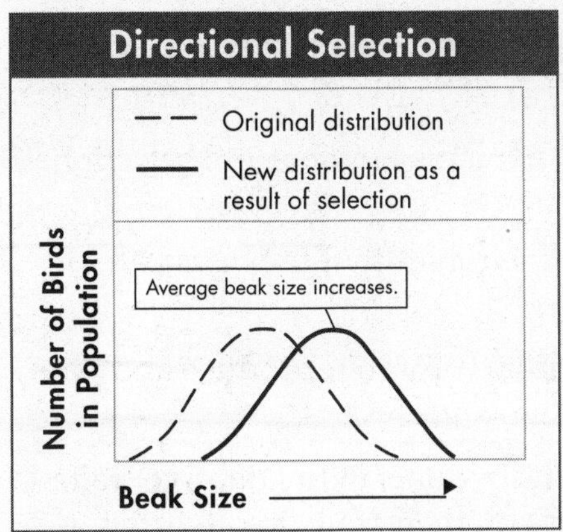

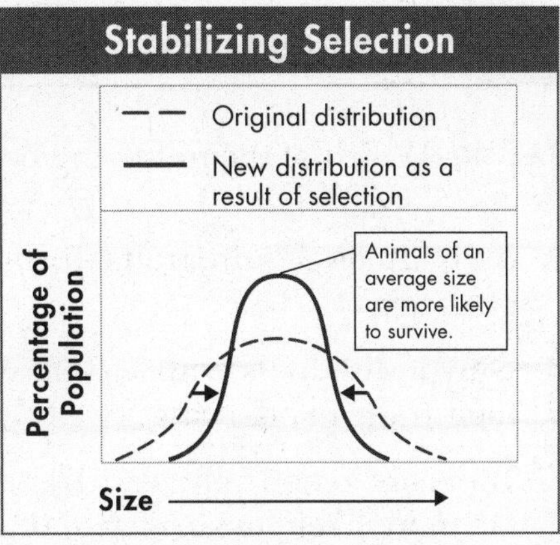

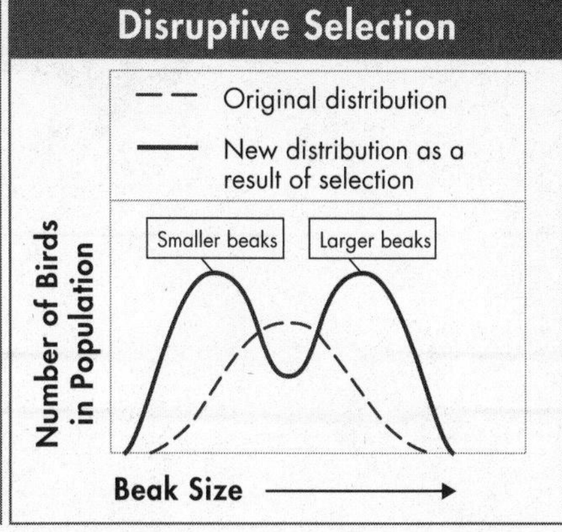

Figure 2
Different Types of Selection

How does natural selection produce changes in populations, not individuals?

Natural selection can occur in a variety of ways. Natural selection on a trait controlled by a single gene with two alleles can cause one allele to increase and the other allele to decrease. Polygenic traits are more complicated. Natural selection on polygenic traits can occur as directional selection, stabilizing selection, or disruptive selection. As shown in **Figure 2**, each of these ways causes a distinct type of change to a population.

Directional selection occurs when individuals with a particular phenotype have an advantage in their environment. Often a single gene controls the trait. In the graph above, birds at one end of the curve have a higher fitness than birds in the middle or at the other end. The range of phenotypes shifts because birds with larger beaks are more successful at surviving and reproducing than birds with small or medium-sized beaks. As a result, the average beak size increases in each generation.

Stabilizing selection occurs when extremes in phenotypes give individuals in the population a disadvantage. Often these traits are polygenic—controlled by multiple genes. An example is the body size of an organism. For most animals, very large or very small bodies are not favorable. This provides the population with a stable range of sizes, often with the mean size being the most common. This situation keeps the center of the curve at its current position, but it narrows the curve overall.

Disruptive selection occurs when extreme phenotypes for a trait are adaptive. For example, if beaks of an intermediate size are a disadvantage for survival, birds with either small or large beaks are more likely to survive and reproduce. Disruptive selection acts against individuals of an intermediate type. If the pressure of natural selection is strong and lasts long enough, this situation can cause the single curve to split into two. In other words, disruptive selection produces two distinct phenotypes. In the graph above (right), the population is composed of birds with two distinct beak sizes, small or large.

Study Tip

Remember that for natural selection to occur, there must be genetic variation in a population and a struggle for survival.

1. **Define** Which of the following best explains how natural selection occurs?

   A Individuals acquire traits during their lives that they pass on to offspring.

   B Only individuals with adaptive traits want to reproduce and pass their traits to offspring.

   C Traits are genetically based, and individuals with adaptive traits are more likely to survive and pass on their traits to offspring.

   D When organisms reproduce, they pass along only their most useful traits to offspring.

2. **Analyze** Based on the data in graphs A and B, which type of natural selection has occurred in the crab population from 1950 to 1990?

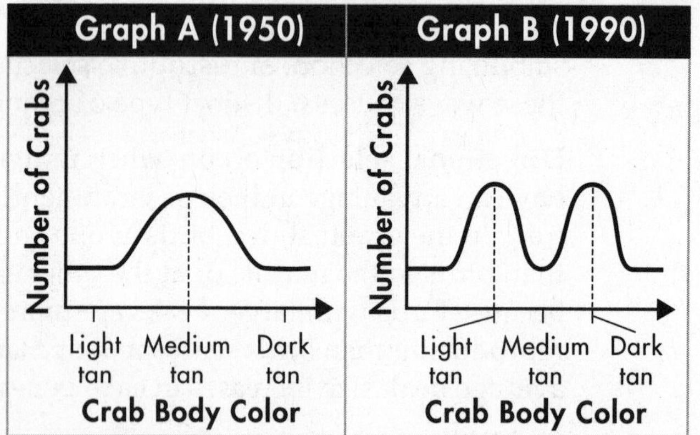

   F distributed selection

   G directional selection

   H disruptive selection

   J stabilizing selection

3. **Evaluate** A grasshopper population has an allele for color that produces green grasshoppers and another allele that produces brown grasshoppers. The numbers of green and brown grasshoppers change from year to year based on the weather. During rainy years, there are more green grasshoppers than brown ones. During years of drought, there are more brown grasshoppers than green ones. Why do you think this is the case? How do you think the grasshopper population would change after several rainy years?

Natural Selection and Fitness

TEKS 7D

Analyze and evaluate how the elements of natural selection, including inherited variation, the potential of a population to produce more offspring than can survive, and a finite supply of environmental resources, result in differential reproductive success.

What causes inherited variation among individuals in a population?

Inherited variation refers to the genetic differences among individuals in a population, such as body size or fur color. Inherited variation can be caused by mutations in DNA that affect the way genes are expressed. Other causes include crossing-over and the independent assortment of chromosomes that occur during meiosis. Variations can also be introduced when individuals migrate from one population to another and mate.

Two components of inherited variation are genotype and phenotype. Genotype is the individual's set of alleles for a trait, while phenotype is the appearance or expression of the trait. In some cases, an allele that appears the most frequently may not be expressed the most frequently.

Knowing the frequency of alleles and phenotypes in a population is important for understanding how natural selection could affect the evolution of a population. For example, a sample population of mice is made up of 48 percent heterozygous black mice (*Bb*), 16 percent homozygous black mice (*Bb*), and 36 percent homozygous brown mice (*bb*). Sixty-four percent of the population has black fur. However, as shown in **Figure 1,** the brown fur allele occurs more frequently in the population than the black fur allele (b = 60%; B = 40%).

Figure 1
Alleles in a Population

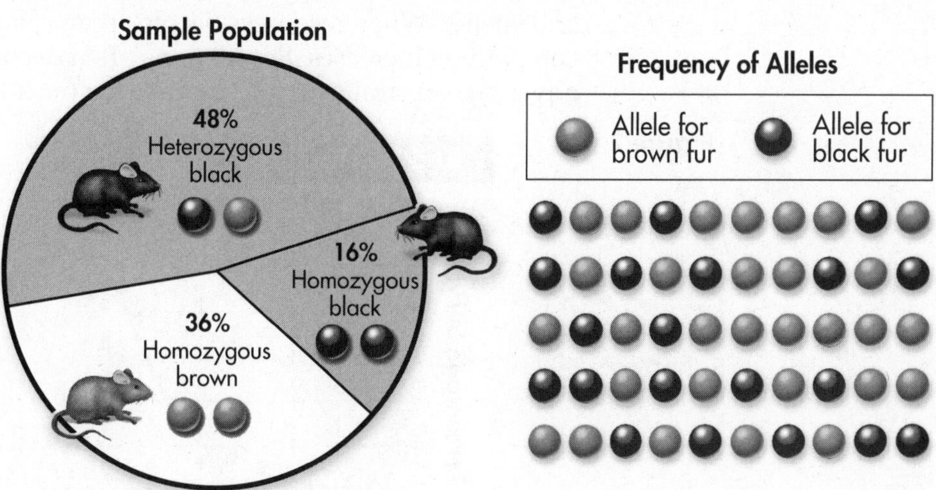

Study Tip

Natural selection is caused by an environmental stressor for which specific phenotypes have a fitness advantage. Over time, the individuals with those adaptive phenotypes survive and reproduce, which makes the allele responsible for the phenotype more common in the population.

What contributes to differential reproductive success?

The environment poses many challenges to individuals. Resources are scarce and predators and competitors are many. Many organisms die before they reproduce. However, certain phenotypes can give some individuals a fitness advantage. Fitness refers to an organism's ability to survive, attract a mate, and reproduce in a particular environment. For example, in some environments, black mice are better camouflaged than brown mice. This could mean that black mice have a fitness advantage, giving them a better chance of surviving long enough to reproduce and produce more offspring than brown mice.

The difference in the number of offspring produced by these two phenotypes can be referred to as *differential reproductive success*. Natural selection is the process by which traits become more or less common in a population due to differential reproductive success. There are several elements of natural selection.

Inherited Variation In an environment that favors black fur, eventually the frequency of the allele for brown fur will decline because mice with black fur have a better chance of surviving and passing on their alleles. If the environment changes, the relative fitness of individuals can change, too. For example, if the environment changed in a way that provided better camouflage to brown mice instead of black mice, then brown mice would have a fitness advantage. Over time, the frequency of the allele for brown fur would increase while the allele for black fur would decrease.

Producing More Offspring Than Can Survive Most populations produce far more offspring than can survive in any given environment due to resource constraints. When populations produce many more offspring than can survive, the likelihood increases that some offspring will reach reproductive age. The ones that do reproduce likely have phenotypes that gave them an advantage within that environment over those that did not survive or reproduce.

Finite Supply of Environmental Resources In any environment, individuals compete for finite, or limited, resources such as space, food, and shelter. When resources become scarce, such as during a drought, then competition increases. Populations often decline, and the individuals with advantageous traits for survival are the most likely to live and reproduce.

Figure 2

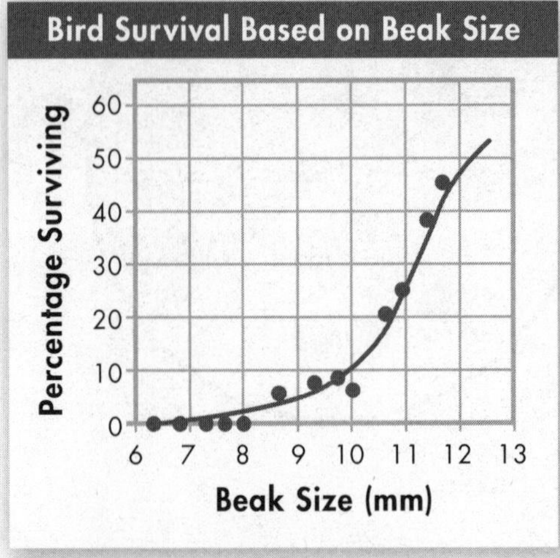

For example, studies on ground finches in the Galápagos Islands show that when seeds become scarce, population sizes of ground finches tend to decrease. However, the finches that are most likely to survive the scarcity of food are those with beaks large enough to eat many types of seeds. In this case, a large beak is a fitness advantage. Populations with small beaks decline the most, while populations with large beaks are better able to survive and reproduce. (See **Figure 2.**)

TEKS End-of-Course Assessment Review

1. Evaluate Which of the following best describes how frequencies of alleles are related to environmental conditions?

- **A** If the environment changes, then new alleles will emerge and become more frequent in a population.
- **B** If the environment changes, the frequency of alleles that give individuals an advantage in the new environment will increase.
- **C** Environmental changes occur in response to changes in allele frequencies.
- **D** Genetic mutations in individuals can give the rest of the population a survival advantage.

2. Analyze How can an environmental pressure such as seed scarcity affect the evolution of a population of birds?

- **F** The population could evolve a higher frequency of alleles for a phenotype that would enable the birds to eat a wider range of seeds.
- **G** The population of birds would likely remain unchanged because of the environmental stress.
- **H** The population would likely migrate to a different location in search of a new food source.
- **J** The population would likely have more mutations in genes that carry traits for efficiency of seed collection.

3. Evaluate Why do some individuals have more reproductive success than others in a population?

- **A** Reproductive success is equal for all individuals within a population.
- **B** Individuals with traits that lead to increased fitness in their environment survive to adulthood and are more likely to reproduce than individuals that lack these traits.
- **C** Individuals that are less fit for their environment mate more frequently in order to pass on their genes as quickly as possible.
- **D** Individuals with traits for increased reproductive rates are less likely to survive in the environment.

4. Analyze How is it beneficial to populations to produce more offspring than can survive?

Natural Selection and Diversity

TEKS 7E

★ READINESS ★

Analyze and evaluate the relationship of natural selection to adaptation and to the development of diversity in and among species.

Vocabulary
speciation
reproductive isolation
geographic isolation
behavioral isolation
temporal isolation

What is the relationship of natural selection to adaptation?

An adaptation is a heritable trait that increases an organism's ability to survive and reproduce in its environment. Adaptations include inborn behaviors, such as web spinning in spiders, as well as physical traits, such as fur or skin color that provides camouflage. An organism's genes determine its adaptations.

Due to natural selection, individuals with adaptations that give them an advantage over other individuals in the same environment are more likely to reproduce and pass the adaptations on to their offspring. If the adaptation continues to be beneficial, then over time, as the trait is passed on to successive generations, a larger portion of the population will have the adaptation.

Study Tip

Recall that natural selection acts on phenotypes rather than genotypes.

What is the relationship of natural selection to the development of diversity in a species?

Individuals within a species vary genetically. This genetic diversity can arise in several ways, including mutations and the random assortment of chromosomes during meiosis. Natural selection cannot change the genetic diversity of a species or population, but the outcome of natural selection may result in a change in frequency of the genes that already exist. For example, polar bears could not respond to a warmer, less snowy Arctic by producing thinner or brown fur. But if the genes for thinner or brown fur already exist in the population, they will likely be selected for in a warmer and less snowy environment, leading to a more diverse polar bear population.

What is the relationship of natural selection to the development of diversity among species?

Species diversity refers to the number of species that exist at a given time. The process of natural selection and other mechanisms of evolution have lead to the millions of species living on Earth today and the millions of different species that lived in the past. Natural selection and many other factors have a role in **speciation**, the formation of a new species.

Tortoises of the Galápagos Islands can be used to describe how speciation may occur. At some point in time, there was one species of tortoise living on one island. Within that one population there was genetic diversity.

An event occurred, perhaps a storm that stranded some tortoises on a different island. These individuals started a new population in a slightly different environment. Over time, the two populations were subjected to different pressures from the environment, and the genetic variation between the two populations increased. Once the genetic variation reached the point that individuals from the different populations could no longer mate and produce offspring, the populations became different species. **Figure 1** shows how speciation may occur.

Figure 1
Speciation

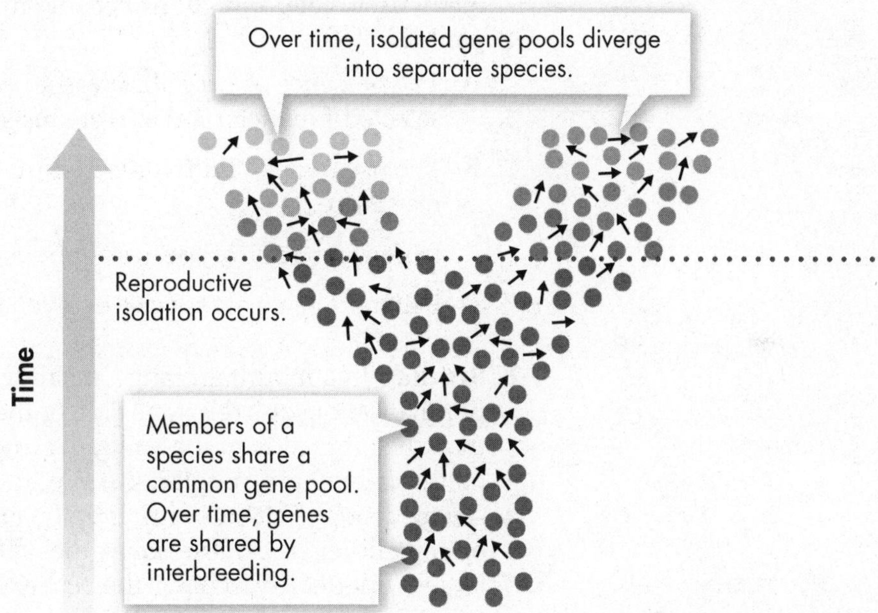
Over time, isolated gene pools diverge into separate species.
Reproductive isolation occurs.
Time
Members of a species share a common gene pool. Over time, genes are shared by interbreeding.

Reproductive isolation occurs when members of a population no longer interbreed. There are several ways in which reproductive isolation may occur, including geographic isolation, behavioral isolation, and temporal isolation.

Geographic Isolation **Geographic isolation** occurs when a physical barrier such as a body of water or a mountain range separates members of a population. For example, a small population of squirrels became isolated on the north rim of the Grand Canyon. Separate gene pools formed, and genetic changes that appeared in one group were not passed to the other. Natural selection worked separately on each group and led to the formation of a distinct subspecies of squirrel.

Behavioral Isolation **Behavioral isolation** occurs when members of a species develop different behaviors that interfere with their ability to interbreed. For example, if a difference in courtship ritual develops between members of a population, only certain members of the population will breed together.

Temporal Isolation When species breed at different times of the year, this is called **temporal isolation.** Temporal isolation occurs in many plant populations because flowers tend to bloom for a short period and during a specific time of year, which strictly limits the time when reproduction is possible.

TEKS End-of-Course Assessment Review

1. Analyze For many decades, doctors prescribed penicillin to fight bacterial infections. As explained by natural selection, how did so many bacterial populations become resistant to the original form of penicillin?

A The presence of penicillin was an environmental pressure that selected for bacteria that were resistant to it.

B The use of penicillin induced mutations that promote penicillin resistance.

C Different bacterial species evolved due to reproductive isolation.

D Different bacterial species evolved due to geographic isolation.

2. Predict In a mountain range, a valley forms that separates a population of squirrels. One side of the valley receives far less rainfall than the other side of the valley. At first the population of squirrels on the drier side struggles. But eventually it grows and flourishes. A severe drought hits the entire region and the population of squirrels on the rainier side of the valley dies off, while the other population is largely unaffected. What is the best explanation for this sequence of events?

F The original intact population of squirrels had no alleles for resistance to drought.

G By chance, the population that ended up on the drier side of the valley had a high frequency of an allele that provided resistance to drought.

H Living on the drier side of the valley caused the squirrels to acquire a genetic variation that allowed them to be resistant to drought.

J Temporal isolation changed the genetic variations of the two populations.

3. Evaluate How does the different species of tortoise living on different islands in the Galápagos Islands demonstrate the relationship between natural selection and genetic diversity among species?

4. Explain How do changes in the environment affect the genetic variation within a species?

5. Describe Explain some factors that need to exist for speciation to occur.

Genetic Drift, Gene Flow, Mutation, and Recombination

TEKS 7F

Analyze and evaluate the effects of other evolutionary mechanisms, including genetic drift, gene flow, mutation, and recombination.

Vocabulary
genetic drift
bottleneck effect
founder effect
gene flow
recombination

How does genetic drift affect evolution of species?

Genetic drift is an evolutionary mechanism in which allele frequencies change in a population. Unlike natural selection, the allele frequencies do not change due to selective pressures. Instead, the changes may be due to a natural disaster, such as a flood or forest fire, that randomly eliminates members of the population. It is possible that the remaining population has a different allele frequency than the larger population had. Only the genes of the surviving population members can be passed to future generations. This change in allele frequency is called the **bottleneck effect**.

Genetic drift may also occur if a small number of individuals are separated from a larger population, as shown in **Figure 1.** The gene pool of this small population could be very different from that of the larger population. This change in allele frequency is called the **founder effect**. The founder effect is an important part of the evolution of island species, because often island populations are formed from a very small number of individuals.

Figure 1
The Founder Effect

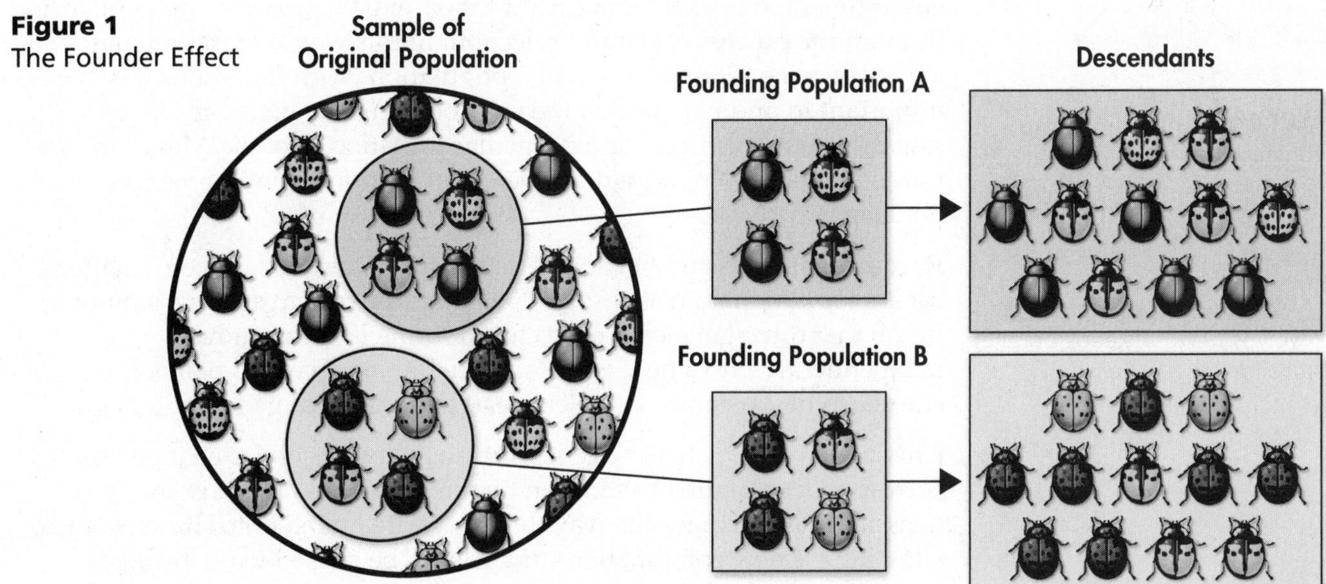

Study Tip

Remember that gene flow tends to reduce genetic variability between populations, and mutations and recombination tend to increase it.

How does gene flow affect evolution of species?

Gene flow occurs when the genes of one population flow to a different population. This can happen if members of a species arrive in a new habitat and mate with members of an existing population. The genes of these new members may cause a shift in allele frequency of the existing population. In populations that do not experience a lot of immigration (addition of members) or emigration (loss of members), the amount of gene flow will be low. Gene flow increases the genetic variation within populations, but reduces the genetic differences from one population to another.

Gene flow slows the evolution of new species because it makes two populations more similar. In this process, the flow of genes from one population to another makes the populations more similar genetically.

If two populations of a species are isolated geographically, there will be a lack of gene flow between the populations. Eventually, the two populations might evolve into separate species.

How do mutations and recombination affect evolution?

Figure 2
How Mutations Enter Populations

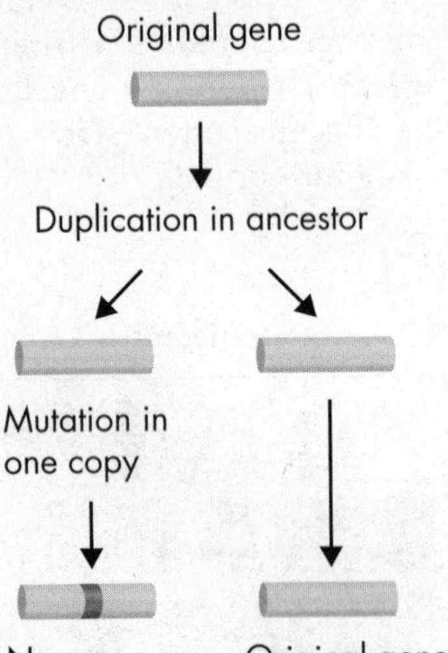
Original gene
Duplication in ancestor
Mutation in one copy
New gene evolves new function.
Original gene keeps original function.

A mutation is any change in the genetic material of a cell. Mutations can occur within individual genes, as shown in **Figure 2,** or they can involve changes in pieces of chromosomes. A mutation can occur in any cell of an organism. However, for a mutation to be passed on to offspring, it must affect reproductive cells, which are the cells that produce sperm and egg cells.

Genetic mutations give individuals differences in traits that may be beneficial, may be harmful, or may have no effect in a particular environment. If the mutation is beneficial for survival in a given environment, it is likely that the mutation will be passed to more offspring through the process of natural selection. In this way, a mutation may slowly become more common in a population. With mutations it is important to understand that the environment can affect the rate of mutation, but it can't cause a particular mutation to occur. Mutations are random and exist in individuals before evolutionary mechanisms can act on them.

Recombination is another source of heritable variation. Recombination occurs for two main reasons: independent assortment and crossing-over. Recall that during meiosis, each chromosome in a pair moves independently into a new gamete. Since humans have 23 pairs of chromosomes, recombination can lead to millions of gene combinations.

Crossing-over, which also occurs during meiosis, is the exchange of corresponding segments between two homologous chromosomes. Crossing-over changes the way that genes are linked onto chromosomes, allowing for new combinations of alleles to be passed to offspring.

TEKS End-of-Course Assessment Review

1. **Analyze** A fire kills all but a few of the deer that live in a forest. The surviving deer have a significantly different genetic makeup than did the average deer in the original, larger population. What best describes the evolutionary changes that will likely occur to the deer population?
   - **A** Selective pressures caused advantageous traits to become more common in the population.
   - **B** Selective pressures changed the population in random ways that may not be to the deer's advantage.
   - **C** Genetic drift has altered the deer population due to the bottleneck effect.
   - **D** Genetic drift has altered the deer population due to the founder effect.

2. **Infer** A plant breeder mates two pea plants from the same strain, and then plants the seeds they produce. Which observation of the offspring suggests that a mutation occurred in the genes of one of the parent plants?
   - **F** plants that produce orange peas, a color never before observed in this strain
   - **G** plants that produce peas that are green and wrinkled, a combination that is rare in this strain
   - **H** several plants that have a combination of the traits of the two parents
   - **J** a plant that is nearly identical to one of its parents

3. **Analyze** Which of the following mechanisms of evolution usually causes an increase in genetic diversity within a species?
   - **A** competition
   - **B** genetic drift
   - **C** mutation
   - **D** gene flow

4. **Evaluate** Explain how mutations can be a mechanism of evolution.

5. **Infer** Why might a species that has 94 chromosomes per cell be able to evolve more quickly than a species that has 12 chromosomes per cell, even if both species depend on about the same number of genes?

Cell Complexity

TEKS 7G

Analyze and evaluate scientific explanations concerning the complexity of the cell.

Vocabulary
endosymbiotic theory

What do scientists think ancient cells were like?

No one knows precisely when the first cells lived on Earth. But microscopic fossils that resemble bacteria have been found in rocks more than 3.5 billion years old. Some scientists think that these ancient fossils were the ancestors of prokaryotes.

The first cells lived when Earth's atmosphere lacked oxygen. Compared to prokaryotes alive today, they were most similar to those that live in extreme environments, such as near hot springs or hydrothermal vents in the ocean.

Over time, cellular processes such as photosynthesis and cellular respiration developed. Photosynthetic bacteria were the first organisms to perform photosynthesis. Based on the fossil record, these bacteria arose at least 2.7 billion years ago and became common about 2.2 billion years ago. Rocks from this time contain oxidized iron, suggesting that these organisms released oxygen during photosynthesis.

Figure 1
History of Life

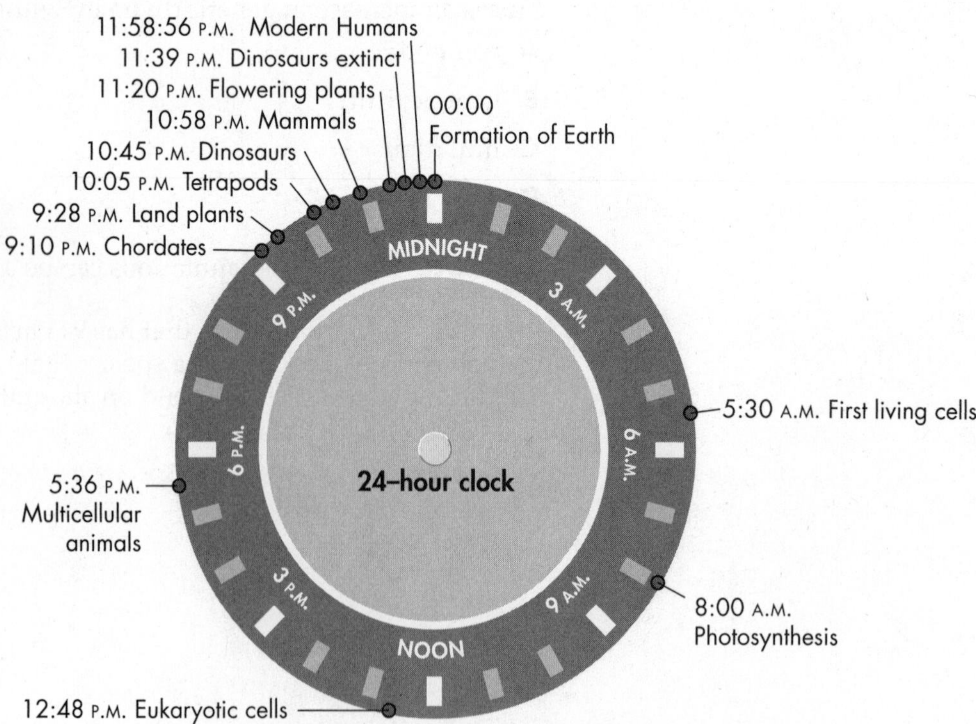

Photosynthesis may have increased oxygen levels so much that oxygen became more prominent in Earth's atmosphere, making it possible for organisms who rely on oxygen for cellular respiration to exist on land.

Study Tip

The meaning of endosymbiosis can be remembered by considering its root word parts: *endo-* means "inside," *sym* means "with," *bio* refers to "life," and *sis* means "process." Endosymbiosis is the process in which one organism comes to live entirely within another, and both organisms benefit from the relationship.

What are some scientific explanations for how the complexity of cells has changed over time?

Cellular respiration and photosynthesis involve complex pathways that depend on many intermediate steps and enzymes. How could these pathways have evolved? To explain the origin of the Krebs cycle, a major step of cellular respiration, scientists cite evidence that the enzymes were "borrowed" from genes and proteins that cells were using for other purposes. Evidence also suggests that cell structures such as cilia and flagella, which are used for movement, might also have been first assembled from proteins that cells were using for other functions.

The oldest known fossils of eukaryotic cells, which resemble modern green algae, are about 2.1 billion years old. Eukaryotic cells have a nucleus and many other structures that prokaryotes lack. How did these cells arise? Although the fossils lack details of internal structure, scientists have developed theories that are supported by other evidence.

In the 1960s, Lynn Margulis proposed the **endosymbiotic theory,** which states that some organelles in eukaryotic cells formed from symbiotic relationships between early eukaryotes and prokaryotes. *Endosymbiosis* is a process in which one organism lives inside another organism to the benefit of both. According to endosymbiotic theory, free-living aerobic bacteria became endosymbionts inside larger, anaerobic cells. Over time, they evolved into the organelles that we now observe as mitochondria. In another endosymbiotic process, free-living photosynthetic bacteria became chloroplasts.

Figure 2
Endosymbiotic Theory

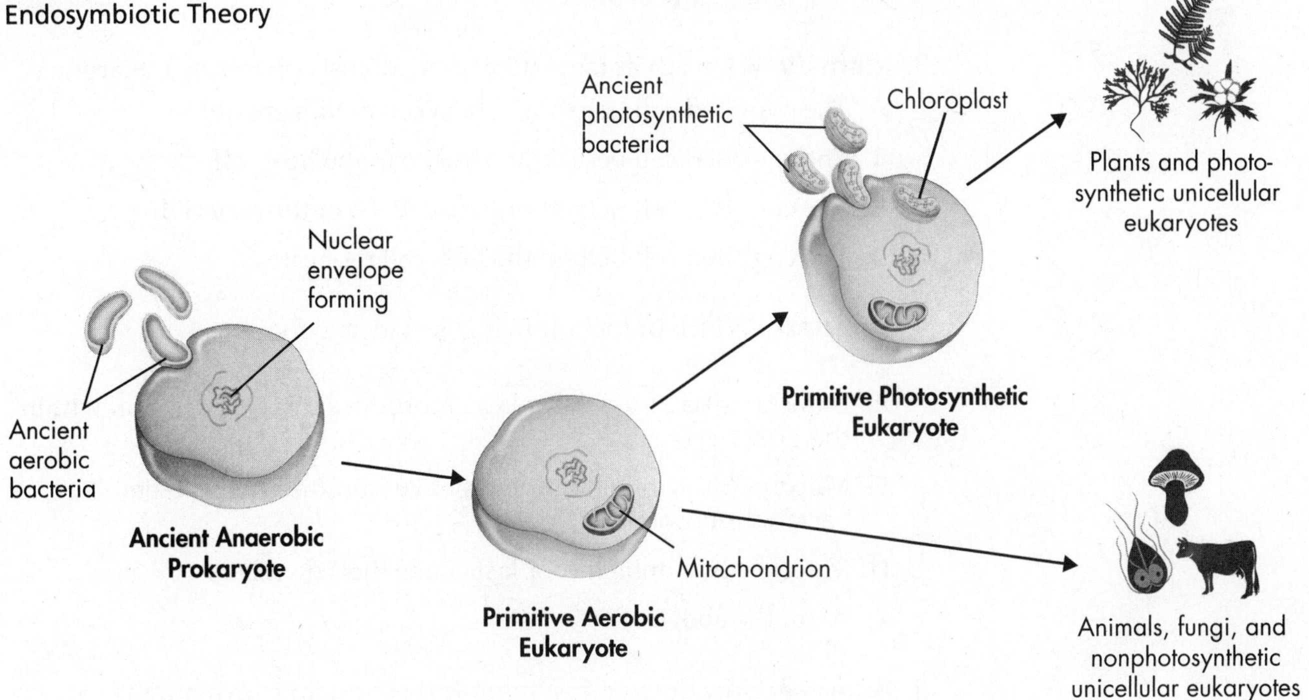

Evidence for the endosymbiotic theory comes from observations of mitochondria and chloroplasts in cells today. The following observations all support the theory that these organelles evolved from free-living cells:

- Mitochondria and chloroplasts have their own DNA and their own mechanisms for making proteins, including ribosomes.
- They are surrounded by double membranes. The inner membrane is thought to be a remnant from their original cell membrane.
- They replicate within the cell by binary fission, the same process used by free-living bacteria.

End-of-Course Assessment Review

1. Evaluate Which of the following best describes early cellular life?

A The first cells were photosynthetic and did not require oxygen.

B The first cells were anaerobic and broke apart small molecules for energy.

C The first cells took in oxygen from fresh water.

D The first cells were very similar to present-day eukaryotic cells.

2. Sequence According to scientists' explanations, which event occurred first?

F The first photosynthetic eukaryote evolved.

G Oxygen levels in Earth's atmosphere began to rise.

H The first bacteria to perform photosynthesis evolved.

J The first plants evolved.

3. Identify What advantage did endosymbiosis give early eukaryotes?

A The engulfed cell helped the host cell obtain energy.

B The engulfed cell became a parasite in the host cell.

C The engulfed cell helped organize DNA in the host cell.

D The engulfed cell helped the host cell replicate.

4. Evaluate Which of the following is evidence for endosymbiotic theory?

F Mitochondria and chloroplasts reproduce by binary fission within their host cells.

G Mitochondria and chloroplasts have ribosomes that resemble bacterial ribosomes.

H Mitochondria and chloroplasts have their own DNA.

J All of the above

5. Analyze How does endosymbiotic theory help to explain the complexity of modern cells?

Taxonomy

TEKS 8A

Define taxonomy and recognize the importance of a standardized taxonomic system to the scientific community.

Vocabulary
taxonomy
binomial nomenclature
genus
species

What is taxonomy?

Taxonomy is the scientific system of naming and classifying organisms. Taxonomy allows scientists to organize millions of types of organisms into logical groups based on their similarities, differences, and ancestry.

An important taxonomist was Swedish botanist Carolus Linnaeus, who developed his taxonomy system in the mid-1700s. Linnaeus's naming system, called binomial nomenclature, remains the basis of the system that scientists use today. **Binomial nomenclature** comes from Latin words for "two-word naming system."

In this naming system, each species is given a two-word Latin name. The first word is the organism's **genus**, or the group to which it and other similar species belong. The second word is a species name. A **species** is now typically defined as a group of organisms that can breed with one another and produce fertile offspring. The two names make up a unique *binomial* that identifies the species of the organism.

Linnaeus's classification system grouped organisms into levels called taxa (singular: taxon) based on similarities and differences in anatomical structures. The taxa progress from larger more general groups to smaller more specific groups. There are seven main classification levels: kingdom, phylum (plural: phyla), class, order, family, genus (plural: genera), and species. **Figure 1** on the next page shows the classification of *Camelus bactrianus* (the Bactrian camel) using these seven taxa.

Why is a standardized taxonomic system important to the scientific community?

Today's standardized naming system allows scientists to communicate precisely about the species they are studying. The use of common names causes far too much confusion. Even among English speaking scientists, for example, the name *camel* may refer to different species of camel, depending on what the local camel species is. But a scientific name such as *Camelus bactrianus* is recognized by scientists around the world as referring to only one type of camel.

Figure 1
Taxonomic Groups

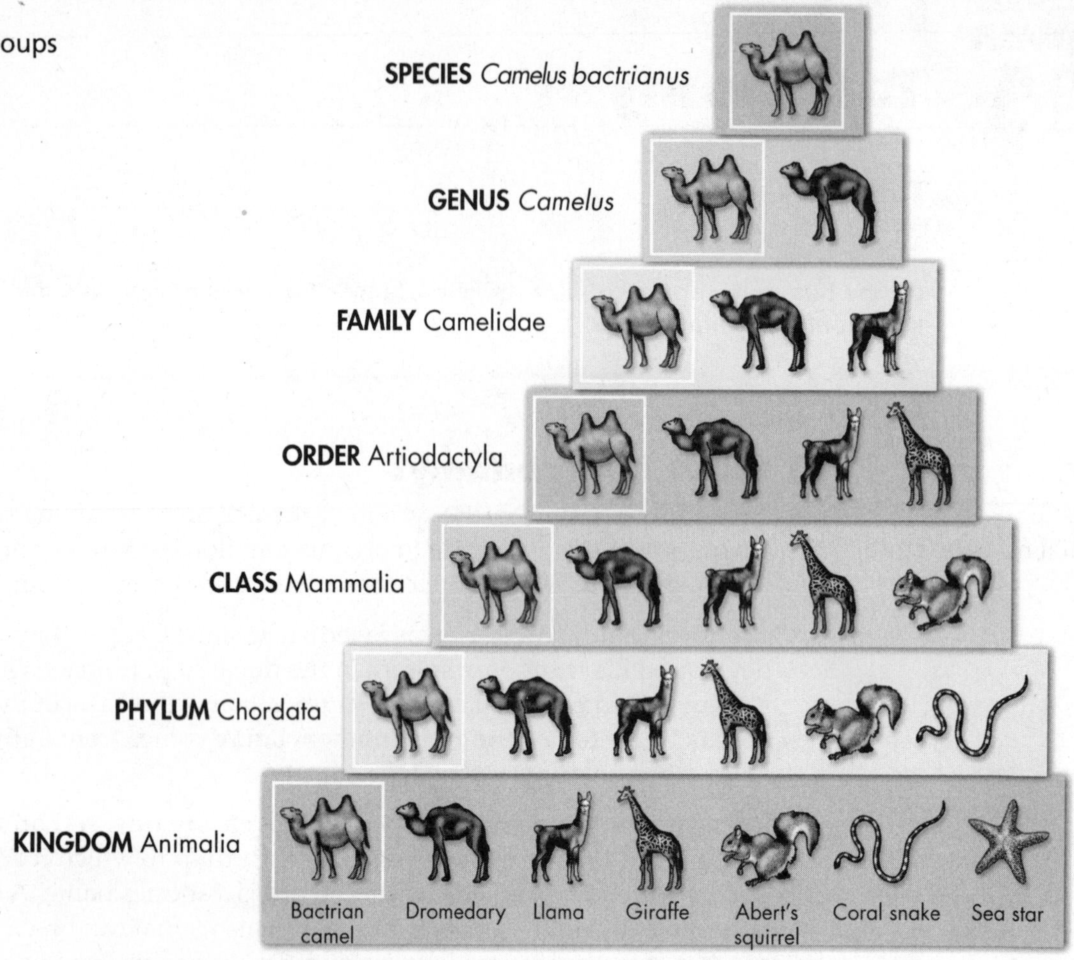

Before Linnaeus developed his system of taxonomy, naturalists devised scientific names in a variety of ways. "Scientific" names sometimes contained as many as seven words, and often a species had more than one "scientific" name. For example, the wild briar rose was known as *Rosa sylvestris alba cum rubore, folio glabro*. It was also known as the woodland dog rose, with the Latin name *Rosa sylvestris inodora seu canina*. Linnaeus recognized that the wild briar rose and the woodland dog rose were the same species. He gave the plant one name, *Rosa canina,* which all scientists can use no matter what part of the world they come from.

In addition to a naming system, a standardized classification system is also important. Scientists communicate better with each other if they are referring to the same groups and their characteristics.

Study Tip

To help remember the order of levels in classification, use the following sentence as a mnemonic device: **K**ing **P**hilip **C**ame **O**ver **F**or **G**rape **S**oda. That stands for **K**ingdom, **P**hylum, **C**lass, **O**rder, **F**amily, **G**enus, **S**pecies.

How has taxonomy changed over time?

Modern taxonomists, often called systematists, use more than anatomical similarities and differences to classify organisms. They use evidence from the fossil record and DNA and other molecular comparisons to develop hypotheses about evolutionary relationships. The goal of evolutionary classification is to assign species to higher taxa according to how closely related those species are to one another.

In the modern taxonomic system, all species within a genus are more closely related to one another than they are to members of any other genus. In the same way, all genera in a family are more closely related to one another than to members of any other family, and so on. The larger a taxon, the further back in time is the common ancestor of all the organisms in that taxon.

TEKS End-of-Course Assessment Review

1. Define Which of the following is the best description of taxonomy?

A Taxonomy is the study of grouping organisms based on traditional naming systems.

B Taxonomy is the study of giving organisms a two-word name in Latin.

C Taxonomy is the study of classifying and naming organisms based on shared characteristics.

D Taxonomy is the study of classifying organisms based on similar structures and DNA sequences.

2. Identify Why do scientists use binomial nomenclature to name species?

F Binomials are specific and universally understood by scientists.

G A single binomial can be used for many species, making it easier to name different animals.

H Binomials tell scientists how a species looks, relative to others in the same genus.

J A binomial is easier to remember than a long name with multiple Latin words.

3. Infer Class Mammalia includes all mammals, which are animals that have hair or fur and that make milk for their young. Many mammals, called placental mammals, complete their development within their mother. Marsupials, which include kangaroos and koalas, are mammals that complete their development in their mother's pouch. In which group are marsupials classified?

A a class other than class Mammalia

B an order of class Mammalia

C a kingdom that does not include class Mammalia

D a phylum that does not include class Mammalia

4. Interpret Visuals Look at **Figure 1** on the previous page. What parts of the diagram would need to change to show the classification of the giraffe?

Classification Systems

TEKS 8B

READINESS

Categorize organisms using a hierarchical classification system based on similarities and differences shared among groups.

Vocabulary
cladogram
derived character
clade
dichotomous key

How do scientists categorize organisms?

Scientists may use several hierarchical classification systems to categorize organisms. A cladogram is a diagram that shows relationships among groups of organism. A dichotomous key can be used to determine the identity of a single organism.

What is a cladogram?

Scientists make charts called **cladograms** to show the evolutionary relationships among species. Cladograms show how members of a group change over time, giving rise to new groups. In a cladogram, more closely related groups appear closer to each other, while more distantly related groups are farther away.

To construct a cladogram, scientists compare many types of information including DNA, proteins, anatomical structures, biogeography, and behavior. This combination of information makes cladograms more accurate than traditional taxonomy in determining how species are related.

A cladogram looks like a tree with a common "trunk" that represents the ancestral line of all the organisms. The branches indicate when a modification to the ancestral form occurs. There are a few rules to follow when building or interpreting a cladogram.

- All groups on a cladogram share a common ancestor.
- Branches divide into two branches at a point called a node.
- At a node, a group that branches off has a characteristic its ancestors do not have, known as a derived character.

Figure 1
Derived Characters of Plants

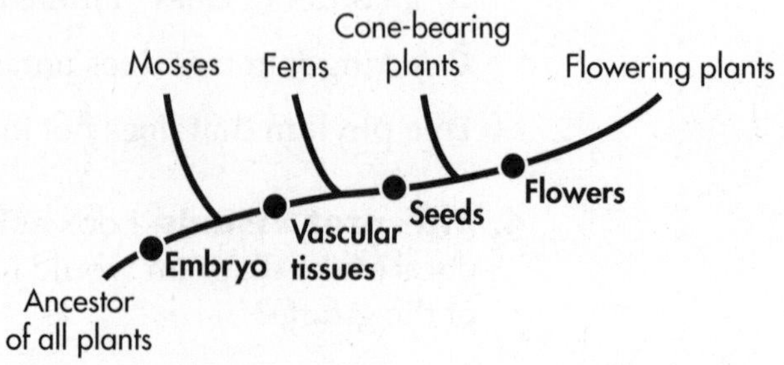

A **derived character** is a trait found in a new species but not in the ancestral species. For example, the derived characters in the cladogram in **Figure 1** are *embryo*, *vascular tissues*, *seeds*, and *flowers*. The cladogram is divided into branches representing organisms that *do* or *do not* have the derived character. In this case, all of the plants in the lineage develop from an embryo. However, only ferns, cone-bearing plants, and flowering plants have vascular tissue (tissue that circulates liquids).

Cladograms reveal clades. A **clade** includes a single common ancestor and all of its living and extinct descendants. Organisms that are in the same clade are more closely related than organisms in different clades. A clade may be different from a group in Linnaean taxonomy (kingdom, phylum, class, etc.). For example, class Reptilia is different from clade Reptilia. As you can see in **Figure 2**, class Reptilia does not include birds. However, clade Reptilia is determined by common ancestry and includes birds, which have the same common ancestor as reptiles. Individual branches of cladograms are also clades. Birds belong to the clade Aves.

Figure 2
Class vs. Clade

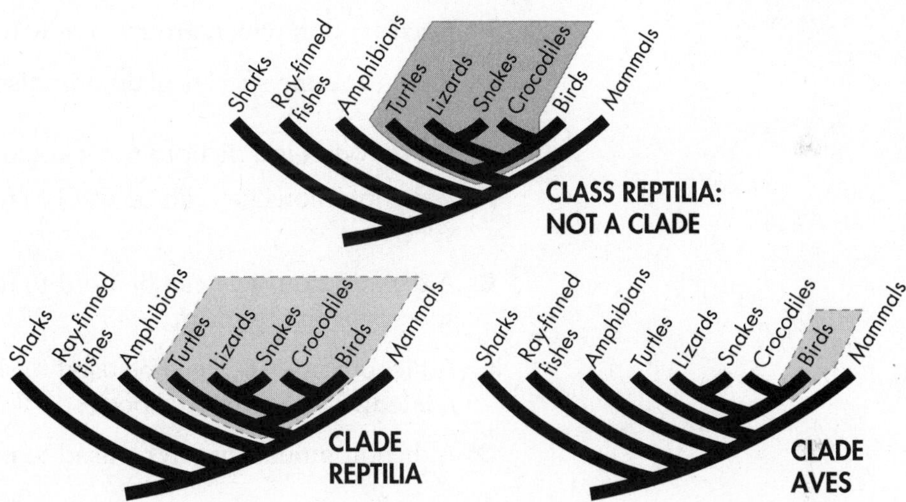

What is a dichotomous key?

A **dichotomous key** is a series of ordered steps you follow to identify an organism. Here are a few principles of dichotomous keys.

- Each step in the key refers to one physical characteristic, for example, the arrangement of veins in a leaf.
- There should be only two variations of the characteristic in the key for each step, for example, parallel veins or branched veins.
- The characteristics in the key should be arranged in steps from most general to most specific.

To use a dichotomous key, you read both of the options given, then decide which variation of the characteristic best fits the organism, then move on to the next question if applicable.

Study Tip

When determining if a group is a clade, remember to ask the question, "Does this group include an ancestor and all of its descendants?"

TEKS End-of-Course Assessment Review

1. Classify Based on the cladogram in **Figure 1**, which plants develop from an embryo and have vascular tissues but do not have seeds or flowers?

A mosses

B ferns

C cone-bearing plants

D ancestors of plants

2. Infer In a cladogram, what does the appearance of a derived character tell you?

F It tells you the name of the ancestral group.

G It tells you which traits were exhibited in the ancestral group but are not seen in more modern groups.

H It tells you in which groups a new trait arose.

J It tells you the species of an organism.

3. Identify What is a dichotomous key used for?

A A dichotomous key can be used to find the ancestral form of a species.

B A dichotomous key can be used to find the classification and species of an organism.

C A dichotomous key can be used to show the evolutionary relatedness of different species.

D A dichotomous key can be used to make a cladogram.

4. Evaluate Based on the cladogram below, are X, Y, and Z a clade? Would Y and Z represent a clade without X? Explain your answers.

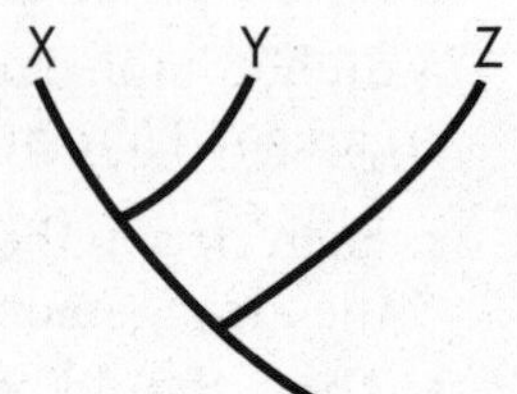

Six Kingdoms of Classification

TEKS 8C

Compare characteristics of taxonomic groups, including archaea, bacteria, protists, fungi, plants, and animals.

Vocabulary
domain
kingdom
bacteria
archaea
protist
fungi
plant
animal

What are the three domains and six kingdoms of organisms?

Taxonomists divide living things into three domains: Archaea, Bacteria, and Eukarya. A **domain** is one of the largest, most inclusive taxonomic categories into which biologists classify organisms. Evidence for placing organisms into three domains comes from comparing ribosomal RNA. Domains Bacteria and Archaea both contain prokaryotic organisms, but the members of each domain differ in cell wall structure and DNA organization. Bacteria have a molecule called peptidoglycan in their cell walls, while Archaea do not. Some Archaea have histones that organize their DNA, but Bacteria do not have histones. Histones are proteins that bind to DNA. Domain Eukarya is made up of all the eukaryotic organisms.

Organisms can be further classified into six kingdoms: Eubacteria, Archaebacteria, Protista, Plantae, Fungi, and Animalia. A **kingdom** is the largest and most inclusive traditional taxonomic classification category. **Figure 1** shows how domains and kingdoms correspond, as well as a comparison of their characteristics.

Figure 1

Characteristics of Taxonomic Groups						
DOMAIN	**Bacteria**	**Archaea**	**Eukarya**			
KINGDOM	**Eubacteria**	**Archaebacteria**	**Protista**	**Fungi**	**Plantae**	**Animalia**
CELL TYPE	Prokaryote	Prokaryote	Eukaryote	Eukaryote	Eukaryote	Eukaryote
CELL STRUCTURES	Cell walls with peptidoglycan	Cell walls without peptidoglycan	Some: cell walls of cellulose; some: cilia	Cell walls of chitin	Cell walls of cellulose; chloroplasts	No cell walls or chloroplasts
NUMBER OF CELLS	Unicellular	Unicellular	Most unicellular; some colonial; some multicellular	Most multicellular; some unicellular	Most multicellular: some green algae unicellular	Multicellular
NUTRITION	Autotroph or heterotroph	Autotroph or heterotroph	Autotroph or heterotroph	Heterotroph	Autotroph	Heterotroph
REPRODUCTION	Asexual	Asexual	Asexual or sexual	Asexual or sexual	Sexual or asexual	Usually sexual
METABOLISM	Aerobic or anaerobic	Anaerobic	Most are aerobic	Anaerobic or aerobic	Aerobic	Aerobic
EXAMPLES	*Streptococcus, Escherichia coli*	Methanogens, halophiles	*Amoeba, Paramecium,* slime molds, giant kelp	Mushrooms, yeasts	Mosses, ferns, flowering plants	Sponges,worms, insects, fishes, mammals

Study Tip

One way to remember which types of organisms are Archaebacteria and which are Eubacteria is to remember the rhyme "Eubacteria are the true bacteria." Most prokaryotes you hear of are Eubacteria. Most Archaebacteria inhabit only the most extreme habitats on Earth.

What are the characteristics of organisms in the kingdom Eubacteria?

Eubacteria, or **bacteria**, are single-celled prokaryotes that reproduce by a type of asexual reproduction called binary fission. Eubacteria is an extremely diverse kingdom whose members utilize various forms of metabolism. Organisms in this kingdom may be *aerobes*, which require oxygen for respiration, or *anaerobes*, which do not require oxygen for respiration. Eubacteria may be *autotrophs* (producing their own energy source from sunlight or chemicals) or *heterotrophs* (acquiring energy by consuming other organisms). The bacteria you are most familiar with, from the *L. acidophilus* in yogurt, to the *E. coli* living in your digestive tract, to the *Streptococcus* that can give you a severe sore throat, are all Eubacteria.

What are the characteristics of organisms in the kingdom Archaebacteria?

Archaebacteria, or **archaea**, are also single-celled prokaryotes that reproduce asexually by binary fission. They are different from Eubacteria because they have histones that compact DNA, and their cell walls lack peptidoglycan. Organisms in this kingdom are found in some of the most extreme environments on Earth, such as deep ocean vents, hot springs, and salt lakes. Archaea are anaerobic and autotrophic and often have unusual processes for obtaining energy that allow them to survive in extreme environments.

What are the characteristics of organisms in the kingdom Protista?

Protista is such a diverse kingdom that many biologists question the validity of the kingdom. Some of the organisms within Protista are more different from each other than they are from organisms in other kingdoms. The only true similarity of all **protists** is that they are eukaryotes. Most protists are unicellular, others live in colonies, and some are multicellular. Many have complex life cycles. Protists may reproduce asexually—by budding or binary fission—or sexually. Some are heterotrophs and some are autotrophs. Protists range in size from the microscopic amoeba to 50-meter-long kelp.

What are the characteristics of organisms in kingdom Fungi?

Fungi are heterotrophic eukaryotes whose cell walls contain chitin. They are usually decomposers or parasites. Fungi obtain nutrients by digesting material from other organisms outside of their cells and then absorbing the organic molecules that have been digested. Animals, on the other hand, directly ingest organisms for nutrients. Fungi may be aerobic or anaerobic. Different fungi may reproduce asexually by budding or binary fission or sexually or asexually by spores.

What are the characteristics of organisms in the kingdom Plantae?

Plants are autotrophic eukaryotes whose cell walls contain cellulose. Most are multicellular. All plants are photosynthetic autotrophs, meaning they convert the energy in sunlight to chemical energy in food. Plants are aerobic organisms. Plants can reproduce either asexually or sexually.

What are the characteristics of organisms in the kingdom Animalia?

Animals are heterotrophic multicellular eukaryotes whose cells lack cell walls. Organisms in this kingdom include invertebrates and chordates, and they range in complexity from sponges to humans. The kingdom Animalia may seem diverse to us because it is the one with which we are most familiar, but it has the fewest known species of the eukaryotic kingdoms.

TEKS End-of-Course Assessment Review

1. **Compare and Contrast** What characteristic applies to all members of the kingdoms Protista, Fungi, Plantae, and Animalia but not to members of the other kingdoms?
   - **A** Protista, Fungi, Plantae, and Animalia are heterotrophs.
   - **B** Protista, Fungi, Plantae, and Animalia are multicellular.
   - **C** Protista, Fungi, Plantae, and Animalia are prokaryotes.
   - **D** Protista, Fungi, Plantae, and Animalia are eukaryotes.

2. **Contrast** What is one way in which archaea are different from bacteria?
   - **F** Archaea lack peptidoglycan in their cell wall.
   - **G** Archaea do not have a nucleus.
   - **H** Archaea are eukaryotes.
   - **J** Archaea are heterotrophs.

3. **Classify** You have a unicellular heterotrophic eukaryote under your microscope. To which kingdom does it belong?
   - **A** Eubacteria
   - **B** Protista
   - **C** Archaebacteria
   - **D** Animalia

4. **Identify** Which of the following lists includes all the kingdoms with autotrophic organisms?
   - **F** Bacteria, Archaebacteria, Plantae
   - **G** Plantae
   - **H** Bacteria, Archaebacteria, Fungi, Plantae
   - **J** Bacteria, Archaebacteria, Protista, Plantae

5. **Distinguish** What are two characteristics by which you can distinguish fungi from plants?

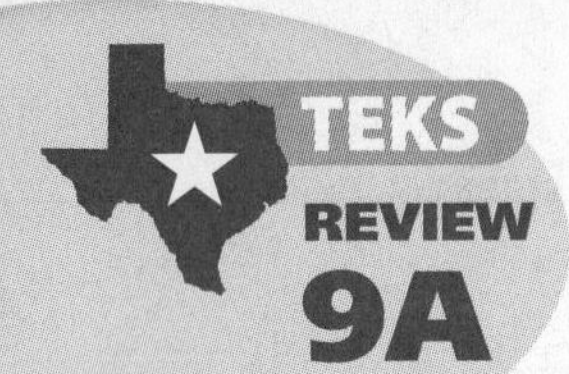

Biomolecules

TEKS 9A

READINESS

Compare the structures and functions of different types of biomolecules, including carbohydrates, lipids, proteins, and nucleic acids.

Vocabulary
biomolecule
polymer
monomer
carbohydrate
lipid
protein
nucleic acid

What are the different types of biomolecules found in living things?

All living things make and use biomolecules, which include large organic molecules. A **biomolecule** consists of a chain of carbon atoms that bond with hydrogen, nitrogen, oxygen, phosphorus, or some combination of these elements. The four main types of biomolecules are carbohydrates, lipids, proteins, and nucleic acids.

Many biomolecules are polymers. A **polymer** is a large molecule made from repeated units of smaller molecules. Repeated units of smaller molecules that join together to make a polymer are called **monomers.** Remember that "mono" means "one" and "poly" means "many."

What are the structures and functions of carbohydrates?

Carbohydrates are made of carbon, hydrogen, and oxygen. Cells break down carbohydrates for energy. Carbohydrates are also important structural components in cell membranes and in cell walls. For example, lignin is a carbohydrate that strengthens plant cell walls. A carbohydrate monomer may consist of five or six carbon atoms bonded in a ring with an oxygen atom. The structure of glucose, a common carbohydrate monomer, is shown in **Figure 1**.

Figure 1
Structure of Glucose

Starch

Glucose

CH_2OH

Sugars, such as glucose and sucrose, are called simple carbohydrates because they include only one or two monomers. Glucose is a monosaccharide, meaning it is made of one ("mono") unit of a sugar ("saccharide"). Sucrose is a disaccharide, meaning it is made of two ("di") monomers bonded together. When large numbers of monosaccharides join, they form complex carbohydrates called polysaccharides. An example of a polysaccharide is glycogen, which animals use to store excess glucose.

What are the structures and functions of lipids?

Lipids are compounds made up of mostly of carbon and hydrogen. They make up a diverse group that include fats, oils, phospholipids, steroids, and waxes. As shown in **Figure 2**, lipids have many roles. They are found in hormones and some vitamins; serve as energy storage and transport molecules; and play structural roles within cells. Lipids do not dissolve in water or the cytoplasm of the cell.

Figure 2

Lipids

Lipid type	Characteristics	Examples
Fats and oils	Store energy, which is released when they burn; hydrocarbons with chemical structures similar to gasoline	Animal fats, vegetable oils, petroleum
Phospholipids	Primary component of cell membranes; similar to fats	Primary component of lecithin, a fatty substance found in egg yolks and some seeds
Steroids and steroid hormones	Cell membrane component (steroids); produce bodily changes, such as sexual development (steroid hormones)	Cholesterol (steroid); androgens, estrogen, testosterone (steroid hormones)

Unlike other biomolecules, lipids are not polymers. Many lipids are formed when fatty acids, which consist of long chains of carbon and hydrogen atoms, are combined with glycerol molecules. Fatty acids are important fuels for cellular processes, particularly those in the heart and skeletal muscles. Triglycerides (fats) are composed of three fatty acid chains connected to a glycerol molecule. Triglycerides store energy and transport molecules in cells. Phospholipids have two fatty acids attached to a glycerol molecule. Glycerol also binds to a phosphate group.

What are the structures and functions of proteins?

Proteins are polymers of amino acids that are made up of carbon, hydrogen, oxygen, nitrogen, and sometimes sulfur. Two amino acids can join together with a *peptide bond*. Long chains of amino acids, called polypeptides, fold and combine into functional proteins.

Study Tip

Build a table similar to Figure 2 and populate it with similar information about the other three types of biomolecules.

Proteins play an important role in nearly every cell function. Some act as enzymes, which increase the rate of chemical reactions in cells. Other proteins play critical structural roles—they support and maintain cell shape, and they make up key parts of the cell membrane. Muscle cells depend on two proteins—actin and myosin—for their structure and function. Proteins also store energy, transport substances, and have roles in the immune system.

What are the structures and functions of nucleic acids?

Nucleic acids include DNA (deoxyribonucleic acid) and RNA (ribonucleic acid). Nucleic acids carry genetic information, code for the production of proteins, and are involved in gene expression.

The monomer of a nucleic acid is called a *nucleotide*. A nucleotide is made of three parts: a five-carbon sugar, a nitrogenous base, and a phosphate group. The nitrogenous bases include adenine, thymine (in DNA only), uracil (in RNA only), guanine, and cytosine. DNA contains the sugar deoxyribose, and RNA contains the sugar ribose.

TEKS End-of-Course Assessment Review

1. Identify Which of the following biomolecules are major energy sources for cells?

A carbohydrates

B lipids

C proteins

D nucleic acids such as DNA

2. Explain Certain processes in the human body must be sped up in order to occur fast enough to sustain life. Why does the timeliness of these processes depend on proteins?

F Some proteins store energy as muscle tissue.

G Some proteins are enzymes that increase the rate of reactions.

H Some proteins support and maintain cell shape.

J Some proteins are important fuels for cellular processes.

3. Compare and Contrast What do all biomolecules have in common? How do the structure of lipids differ from all other biomolecules?

Photosynthesis and Cellular Respiration

TEKS 9B

Compare the reactants and products of photosynthesis and cellular respiration in terms of energy and matter.

Vocabulary
photosynthesis
chlorophyll
cellular respiration
fermentation

What are the reactants and products of photosynthesis?

Photosynthesis is the process by which plants and other autotrophs use light energy to make sugar (glucose) from water and carbon dioxide.

- The reactants of photosynthesis are carbon dioxide (CO_2) and water (H_2O).
- The products of photosynthesis are glucose ($C_6H_{12}O_6$) and oxygen (O_2).
- The chemical equation for the overall reaction is:

$$6CO_2 + 6H_2O \rightarrow C_6H_{12}O_6 + 6O_2$$

Photosynthesis is a series of reactions. It involves light-dependent reactions and light-independent reactions. The light-dependent reactions begin when **chlorophyll**, a pigment found in plants, absorbs light energy and converts it to chemical energy. The energy is stored in molecules called ATP and NADPH. These molecules are used in the light-independent reactions, also called the Calvin cycle, to produce glucose that plant cells can use for energy. Oxygen is released as a by-product.

What are the reactants and products of cellular respiration?

Cellular respiration is the process by which cells obtain energy from organic molecules. Both plant and animal cells perform cellular respiration. The process involves a series of chemical reactions that break down a simple carbohydrate, such as glucose ($C_6H_{12}O_6$), in the presence of oxygen.

- The reactants of cellular respiration are glucose ($C_6H_{12}O_6$) and oxygen (O_2).
- The products of cellular respiration are carbon dioxide (CO_2), water (H_2O), and energy.
- The chemical equation for the overall reaction is:

$$C_6H_{12}O_6 + 6O_2 \rightarrow 6H_2O + 6CO_2 + \text{energy}$$

The energy released by cellular respiration is captured in ATP or lost to the environment as heat. For every glucose molecule consumed, a total of 36 ATP molecules are formed. Cells can break bonds in ATP to access energy.

Study Tip

The suffix *-lysis* means "the breaking apart of." Glycolysis is the process that breaks apart glucose.

Cellular respiration is a series of reactions that break down glucose. The first step is glycolysis. The reactions of glycolysis break down glucose into smaller molecules, which are transported to mitochondria. In the mitochondria, reactions of the Krebs cycle break down the molecules into carbon dioxide and water. Other products of the Krebs cycle enter a process called electron transport. Electron transport concludes with the combining of hydrogen and oxygen into water.

The Krebs cycle and electron transport are together described as aerobic respiration because they depend on oxygen. If oxygen is not available, cells can perform glycolysis only for a short period of time. This process is called **fermentation**. Fermentation is not as efficient as aerobic respiration because it produces only 2 ATP molecules per molecule of glucose.

How do the reactants and products of photosynthesis and cellular respiration compare?

Compare the chemical equations for photosynthesis and cellular respiration on the previous page and in **Figure 1**. The products of photosynthesis are the reactants in cellular respiration. And the products of cellular respiration are the reactants in photosynthesis.

Figure 1
Reactants of Photosynthesis and Cellular Respiration

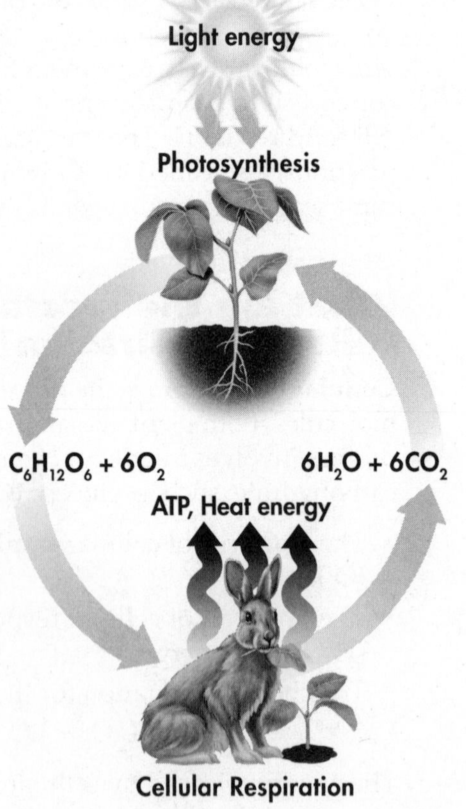

Notice that the two reactants of photosynthesis—water and carbon dioxide—are small molecules that come from the environment. Plants take water from the soil and carbon dioxide from the air, and they receive light energy from the sun. During photosynthesis, plant cells combine the small molecules to produce glucose, a larger molecule.

In contrast, cellular respiration involves the breaking apart of a large molecule into smaller molecules, and energy is released in the process. To perform cellular respiration, plants rely on the glucose they make during photosynthesis. Animals obtain glucose from the food they eat. Both plants and animals take in oxygen from the environment for cellular respiration.

TEKS End-of-Course Assessment Review

1. Compare How are photosynthesis and cellular respiration alike?

A Both occur only in the presence of light energy from the sun.

B Both release energy stored in molecules of glucose.

C Both involve carbon dioxide, water, and oxygen.

D Both take place in plant and animal cell.

2. Evaluate Which of the following best describes the difference between the products and reactants of photosynthesis and cellular respiration?

F The reactants of photosynthesis are made in the cell, while the reactants of cellular respiration come from the environment.

G The products of photosynthesis are the same as the products of cellular respiration.

H All the reactants of photosynthesis come from the environment, while some of the reactants of cellular respiration are made by living things.

J The reactants of photosynthesis are the same as the reactants in cellular respiration.

3. Sequence Describe the correct order of the three main processes of cellular respiration.

4. Compare How do the reactants and products of photosynthesis compare to the reactants and products of cellular respiration?

Enzymes

TEKS 9C

Identify and investigate the role of enzymes.

Vocabulary
catalyst
enzyme
substrate
active site

What is the role of an enzyme?

A **catalyst** is a substance that speeds up a chemical reaction. A catalyst is not a reactant in a reaction, but it does participate in the reaction. An **enzyme** is an organic catalyst, meaning it speeds up reactions in living things. Without enzymes, the chemical reactions of life would occur too slowly to keep cells alive. For example, the breakdown of glucose for energy requires a series of about 20 chemical reactions, each catalyzed by a different enzyme. In the absence of even one of the enzymes, the process would occur too slowly for the cell to survive.

Most enzymes are proteins. Organisms rely on a huge variety of enzymes to conduct the reactions necessary for life. This is because an enzyme typically catalyzes only one specific chemical reaction. The names of enzymes usually provide a clue as to their role in the body. For example, the enzyme amylase catalyzes the breakdown of the carbohydrate amylose. Most enzyme names end with the suffix *-ase.*

Figure 1

Examples of Enzymes	
Enzyme	**Catalyzes the...**
Catalase	Breakdown of hydrogen peroxide to oxygen and water
Cellulase (found mainly in fungi and microorganisms)	Breakdown of cellulose
DNA polymerase	Production of DNA molecules
Kinase	Transfer of phosphate groups from ATP to other molecules
Lactase	Breakdown of lactose
Lipase	Breakdown of lipids
Protease	Breakdown of proteins
Sucrase	Breakdown of sucrose

Study Tip

In everyday language, to *catalyze* means to bring about or inspire. You can think of an enzyme or other catalyst as "inspiring" a chemical reaction to occur.

How do enzymes work?

To remember how enzymes function, think of a lock and key. The lock is the enzyme. The key is the molecule or molecules that bind to the enzyme. These molecules are called **substrates**. As shown in **Figure 2,** a substrate binds to the enzyme at a location called the **active site**, which you can compare to the keyhole of the lock.

Figure 2
An Enzyme at Work

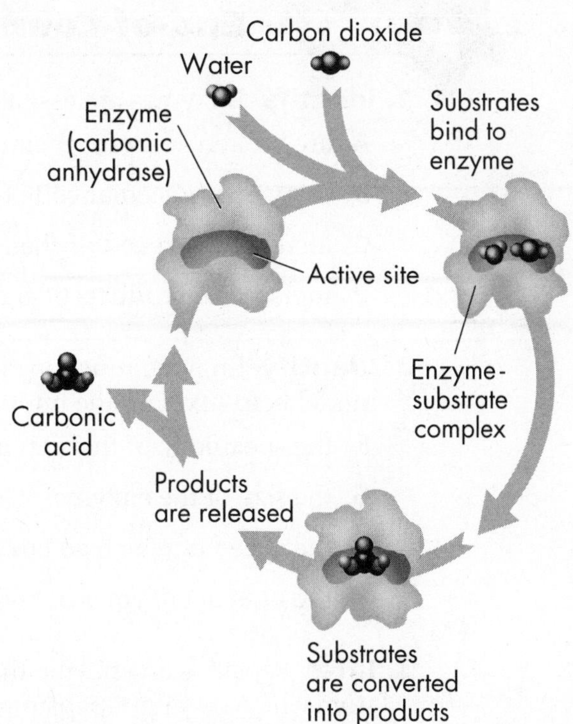

When a substrate binds to the active site, it is positioned for a reaction. The reaction might join two substrate molecules together. Or it might split a single substrate into two parts. In either case, products are released, and the enzyme is then free to catalyze another reaction.

What factors affect enzyme function?

Enzymes work because of the shape of the active site. Because both pH and temperature can change the shape of (denature) proteins, enzymes work best at very specific pH and temperature conditions.

Different enzymes have different optimal conditions. For example, pepsin is a digestive enzyme that helps break down proteins in the stomach. It works optimally in the low acidic pH of stomach fluid. In contrast, the digestive enzymes produced by the pancreas and released into the small intestine work optimally at higher, more alkaline pH values.

How do organisms control enzyme function?

Cells control the function of enzymes in many ways. For example, the body can respond to the presence of food by producing digestive enzymes. Chemical messengers called *hormones* can signal a cell to start or stop enzyme production, either temporarily or permanently. Cells also make and use a variety of inhibitors. An *inhibitor* either prevents or slows the catalytic action of an enzyme. For example, ATP can act as an enzyme inhibitor by binding to enzymes that build compounds. When ATP is abundant in a cell, the ATP inhibits production of more ATP.

End-of-Course Assessment Review

1. **Identify** Enzymes are essential for life because they
   - **A** are broken apart for their energy.
   - **B** carry the molecular code for producing proteins.
   - **C** increase the speed of chemical reactions.
   - **D** replace the products of chemical reactions.

2. **Identify** Enzyme function is often compared to a lock and key. The model helps explain the importance of which property of an enzyme?
   - **F** the specificity of the enzyme
   - **G** the size of the enzyme
   - **H** the speed at which an enzyme catalyzes reactions
   - **J** the uses of enzymes outside of organisms

3. **Infer** Pepsin is an enzyme that helps break apart proteins in the stomach. Why might pepsin work poorly after it moves from the stomach to the small intestine?
   - **A** It is denatured in the alkaline pH of the small intestine.
   - **B** It is used up by proteins in the stomach.
   - **C** It is inhibited by the alkalinity of stomach pH.
   - **D** It is replaced by proteins in the stomach.

4. **Infer** Why is it important for enzyme function to be controlled?

Origins of Cellular Life

TEKS 9D

Analyze and evaluate the evidence regarding formation of simple organic molecules and their organization into long complex molecules having information such as the DNA molecule for self-replicating life.

Vocabulary
organic molecule

What evidence supports the formation of simple organic molecules on early Earth?

Organic molecules are molecules that contain bonds between carbon atoms. These molecules follow the same rules as all molecules, but they are significant because many of them are made by, or are otherwise important to, living things. Examples of organic molecules include nucleic acids, ATP, amino acids, and proteins.

Scientists can only hypothesize about the conditions on the early Earth, and these hypotheses change frequently due to new evidence. Evidence suggests that Earth formed 4 to 5 billion years ago. For millions of years volcanic activity and strikes from meteors and comets kept Earth's crust unstable. About 3.9 billion years ago, the strikes slowed and oceans formed. The atmosphere developed from gases emitted by volcanoes.

There is no accepted theory of how organic molecules first formed, but there are many hypotheses. Many of these hypotheses state that the formation of organic molecules requires an external energy source, such as lightning, geothermal heat, or ultraviolet radiation.

In 1953, American scientists Stanley Miller and Harold Urey conducted an experiment to investigate how simple organic molecules may have formed. The experiment involved a chamber containing methane, ammonia, hydrogen, and water vapor. The mixture was chosen to mimic the composition of Earth's early atmosphere (as it was hypothesized in 1953). The researchers sent sparks of electricity through the chamber to simulate lightning. The gases were then cooled and condensed into droplets. The liquid contained a mixture of small organic molecules found in living organisms, including amino acids.

Scientists have since revised the list of gases that they think made up Earth's early atmosphere. In 1995, scientists revisited Miller and Urey's experiment with the revised hypothesis about the atmosphere and with the use of modern technology. These scientists also found amino acids, along with cytosine and uracil, two of the nitrogenous bases in RNA.

Evidence from space supports the conclusions of this experiment. For example, the Murchison meteorite, found in Australia in 1969 and dated as over 4 billion years old, contains many organic molecules. If these molecules formed in other areas of the universe, then they could have also formed on Earth.

Study Tip

Remember the chain of events that are hypothesized to have formed cells: the formation of simple molecules, complex molecules, self-replicating molecules, metabolic processes.

How might complex molecules and cells have formed?

Many scientists agree that the steps from simple organic molecules to life probably occurred in the following order: simple organic molecules, polymers (repeated units of simple organic molecules), self-replicating molecules, metabolic processes.

There is evidence in 3.8 billion-year-old rocks of chemical reactions that take place in living things. Remains of organisms similar to bacteria have been found in rocks that are 3.5 billion years old.

Miller and Urey conducted their experiment to test the first part of a hypothesis called the Oparin-Haldane hypothesis. The first part of the hypothesis proposed that simple organic molecules could form in the conditions of early Earth. The hypothesis went on to propose that once these simple organic molecules formed, they accumulated in oceans in a "soup." Eventually more complex organic molecules formed from the simple ones, followed by systems of molecules. Over time, anaerobic heterotrophs developed from these molecular systems.

Many hypotheses exist regarding how the first cells developed and in which environment. Some scientists propose the first cells formed around deep-sea hydrothermal vents, which are a source of geothermal energy and mineral-rich compounds. Others propose they developed in aquifers near volcanoes. Both hypotheses are supported by good evidence.

How did DNA become the molecule that directs cell activity?

In all organisms, DNA directs cell activity, growth and development, and certain behaviors. How did DNA come to fill its central role in life? Scientists continue to investigate this question.

Figure 1
The "RNA World" Hypothesis

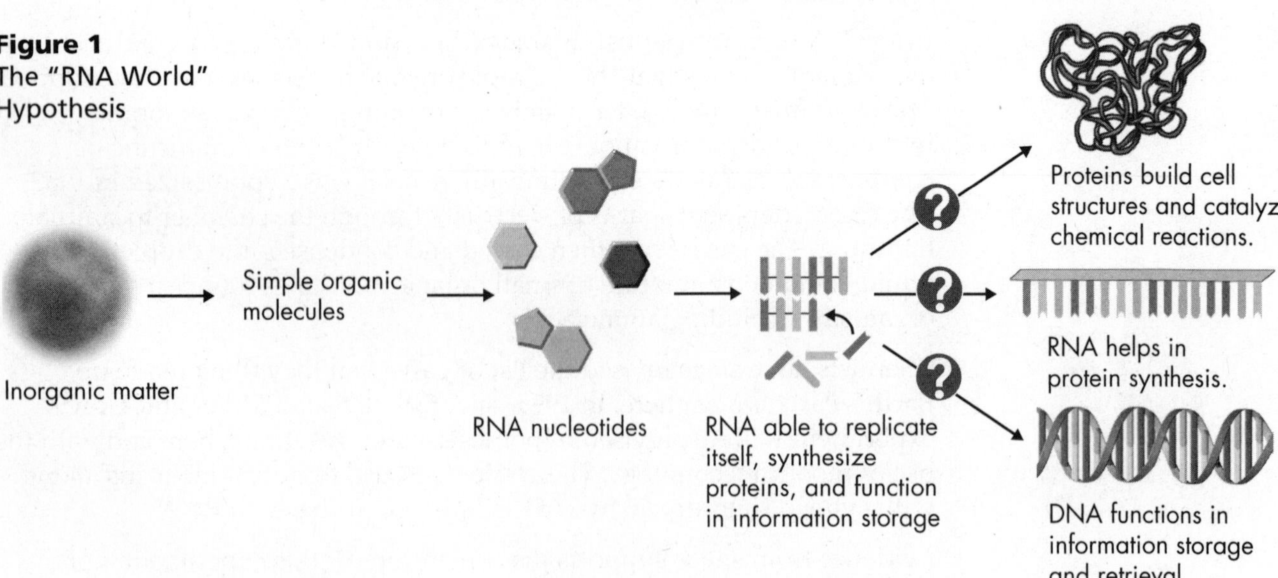
Inorganic matter
Simple organic molecules
RNA nucleotides
RNA able to replicate itself, synthesize proteins, and function in information storage
Proteins build cell structures and catalyze chemical reactions.
RNA helps in protein synthesis.
DNA functions in information storage and retrieval.

In 1968, Carl Woese introduced the hypothesis that DNA arose from RNA, known as the "RNA world" hypothesis (**Figure 1**). Many characteristics of RNA support this hypothesis. For example, one type of RNA, called catalytic RNA, can self-replicate without additional enzymes. Catalytic RNA can also code for amino acids to form a protein. Some scientists hypothesize that one of these proteins allowed RNA to convert into DNA. DNA is a more stable molecule than RNA and better able to store genetic material. Early cells that contained DNA would have had an advantage over those that did not.

TEKS End-of-Course Assessment Review

1. Explain Miller and Urey performed their experiment to determine if they could form

A small, organic molecules from nonorganic molecules.

B large, organic molecules from simple organic molecules.

C Earth's early atmosphere.

D Earth's oxygen-rich atmosphere.

2. Analyze Which observation of cells today supports the hypothesis that RNA, and not DNA, was the first genetic material?

F DNA is double-stranded, while RNA is single-stranded.

G DNA is transcribed to form RNA.

H RNA is translated to form proteins.

J Catalytic RNA can self-replicate without additional enzymes.

3. Identify Why was the Miller-Urey experiment replicated many decades later?

4. Evaluate Although the hypotheses about Earth's early atmosphere are often revisited and revised, most scientists agree that it did not contain any oxygen, or it contained a very small amount of oxygen. Based on this information, what conclusion can you draw about the first cells?

TEKS
REVIEW
10A

Interactions Among Animal Body Systems

TEKS 10A

★ READINESS ★

Describe the interactions that occur among systems that perform the functions of regulation, nutrient absorption, reproduction, and defense from injury or illness in animals.

How do systems interact to regulate an animal's body?

Animals have many different body systems that perform specific tasks. Although each body system may have unique tasks, overall they must work together as one system to maintain homeostasis throughout the body.

The nervous system is the master control center for regulation. Nervous system complexity varies among animals. Most chordates have a concentrated nerve center called a brain. Some invertebrates have just a loose network of nerves. All nervous systems collect information from the internal and external environment and send out commands to the rest of the body. **Figure 1** shows how a mouse's nervous system interacts with its muscular and skeletal systems as the mouse tries to escape from a cat.

Figure 1
Interaction of Systems

NERVOUS SYSTEM
Sensory receptors gather information.
SENSORY RECEPTORS
Sound, Odor, and Visual Cues
BRAIN CELLS
Interneurons process information and determine necessary response.
NERVOUS AND MUSCULOSKELETAL SYSTEMS
Nervous system stimulates muscles.
BRAIN CELLS
MUSCLES
Brain coordinates muscle action for escape response.

Study Tip

Remember that body systems are constantly interacting, even to complete relatively simple tasks such as picking up a pencil from the floor.

For another example, in humans sensory nerves carry information about body temperature to the brain. The brain processes this information and decides whether to raise or lower body temperature. The brain then stimulates the release of chemical signals (hormones) that affect things such as sweating, shivering, and cellular metabolism. To regulate temperature, the nervous system interacts with the endocrine system, which interacts with the circulatory system. Hormones travel in blood from glands of the endocrine system to other parts of the body.

The regulatory effects of the nervous system tend to be rapid but short-lived. Other examples of nervous system regulations include the control of muscle movements, stimulation of the heart and lungs during exercise, and relaxation of the body during rest and sleep.

The endocrine system works more slowly than the nervous system, but its effects often last longer. Many hormones help prepare the body for physical exertion. One example is adrenaline, which quickens the heart rate and makes more glucose available for cells to access energy.

How do systems interact to absorb nutrients?

All animals are heterotrophs, which means they obtain their energy by eating food. To locate and obtain food, animals must use their nervous, muscular, and skeletal systems to some degree. Sensory clues such as sights and smells may alert an animal that food is near. Muscles pull on bones or other skeletal structures to move the animal toward the food.

Figure 2
Example of a Digestive System

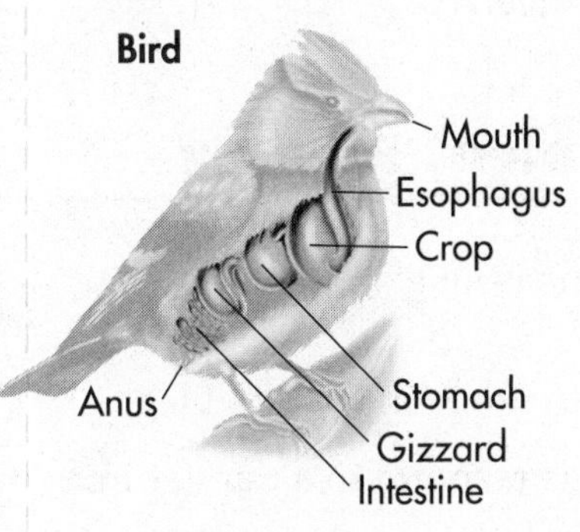

The shape and size of teeth and jaws provide clues about an animal's diet. Those that eat meat (carnivores) will likely have powerful jaws and sharp teeth that can slice and tear. Those that eat plants (herbivores) will likely have jaws that move from side to side and flatter teeth that grind plants.

In some less complex animals, such as sponges, digestion occurs within specialized cells. In more complex animals, digestion occurs in a continuum of organs that process and digest food until it can be absorbed and delivered to cells throughout the body by the circulatory system. To a certain degree, the nervous and endocrine systems also regulate functions of the digestive system. For example, the nervous system controls the muscles that move food through digestive organs. Hormones stimulate the pancreas to release enzymes critical in breaking down food.

How do systems interact in reproduction?

Most animals reproduce sexually, which maintains genetic diversity in a population. Some invertebrates and a few vertebrates reproduce asexually, which allows for rapid reproduction, but little genetic variation.

The main job of the reproductive system is to produce haploid gametes. Males typically produce sperm and females typically produce eggs. When a sperm and egg join, the result is a diploid zygote.

The reproductive system is largely influenced by the nervous and endocrine systems, which send signals to the reproductive system when conditions are right for reproduction. In many environments, offspring need to be born during a certain season to have a chance at survival.

In many animals, the female lays eggs. But in most mammals, known as placental mammals, offspring develop inside the female. The developing offspring is called an embryo. Many systems interact in the mother's body to allow an embryo to develop. A placenta grows from the tissues of the mother and the embryo. Blood vessels in the placenta carry food and oxygen to the embryo and wastes away from it. The endocrine system also stimulates milk production in the mother to feed the offspring after birth.

How do systems interact to defend the body?

The immune system defends the body from illness. It includes a variety of white blood cells that recognize and attack pathogens.

Other systems also defend the body against pathogens. In the digestive system, acid in the stomach helps kill pathogens that enter the body with food and saliva. In the integumentary system, skin acts as the main barrier between pathogens and internal body tissues. Mucous membranes line the nose, mouth, and other body cavities, and the mucus that they secrete helps trap pathogens and small foreign objects.

The nervous system also protects the body from injury. The brain can process sensory information to recognize danger and react accordingly. When an animal feels threatened, body systems interact for the sake of protection. Adrenaline from the endocrine system and messages from the nervous system help the animal fight or flee its attacker. The circulatory, respiratory, and muscular systems all work harder and faster than normal to give the animal oxygen and energy to fight or flee.

TEKS End-of-Course Assessment Review

1. Describe Which interaction of body systems is an example of homeostasis?

A The nervous system stimulates muscles to move in the right leg.

B The endocrine system helps other systems respond to a danger in the environment.

C When blood sugar is high, hormones stimulate cells to take up sugar from the blood.

D None of these

2. Describe Which process involves the nervous system and endocrine system working together?

F moving the hand and fingers to scratch an itch

G jerking the arm away when the hand touches something hot

H digesting food after it is swallowed

J swallowing food after it is chewed

3. Apply Concepts How is it helpful for the body to have more than one system defend it from injury and illness?

10B Interactions Among Plant Systems

TEKS 10B

READINESS

Describe the interactions that occur among systems that perform the functions of transport, reproduction, and response in plants.

Vocabulary
xylem
phloem
phototropism
gravitropism
thigmotropism

How do systems interact in plants to transport water, minerals, and food?

Seed plant cells are organized into tissues, organs, and systems. The three types of tissues found in seed plants are vascular, dermal, and ground. The three main types of organs are roots, stems, and leaves. All are involved in the transport of materials throughout the plant.

Vascular tissues have a central role in transport. Water and dissolved minerals from the soil are transported by vascular tissue called **xylem**. Root hairs, which are part of dermal tissue, use active transport to bring in minerals. Osmosis causes water to follow the minerals. Once the fluid is in the xylem, it rises through the roots, stems, and leaves. Fluid exits the plant when it evaporates from the leaves through pores called *stomata*.

Specialized cells allow a plant to control the flow of xylem fluid. For example, *guard cells* open and close stomata in leaves, which allows the plant to conserve water. In roots, the *Casparian strip* works like a one-way valve to ensure that water does not flow back into the soil.

Figure 1
Cross Section of a Root

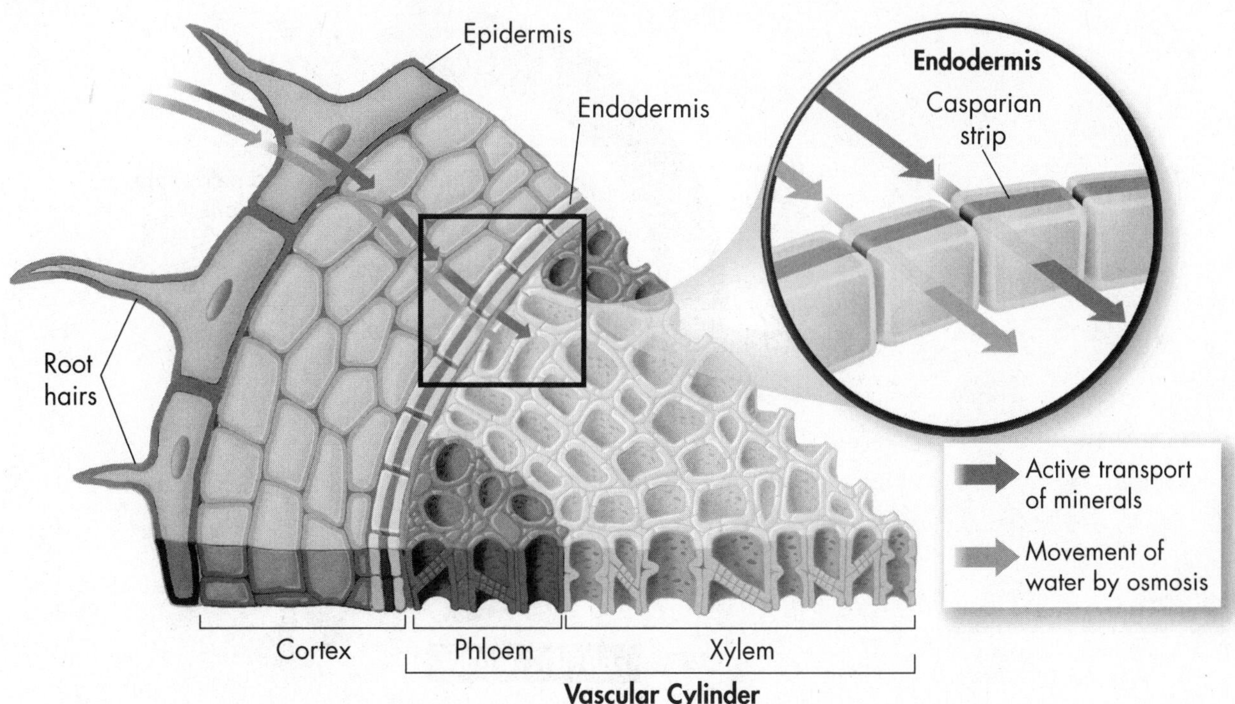

Sugars, which are food produced and used by the plant, are carried in a vascular tissue called **phloem**. Phloem may also carry minerals, amino acids, and hormones. The fluid travels from an organ that produces sugar, such as a leaf, to an organ that uses sugar, such as a growing stem, root, or fruit.

How do systems in plants interact in reproduction?

Many plants can reproduce both asexually (vegetative reproduction) and sexually. Vegetative reproduction requires the interaction of all the systems of a plant normally involved in growth and development.

Figure 2 shows the general life cycle of sexually reproducing plants. In angiosperms, flowers are the reproductive organs. Flowers consist of dermal, ground, and vascular tissue. They also have four types of leaves: sepals (protect buds and developing flowers), petals, stamens, and carpels. Stamens and carpels produce gametophytes, which are gamete-producing plants. Pollen grains are male gametophytes, and an ovule with an embryo sac is a female gametophyte. Fertilized gametes grow into sporophytes, which produce spores that grow into gametophytes.

Pollination occurs when pollen is transferred to the female portions of a flower by wind or animals such as bees. Fertilization occurs when a pollen grain lands on a stigma. Then a pollen tube grows into the style and eventually into the ovule. A double fertilization takes place when one of the sperm nuclei fuses with the egg nucleus to form a diploid zygote. The other sperm nucleus fuses with other nuclei of the female gametophyte to form an energy-rich substance that will nourish a growing seedling.

Figure 2
A Plant Life Cycle

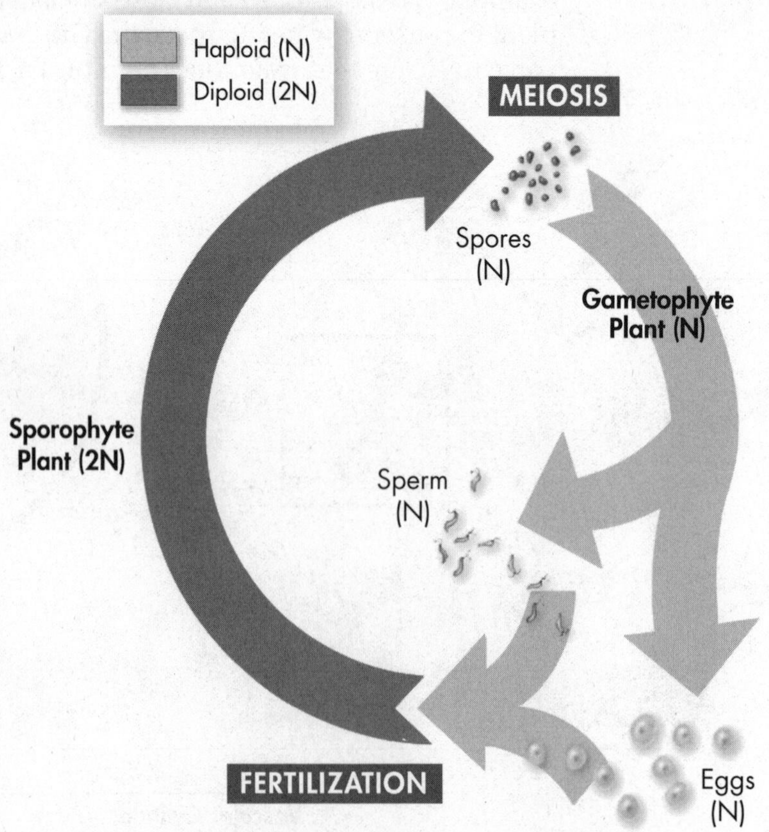

Study Tip

The prefix *trop-*, from the Greek word *tropos*, means "turn" or "change." A tropism is a characteristic change in an organism in response to its environment.

Once fertilization is complete, the plant's vascular system brings a steady flow of nutrients to the flower tissue, which supports the growing embryo within the seed. As the seeds mature, the ovary walls thicken and form a fruit that encloses the developing seeds.

How do systems in plants interact to respond to the environment?

Plants respond to light, gravity, water, and seasonal weather changes. Many of these plant responses are controlled by hormones.

Phototropism is the growth of plants toward a light source. This response is triggered by a hormone called auxin. Auxin accumulates where light is less intense and causes cells to elongate. As a result, cells that receive less light grow longer than cells that receive more light. In a stem, this growth pattern causes the stem to bend toward a light source.

Gravitropism is the growth of plants in response to gravity. Roots show positive gravitropism, meaning they grow in the direction of gravity. Stems show negative gravitropism. Like light, gravity affects the distribution of auxin in a cell. If a plant falls over, auxin accumulates in cells on the lower side of the stem. The stem will respond by growing upward.

Thigmotropism is the growth of plants in response to touch. This response allows morning glory vines to climb up fences. In forests, it allows vines to climb toward the light.

TEKS End-of-Course Assessment Review

1. Contrast In which property does xylem differ from phloem?

- **A** presence in trees and other tall plants
- **B** presence in roots, stems, and leaves
- **C** the direction in which it transports materials
- **D** tubelike organization

2. Explain The gravitropism of a tree's trunk explains which of these observations of a tree?

- **F** The tree develops flowers at the same time every year.
- **G** The tree grows to a certain maximum height and then stops growing taller.
- **H** A tree trunk grows slightly wider every year.
- **J** On a steep hillside, the tree's trunk is upright and vertical, not tilted.

3. Describe Give an example of a plant process that involves an interaction between its systems of roots and shoots. (Shoots include stems and leaves.) Describe the interactions that occur.

10C Levels of Organization

TEKS 10C

Analyze the levels of organization in biological systems and relate the levels to each other and to the whole system.

Vocabulary
tissue
organ
organ system

How are biological systems organized?

Biological systems include systems both outside of and within organisms. An ecosystem, for example, consists of all the living and nonliving things in an area, all of which affect one another. This review, however, examines the organization of systems *within* an organism. Many organisms, including bacteria and most protists, consist of a single cell. But other organisms are multicellular. Some simple multicellular organisms function very efficiently without complex organization. But most large organisms, including all familiar plants and animals, are much more complex. For a complex organism to function efficiently, its cells must be organized into systems that work together to complete essential tasks. You can see the levels of organization that include human stomach muscle cells in **Figure 1**.

Figure 1
Levels of Organization

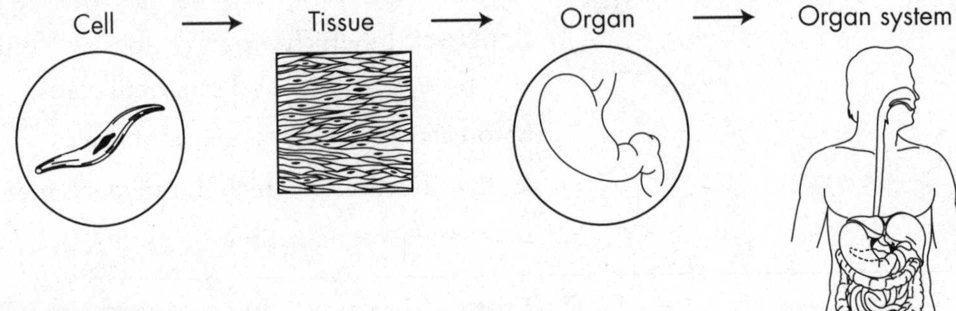

How do cells compare to tissues?

Cells are often referred to as the "building blocks" of multicellular organisms. Cells with similar structures and functions are organized into **tissues.** For example, reddish, spindle-shaped muscle cells are organized together in muscle tissues. The human body relies on three types of muscle tissue: skeletal muscle tissue for moving bones, smooth muscle tissue for the automatic (involuntary) movements of organs such as the stomach, and cardiac muscle in the heart for pumping blood through the body.

Blood is tissue that consists of cells suspended in a liquid called plasma. Red blood cells carry oxygen, and white blood cells defend the body from invading organisms. Other components allow blood to clot at open wounds, which is important to prevent loss of blood. In addition to blood cells, plasma transports dissolved substances, such as gases and nutrients, throughout the body.

How do tissues compare to organs, and how do organs compare to organ systems?

Organs, which contain different types of tissues, are body parts that have a particular function. Examples of organs in animals include the heart, lungs, brain, skeletal muscles, and bones. In plants, organs include roots, stems, and leaves.

The skin is the largest organ of the human body. The skin is composed of different tissue layers, including epithelial tissues and inner dermal layers. Bones also are made of different types of tissues, including a hard tissue on the outside and a spongy tissue on the inside. Tissues in the center of long bones produce blood cells.

A group of organs that work together to fulfill a function make up an **organ system.** The human body has several organ systems. The heart and blood vessels make up the circulatory system. This system delivers oxygen and nutrients to all body cells, and it removes carbon dioxide and other wastes. The brain, sensory organs, and nerves make up the nervous system. This system senses the environment and internal body conditions, processes the information, and sends messages to control body activities.

In plants, the roots make up an organ system that absorbs water and nutrients from the soil. The leaves make up an organ system that performs photosynthesis. The stems and branches make up an organ system that carries water, nutrients, and food through xylem and phloem and that provides support for leaves and flowers.

Study Tip

In multicellular organisms, all cells need food, oxygen, water, and a process to remove wastes. Cells also need to be controlled or coordinated so they work together efficiently. Organ systems meet all of these needs of cells.

How do the levels of organization relate to one another and to the whole system?

In a multicellular organism, no cell, tissue, or organ can function by itself. Their coordination allows the organism to maintain homeostasis and complete a wide variety of tasks. For example, when you see a dollar on the floor and decide to pick it up, the task requires the nervous, muscular, skeletal, circulatory, and respiratory systems—all acting with one another and at the same time.

Without your conscious knowledge, the systems of your body work together quickly, effectively, and continuously. While you might be focusing your attention on a specific task, such as reading this paragraph, a wide variety of coordinated organ systems are performing tasks such as breathing, circulating blood, cleaning your blood of wastes, and digesting food. Even when you are sleeping, they continue performing these tasks.

TEKS End-of-Course Assessment Review

1. **Sequence** Which sequence shows the increasing complexity of levels of organization in multicellular organisms?
   - **A** cell, organ, tissue, organ system, organism
   - **B** cell, tissue, organ, organ system, organism
   - **C** cell, organism, tissue, organ, organ system
   - **D** organ system, organ, organism, cell, tissue

2. **Analyze** The femur is a long bone in the upper leg. The femur is classified as an organ because it
   - **F** functions independently of other organs or organ systems.
   - **G** is larger than a tissue and smaller than an organ system.
   - **H** is made of tissues found nowhere else in the body.
   - **J** is composed of several types of tissues that work together.

3. **Apply Concepts** Muscle tissue that is involved in movement of the body would most likely be associated with the
   - **A** digestive system.
   - **B** circulatory system.
   - **C** respiratory system.
   - **D** skeletal system.

4. **Analyze** Choose a simple activity that you perform every day. Describe the organs and organ systems that are involved in this activity.

TEKS
REVIEW
11A

Feedback Mechanisms and Homeostasis

TEKS 11A

Describe the role of internal feedback mechanisms in the maintenance of homeostasis.

Vocabulary
homeostasis
internal feedback mechanism
hypothalamus

What is homeostasis?

All living things respond to their environment. **Homeostasis** is the relatively constant internal physical and chemical conditions maintained by an organism despite changes that occur inside or outside its body.

Homeostasis is important because an organism functions properly only within a narrow range of internal chemical and physical conditions. Cells depend on a certain range of temperature and pH, as well as a proper supply of oxygen, energy, and water. These conditions are influenced by the external environment, which changes due to weather, the cycle of day and night, and the cycle of seasons. Also, an organism's activities, such as running from a predator, sleeping, or digesting a big meal, change its internal environment.

What are the roles of internal feedback mechanisms in the maintenance of homeostasis?

Internal feedback mechanisms are triggers within a system in which the result of the process controls the process itself. For example, a thermostat maintains a set temperature inside a house using an internal feedback mechanism, as shown in **Figure 1**. If the temperature drops below a particular point, the thermostat responds by turning the heater on. Once the house reaches that set temperature, the thermostat receives this feedback and turns the heater off.

Figure 1
An Internal Feedback Mechanism

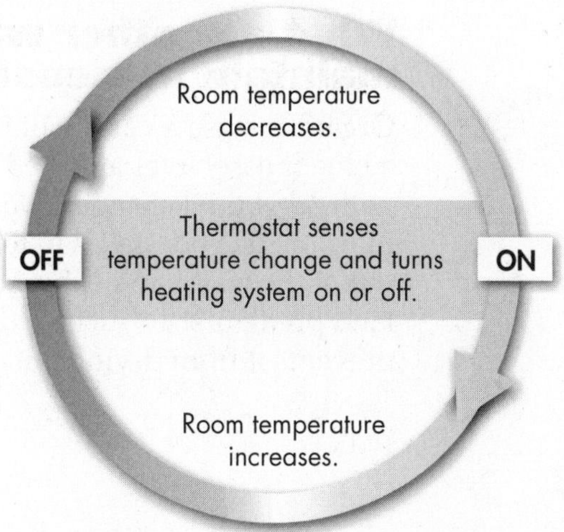
Room temperature decreases.
OFF
Thermostat senses temperature change and turns heating system on or off.
ON
Room temperature increases.

In the human body, the hypothalamus responds to temperature change much like a thermostat. The **hypothalamus** is a structure at the base of the brain that is a control center for recognition of and response to hunger, thirst, fatigue, anger, and body temperature. Sensory nerves in the skin send messages to the hypothalamus about external temperatures. If the air temperature is cold, the hypothalamus responds with messages that cause the body to conserve or produce heat, such as by shivering (**Figure 2a**). When the air temperature is hot, a similar process leads to actions that cool the body, such as sweating (**Figure 2b**).

Figure 2
Temperature Regulation

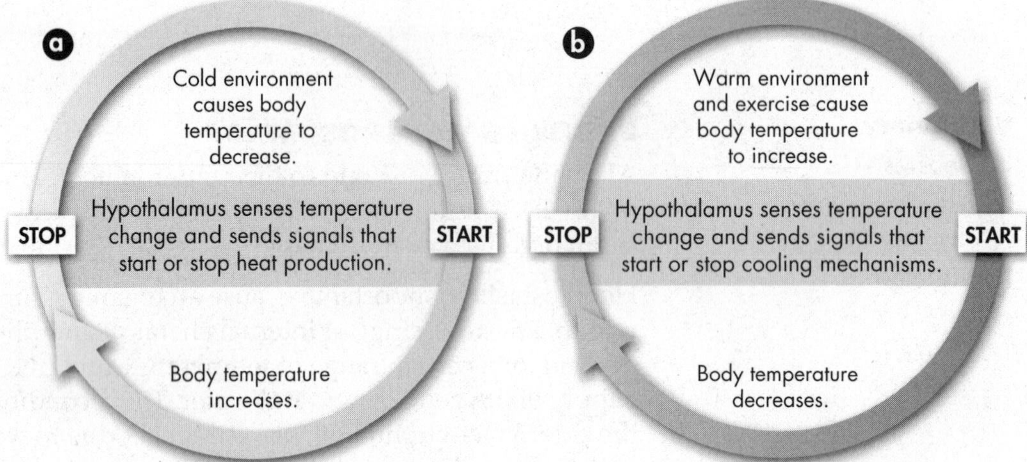

> **Study Tip**
>
> Draw a diagram or flowchart for each positive and negative feedback mechanism discussed in this review.

Internal feedback mechanisms are classified as either negative or positive. Negative feedback mechanisms are more common than positive feedback mechanisms, but both are essential for proper body function.

In a negative feedback mechanism, an increase in the product or the result causes a decrease in the response. An example is the mechanism of temperature regulation in the human body discussed above.

In a positive feedback mechanism, an increase in the product or result causes an increase in the response. You can think of positive feedback as a process of amplification—a small change leads to a much larger change. One example involves childbirth. When uterine contractions begin, the hypothalamus releases more of the hormone oxytocin, which in turn causes more contractions.

What are other ways in which organisms maintain homeostasis?

Organisms use a variety of methods to maintain homeostasis. For example, a blue mussel lives attached to rocks on the ocean coast, where it must withstand tidal changes. During high tide, when the mussel is submerged in water, its body takes in food and oxygen. During low tide, the mussel is out of the water and exposed to sunlight and wind. It also is exposed to land predators. To survive during low tide, the mussel closes its shell. This prevents it from drying out and deters many predators.

In the human body, some methods of maintaining homeostasis involve chemicals in the blood. The body cannot tolerate a blood pH level that varies much from 7.4. An enzyme called carbonic anhydrase allows the blood to convert carbon dioxide gas into soluble substances. These substances keep the pH of blood at about 7.4, even when small amounts of acids or bases are added to the blood.

The nervous system is very involved in maintaining homeostasis. Sensory nerves receive information about internal and external conditions. They send messages to the brain, which analyzes the messages. In response, the brain sends commands through nerves or the blood. Feelings of thirst and hunger or of extreme heat or cold, are examples of messages from the brain. These feelings may promote behavior such as eating or seeking shelter to help the body maintain homeostasis.

TEKS End-of-Course Assessment Review

1. Describe When blood glucose levels increase, the pancreas releases insulin. Insulin causes body cells to take up glucose, and blood glucose levels decrease. In a negative feedback mechanism, what will happen next?

A The pancreas will release more insulin.

B The pancreas will stop releasing insulin.

C Cells will take in more glucose.

D Cells will take in insulin.

2. Describe The hypothalamus acts like a thermostat for the body because it

F can be adjusted to maintain a wide range of body temperatures.

G releases enzymes into the blood that help maintain a constant body temperature.

H sends messages to muscles and glands that help maintain a constant body temperature.

J directly senses the air temperature and adjusts body temperature to match it.

3. Contrast How are negative feedback mechanisms different from positive feedback mechanisms?

4. Describe When a wound causes blood vessel damage, platelets stick to the site of the damage. The platelets release chemicals that attract more platelets to the area and promote the release of the same chemicals from these platelets. Explain if this is a positive or negative feedback mechanism and how the process helps maintain homeostasis.

The Dynamics of Organisms, Populations, and Communities

TEKS 11B

Investigate and analyze how organisms, populations, and communities respond to external factors.

Vocabulary
community
ecosystem
biotic factor
abiotic factor

What is the relationship among organisms, populations, and communities?

The environment can be organized into levels of complexity. An *organism* is an individual living thing, such as a bacterium, protist, fungus, plant, or animal. A *population* is a group of one species of organisms that live together in a certain area. For example, all the tree frogs of one species in a forest make up a population.

A **community** is a group of populations of different species that interact with one another. On a tropical island, the community includes that population of tree frogs as well as all other animal and plant populations. An **ecosystem** includes that community of living things, or **biotic factors**, and the nonliving aspects, or **abiotic factors**, in the environment. The whole tropical island forest is an example of an ecosystem **(Figure 1)**.

Figure 1
Levels of Organization

How do organisms in an ecosystem respond to external factors?

All organisms respond to changes in their environment. Predators are one type of external biotic factor that animals respond to. For example, when a rabbit senses that a hawk or other predator is near, it may run away or hide in a burrow. A skunk will spray a would-be attacker with a foul-smelling liquid, while an opossum will curl into a ball and pretend to be dead.

In order to maintain homeostasis, organisms must also respond to external abiotic factors, such as temperature, precipitation, and soil quality. For example, when the temperature becomes cold, some animals hibernate and some animals migrate to warmer places.

Plants also respond to external biotic and abiotic factors. For example, plants that grow as vines, such as ivy and pumpkins, produce thin tendrils that can wrap around surfaces, including the stems of other plants. Also, the roots of plants tend to grow toward wet soil, while the leaves and stems bend toward sunlight. On the leaves of many plants, pores open during the night and close during the day. This allows the plant to lose less water due to transpiration.

How do populations respond to external factors?

Populations may increase, stay the same, or decrease, depending on how well the organisms that make up the population respond to external factors. Many external factors affect the size of a population. One example is predator-prey relationships. When the population of wolves increases, the population of their prey, such as deer, may decrease. A decrease in the deer population may in turn lower the wolf population, allowing the deer population to increase again.

Two populations may also compete with each other for the same resources, such as food, water, sunlight, or space. Populations can change drastically when new species arrive and begin to compete with established (native) species for the same resources. For example, several types of Asian carp, which were used to control algae in catfish farms, have been introduced into the Mississippi River. These carp grow rapidly, eat a wide variety of foods, and reproduce quickly. As the carp's population increases, the populations of native fishes have been decreasing.

Diseases also affect populations, especially populations that are dense or do not have a lot of genetic variation. For example, for a number of years people planted elm trees in many areas of the United States. Elms were prized for their height and beauty and for the leafy canopies they formed over city streets. But beginning in the late 1920s, the fungus that causes Dutch elm disease spread across the United States. By the 1970s, millions of elm trees had died. Few elms survive today in the United States.

How do communities in an ecosystem respond to external factors?

When a factor affects one population, it affects the whole community. A disease that kills trees in a community affects not only the tree population, but the animals that eat the tree's leaves or make their homes in the tree's branches. At the same time, decomposers benefit from the dead trees and return their nutrients to the soil, which will benefit young growing plants.

Sometimes communities can change drastically because of sudden natural events, such as earthquakes or volcanic eruptions. The ecosystem around Mount St. Helens in Washington State was once home to a thriving community of plants and animals. Then in May of 1980, the volcano erupted in a violent explosion, spewing boiling lava, ash, and dust. Most organisms of the community died or had to relocate. Lava covered many areas and destroyed the upper layer of soil.

Study Tip

From an individual to the largest group, living things are organized into organisms, populations, communities, and ecosystems. Remember these terms in this order.

Over time, however, the communities surrounding Mount St. Helens recovered. This type of ecological recovery is called *primary succession*, in which barren rock gradually evolves into a diverse ecosystem. At Mount St. Helens, gophers and other animals survived underground, and they helped mix fertile layers of soil with less fertile layers. Grasses and wildflowers began growing, followed by trees. Today, the ecosystem is different than it was before the volcanic eruption, but it is diverse and healthy.

Human actions also change communities. All over the world, people are cutting and burning forests and replacing them with houses, farms, and businesses. Prairie and grassland communities have been replaced by crops and grazing animals. On the other hand, abandoned farmland is being replaced by emerging forest communities. Pollution also affects communities, sometimes very suddenly. In April 2010, an oil rig called *Deepwater Horizon* exploded while pumping crude oil from beneath the Gulf of Mexico. Millions of barrels of crude oil were released into the Gulf. Many marine animals and coastal animals, especially birds, were killed. Because oil is difficult to remove from the environment, damage to Gulf communities may persist for many years.

TEKS End-of-Course Assessment Review

1. **Infer** A population of deer belongs to the forest community. Which change to the community would most likely cause the deer population to increase?

   A A new disease strikes mountain lions, a predator of deer.

   B A new beetle arrives that lives in the bark of trees, the food supply for the deer.

   C Human activities divert water away from the forest.

   D Human activities reduce the size of the forest.

2. **Analyze** For the past several decades, a weed called Eurasian water milfoil has been spreading rapidly across lakes, rivers, and other bodies of fresh water in North America. It grows quickly and forms dense mats on the surface of the water. North American fish tend not to eat the milfoil. When Eurasian water-milfoil arrives in a lake, which set of organisms would you expect it to affect?

   F other aquatic plants in the lake

   G fish in the lake that eat plants

   H all fish that live in the lake

   J all members of the lake community

3. **Analyze** How are human activities affecting a natural community in your neighborhood?

4. **Investigate** Some hogs that were domesticated livestock have escaped and established feral hog populations in Texas. The word *feral* means "returned to a wild state." These "newly wild" hogs live in forests, swamps, and brush lands. They eat a wide variety of foods, including insects, amphibians, birds, and other small animals, as well as many types of plants. Form a hypothesis on the effect of feral hogs on various species living in the community.

The Roles of Microorganisms

TEKS 11C

Summarize the role of microorganisms in both maintaining and disrupting the health of both organisms and ecosystems.

Vocabulary
microorganism
pathogen

How can microorganisms maintain the health of other organisms?

A **microorganism** can be defined as any organism that cannot be seen without the aid of a magnifying glass or microscope. Microorganisms are found in almost every habitat on Earth, and they are members of all three domains of life and the six kingdoms.

Many types of microorganisms form mutualistic relationships with animals and plants. A mutualistic relationship is one in which both species benefit from the relationship. The microorganism may gain benefits such as a warm environment to inhabit and nutrients. The animal or plant may gain benefits such as protection from other microorganisms or a supply of enzymes they need but cannot produce.

There are many examples of mutualistic relationships between microorganisms and other organisms. Many types of bacteria live in human intestines and help in digestion. Bacteria (or other single-celled organisms) live in the guts of plant-eating animals such as termites and cows and produce enzymes that help to digest cellulose.

Fungi and plant roots also form mutualistic relationships called *mycorrhizae.* Branching tissues of the fungi, called hyphae, collect water and minerals and deliver them to the plant roots. The plants provide the fungi with nutrients made through photosynthesis. **Figure 1** shows how much some trees can benefit from mycorrhizae.

Figure 1

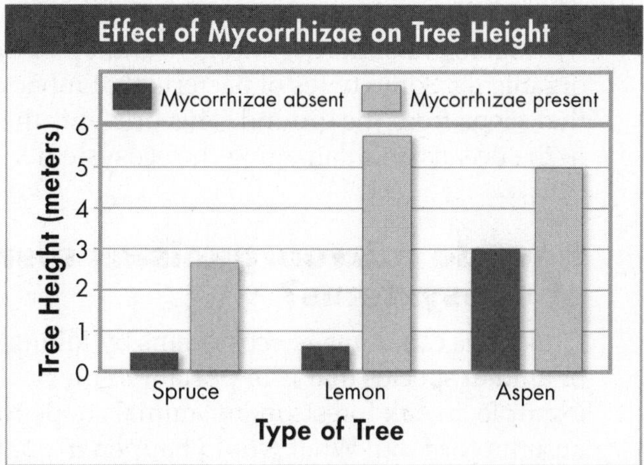

Other plants called legumes contain bacteria of the genus *Rhizobium* in structures on their roots called nodes. The *Rhizobium* fix atmospheric nitrogen so that it is available for plants to use in life processes.

How can microorganisms disrupt the health of organisms?

Some microorganisms enter into parasitic relationships with other organisms that disrupt the health of the other organisms. In this type of relationship, the microorganism is a parasite and the other organism is a host. Microorganisms that cause disease in a host are called **pathogens**. Pathogens usually cause disease by killing host cells, releasing toxins, or interfering with processes within the host's body. Some examples of bacterial pathogens that infect humans are included in **Figure 2.**

Figure 2

Some Human Bacterial Diseases		
Disease	**Effect on Body**	**Transmission**
Lyme disease	"Bull's-eye" rash at site of tick bite, fever, fatigue, headache	Ticks transmit the bacterium
Tetanus	Lockjaw, stiffness in neck and abdomen, difficulty swallowing, fever, elevated blood pressure, severe muscle spasms	Bacteria enter the body through a break in the skin.
Tuberculosis	Fatigue, weight loss, fever, night sweats, chills, appetite loss, bloody sputum from lungs	Bacterial particles are inhaled.
Bacterial meningitis	High fever, headache, stiff neck, nausea, fatigue	Bacteria are spread in respiratory droplets caused by coughing and sneezing; close or prolonged contact with someone infected with meningitis
Strep throat	Fever, sore throat, headache, fatigue, nausea	Direct contact with mucus from an infected person or direct contact with infected wounds or breaks in the skin

How do microorganisms maintain the health of ecosystems?

When microorganisms participate in mutualistic relationships with plants, this benefits not only individual plants, but also entire ecosystems. Microorganisms also recycle nutrients. For example, decomposers break down the organic matter of dead plants and animals. This frees carbon, hydrogen, phosphorus, nitrogen, and other nutrients for use by living organisms. Some types of bacteria that inhabit the ocean floor feed on oil that seeps from the ground. This prevents the leaking oil from building up in the oceans and damaging the ecosystem.

How do microorganisms disrupt the health of ecosystems?

Pathogens can damage ecosystems by killing off large numbers of a plant or animal species that is important to the health of the ecosystem. For example, in oak forests many animals depend on the acorns that fall each autumn for food. What would happen if a pathogen infected the oak trees and prevented them from producing acorns?

Study Tip

Creating a table that summarizes how microorganisms maintain and disrupt the health of organisms and ecosystems will help you recall the information.

Population bursts of green algae and dinoflagellates can lead to algal blooms in aquatic ecosystems that cause harm in various ways. The algal blooms can block sunlight from penetrating water and cause the death of plants along with the organisms that eat the plants. Toxins in dinoflagellates accumulate in the animals that eat the microorganisms and can lead to toxic effects throughout the food chain. When the dinoflagellates die in mass numbers, their decomposition leads to low oxygen levels. Fishes and other aquatic animals cannot live in these oxygen-deprived areas, which are known as dead zones.

TEKS End-of-Course Assessment Review

1. Identify Which of the following best describes a difference between a mutualistic relationship and a parasitic relationship?

A Parasitism harms both organisms, while mutualism harms only one organism.

B Parasitism benefits only one organism, while mutualism benefits both organisms.

C Parasitism involves only two organisms, while mutualism involves many organisms.

D Parasitism continues for many generations, while mutualism is limited to one generation.

2. Summarize Which of the following statements is the best summary of how microorganisms can disrupt the health of organisms?

F Microorganisms live in plant and animal hosts.

G Some microorganisms form mutualistic relationships with plants and animals.

H Some microorganisms form parasitic relationships with plants and animals.

J Some microorganisms break down the organic matter of dead plants and animals.

3. Summarize Write a summary that explains the roles of microorganisms in maintaining and disrupting the health of ecosystems.

Ecological Succession and Changes in Biodiversity

TEKS 11D

★ READINESS ★

Describe how events and processes that occur during ecological succession can change populations and species diversity.

Vocabulary
ecological succession
primary succession
secondary succession

What is ecological succession?

Ecosystems can be drastically altered by volcanic eruptions, severe storms, forest fires, the advance or retreat of glaciers, and human activities such as deforestation. Yet with time, the ecosystem will gradually recover. **Ecological succession** is the natural process of predictable changes that occur in a community following a disturbance. During succession, one community of organisms gradually replaces another community. The ideal end community in any given ecosystem is called its *climax community*. A climax community remains relatively stable until another drastic event disturbs it.

What events and processes occur during ecological succession?

The processes of ecological succession are classified as either primary succession or secondary succession. In both primary and secondary succession, each community produces the conditions that allow a new community to replace it. Typically as succession progresses, the diversity of species increases. The process continues gradually for many years until a climax community is reached.

Primary succession occurs on bare rock or hardened lava on which no soil or organisms exist (**Figure 1**). Typical locations for primary succession include newly formed volcanic islands and the bare rock left behind by a retreating glacier. Primary succession often begins with the arrival of lichens, which are described as *pioneer species*. Pioneer species are able to grow on barren rock. Over time, a thin layer of soil forms as lichens break down rock and add organic matter.

The early stages of primary succession can be very slow. It may take many years, even hundreds of years, for even a thin layer of soil to form. Once soil is established, grasses, wildflowers, shrubs, and other small plants can take root. When these plants die, their remains add more nutrients to the soil. This allows trees and other large plants to grow. As plant communities develop, more animal communities move into the area.

Secondary succession occurs after an event in which the ecosystem is damaged, but not destroyed. Fire, hurricanes, and volcanic eruptions can damage and kill shrubs and trees but leave soil intact. Because soil remains, secondary succession occurs faster than primary succession.

Study Tip

The word *primary* comes from the Latin word for *first*. The process is called *primary* succession because it involves the *first* organisms on that plot of land.

Figure 1 Primary Succession

During secondary succession, new communities form quickly because the soil already contains seeds and nutrients. Insects, birds, small rodents, and other animals will eventually populate the community once plants are established. For example, fires swept through forests of Yellowstone National Park in 1988. But the soil remained intact. Within a year, a variety of small plants were growing on the forest floor among the burnt trees. Today, the region is home to small but healthy trees and to many animals.

In some cases, secondary succession can lead to an ecosystem that is different from the original ecosystem. For example, when tropical rain forests are cleared and the land is used for farming, changes to the soil may prevent the same type of climax community from returning even after the farm land is abandoned.

How does ecological succession change populations and species diversity?

When an event such as a forest fire or volcanic eruption occurs, all populations in the area suffer. The ecosystem loses both populations of organisms and the diversity of species. Over time, however, the numbers and diversity of organisms often recover, especially if the soil is intact. The seeds of some plants survive in the soil, and the death of tall trees provides the space and light that allow seedlings to grow. Insects deposit eggs in the soil, and these eggs may survive and hatch.

If there are still intact habitats, animals may also move into the area from other regions. Previously filled niches may be empty because of the death of species, which reduces competition. This can result in the emergence of entirely new ecosystems. Herbivores, which are plant-eating animals, arrive first because there are only plants to eat in an ecosystem in the early stages of succession. For a while, herbivore populations increase because they have few competitors or predators. Eventually carnivores, or meat eating-animals, arrive to prey on the herbivores, completing the trophic levels in the ecosystem.

How do populations and species diversity change as succession progresses?

As a general rule, population size and species diversity both increase during ecological succession. Very early in succession, very few species can survive in such limited habitat. There are mainly mosses and lichens during primary succession, and grasses and other small plants during secondary succession. These producers provide food for only a few animal species, such as insects and worms.

With time, more species become established. Smaller producers are replaced by larger ones, such as small trees and shrubs. As insects increase, birds and other animals that eat insects arrive. Eventually, the diverse climax community of producers including tall trees, complex undergrowth, and multiple grasses provides food, shelter, and nesting habitat for thousands of species of animals.

TEKS End-of-Course Assessment Review

1. **Classify** Which event would most likely lead to primary succession?
   A A volcanic eruption expands an island in the Pacific Ocean.
   B A rain forest in Brazil is cut down for lumber.
   C A wildfire burns trees across Yellowstone National Park.
   D All of these

2. **Compare and Contrast** In which ecosystem would the species be most diverse and their populations be most numerous?
   F an ecosystem undergoing the first stages of primary succession
   G an ecosystem undergoing the first stages of secondary succession
   H a forest one year after a fire has burned down the trees
   J a forest that has remained unchanged for many years

3. **Describe** When a farm is abandoned, ecological succession usually takes place. Identify what type of ecological succession will occur. Predict how the processes of ecological succession will change populations within the ecosystem.

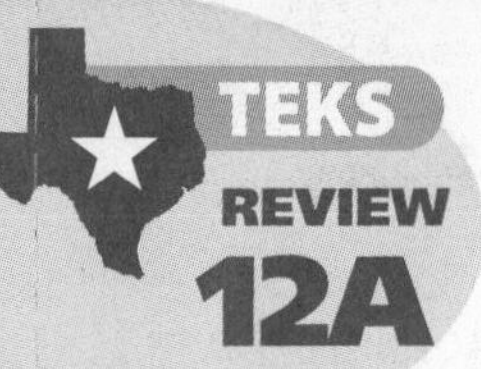

12A Relationships Among Organisms

TEKS 12A

★ READINESS ★

Interpret relationships, including predation, parasitism, commensalism, mutualism, and competition among organisms.

Vocabulary
niche
competition
predation
symbiosis
parasitism
commensalism
mutualism

What is an organism's role in its environment?

An organism's *habitat* is the area where it lives. The same habitat, such as a lake or forest, may be home to hundreds of different types of organisms or species. A *species* is typically defined as a group of organisms that can breed with each other and produce fertile offspring.

In any environment, every species fills a unique niche. A species' **niche** includes the conditions and resources it needs for survival and how it obtains these resources. You can see how different songbird species fill different niches in a spruce tree habitat in **Figure 1**. By living and feeding in different areas of the tree (having unique niches), the bird species avoid competing with each other for the same resources.

Figure 1
Warbler Niches

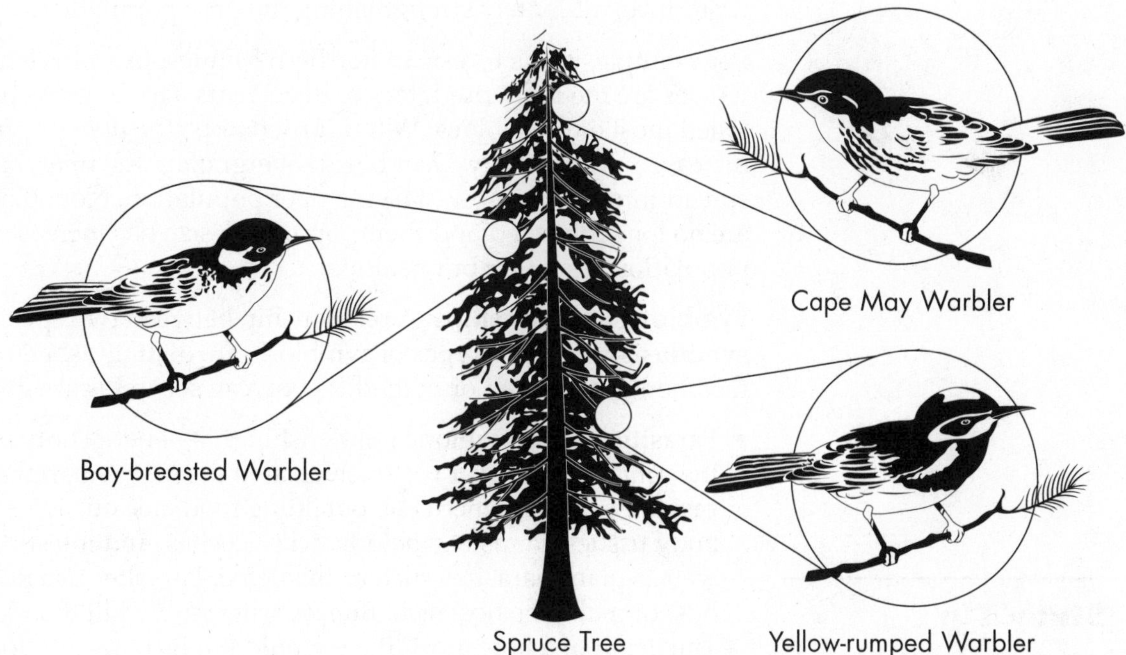

What types of relationships do organisms engage in?

An important part of an organism's niche involves the relationships it engages in with other organisms. These relationships include competition, predation, and various types of symbiosis.

Competition Within a habitat, when more than one organism requires the same resources, **competition** will occur. Birds compete for places to build their nests and for food. Owls, foxes, bobcats, and other predators all compete for the same small animals that are their sources of food. Even animals of the same species compete for food, shelter, and mates. Plants of the same and different species compete, too. For example, in a forest, the branches of mature, tall trees block much of the sunlight from reaching the forest floor. The tall trees outcompete younger, shorter trees for the light, stunting the growth of the younger trees.

If two species try to fill the same niche, one of the species will be better adapted to it. Over time, the other species would develop a new niche, leave, or more likely die out. This rule is called the *competitive exclusion principle*. No two species can occupy the same niche, in the same place, at the same time.

Predation A relationship in which one organism, the *predator*, captures and eats another organism, the *prey* is called **predation.** By killing and eating prey, predators help control the size of the prey population. Predators often kill older, weaker prey that are beyond reproductive age, freeing resources that allow young prey of reproductive age to grow and reproduce, ultimately strengthening the prey population.

For example, in the forests of northern Minnesota and Wisconsin, timber wolves are the main predators of deer. Years ago, humans hunted and killed most of the wolves. Without predators, the deer population increased dramatically. Deer began overgrazing the trees, and disease spread through the now-starving deer population. Now that the wolves are no longer hunted and their population size has increased, the deer population is smaller but healthier.

Symbiotic Relationships A relationship between two species is called **symbiosis**. The three types of symbiosis are distinguished by which members are harmed or helped, as you can see in **Figure 2**.

- **Parasitism** is a symbiotic relationship that benefits only one organism, the *parasite*. The other organism, called the *host*, is harmed. In many cases, a parasite benefits by obtaining food and nutrients from the host's body tissues. Parasites include ticks, leeches, and intestinal worms, as well as plant parasites such as mistletoe. Parasites usually weaken their host or make the host sick. But parasites rarely kill their hosts directly. The death of a host most likely would kill its parasites, too.
- **Commensalism** is a symbiotic relationship in which one organism benefits and the other organism is not affected. For example, barnacles are small marine crustaceans that attach themselves to other marine organisms such as whales, dolphins, clams, and mussels. The barnacles benefit by filtering food from the moving water around them. The larger organism neither benefits nor is harmed in the relationship.

Study Tip

The word *symbiosis* is from the Greek word roots *bios-* meaning "living," and *syn-* meaning "with" or "together."

- **Mutualism** is a symbiotic relationship in which both organisms benefit. Lichens, which often grow on tree trunks or rocks, are examples of mutualism. Lichens consist of algae living inside the tissues of fungi. The algae provide food for the fungi. The fungi protect the algae from losing water and minerals.

Figure 2

Types of Symbiosis		
Symbiotic Relationship	**Organism 1**	**Organism 2**
Parasitism	Benefits	Harmed
Commensalism	Benefits	Not affected
Mutualism	Benefits	Benefits

End-of-Course Assessment Review

1. **Analyze** Bees fly from flower to flower to gather nectar. In the process, they help the plants reproduce by spreading pollen. The relationship between bees and flowering plants is an example of
   A competition.
   B commensalism.
   C mutualism.
   D parasitism.

2. **Infer** Which of these relationships is an example of competition?
   F a bird that picks and eats insects off cattle
   G squirrels and chipmunks living in the same habitat and eating the same seeds
   H a tapeworm living inside an organism and absorbing nutrients from the organism
   J a lion that hunts hyenas for food

3. **Interpret Visuals** Based on **Figure 1**, what would be three possible results if the yellow-rumped warbler and Cape May warbler were forced to compete within the same part of the spruce tree habitat? What principle rules this interaction?

4. **Apply** A drought has lowered the water level in a pond. Explain how the drought can affect two different types of relationships within the community of organisms that live in the pond.

12B Variations and Adaptations

TEKS 12B

Compare variations and adaptations of organisms in different ecosystems.

What is genetic variation?

Within a population, individuals differ from one another. Many of these differences are genetically based. Environmental factors can also lead to individual differences because they influence how genes are expressed.

Genetic variation is the difference in the genotypes within a population. Ladybugs, for example, have a genetic variation in the number of spots on their wings. Humans have genetic variation in traits such as hair and eye color, the shape of the face, and certain health disorders.

Genetic variation helps species survive. If all organisms within a population were genetically identical, then all would be equally vulnerable to a change in the environment. The entire population could die off due to events such as the arrival of a new disease, a new competitor, or a new predator. If a species were to lose individual populations, the entire species could be in danger.

What are adaptations?

An adaptation is a heritable trait that helps an organism survive in its environment. An adaptation may be a physical trait, such as a bird's longer beak or the sharp needles of cacti, or it may be a behavioral trait, such as one that helps an animal find food or protect itself. For example, when a blowfish feels threatened, it puffs up and expands its spines. This behavior makes its body larger and pricklier and less appealing to predators.

Some adaptations are specific to certain ecosystems. An example is *camouflage*, which is an adaptation that helps organisms blend in with their surroundings. The orange and black stripes of a Bengal tiger provide camouflage in forests and grasslands, where sunlight filters through trees, vines, and grasses. In other ecosystems, such as the tundra, the tiger's stripes would stand out and be more visible to the tiger's prey.

How do variations and adaptations of organisms compare in different ecosystems?

Scientists have observed certain patterns in the genetic variation and adaptations in populations. For example, genetic variation tends to increase with the size of a population and the rate at which the species reproduces.

Study Tip

Think of adaptations as structures or behaviors that help organisms *adapt* to their environment. Genetic variation helps explain the *variety* within a population or species.

Bacteria, which are by far the most numerous group of species on Earth, are also the most genetically varied. In contrast, large mammals that have relatively small populations have much less genetic variation.

Scientists have also observed that certain organisms in different ecosystems have similar adaptations. Herbivores that graze on grasslands, for example, include buffalo in North America, zebras in Africa, and llamas in South America. These animals have many similar adaptations, including flat teeth for grinding grass, a long and complex digestive system for breaking down grass, and sturdy hooves for walking and running.

Carnivores throughout the world also have similar characteristics. These adaptations may include keen eyesight and sense of smell, sharp claws or talons, and sharp teeth for cutting and tearing skin and flesh. Even carnivores who are very different from each other, such as a shark and a tiger, may share some general characteristics of a carnivore.

It is also true that many adaptations of a plant or animal are specific to the ecosystem in which it lives. The following are examples of different biomes and ecosystems and the adaptations that help organisms live in them.

Deciduous Forest This biome is characterized by a wide yearly range of temperatures and precipitation. The organisms are adapted to survive the seasonal weather changes. During the spring and summer, deciduous trees grow broad leaves that maximize the amount of sunlight they receive for photosynthesis. They drop their leaves in autumn, which helps them conserve water and energy during the winter.

Animals of the forest survive cold winter weather in a variety of ways. Some reduce their activity, such as by entering a deep sleep called hibernation. Other animals migrate, meaning they travel to warmer climates until warm weather returns to the forest.

Desert Plants and animals of the desert have adaptations that help them conserve water. The leaves of cacti, for example, are protective spines. Their thick stems are adapted for storing water and for photosynthesis. Broad-leafed trees would lose too much water to survive in the desert.

Daytime temperatures in the desert can be extremely high. For this reason, many desert animals are nocturnal, meaning they are active mostly at night. Physical adaptations for keeping cool include the large ears of rabbits and foxes. Large ears help the animals lose more body heat to the environment than smaller ears do.

Coral Reef Coral reefs are formed from the skeletons of coral animals. Many coral reefs are found in shallow tropical waters, but deep-sea coral reefs also exist. A healthy coral reef is home to a wide variety of animals, including corals, anemones, fish, and shellfish. Organisms that live on shallow coral reefs are adapted to warm, relatively shallow salt water. Many of the fishes have disklike shapes that allow them to dart in and out of the reef. Parrotfish have large flat teeth that they use to scrape algae from the reef. Triggerfish have powerful jaws, an adaptation that allows them to feed on sea urchins and mollusks that live on the reef.

TEKS End-of-Course Assessment Review

1. **Compare** Which pair of organisms is most likely to have the most similar adaptations?
   - **A** a hawk and a mouse that both live on North American grasslands
   - **B** two fish-eating birds, such as a pelican and a gull, that live along different parts of the Atlantic Ocean coastline
   - **C** an ocean predator and its prey, such as a shark and a seal
   - **D** a large herbivore, such as an elephant, and a large carnivore such as a lion that live in the same habitat

2. **Infer** Rhinoceroses are large herbivores that live on grasslands in Africa. What combination of teeth and toe types would you expect them to have?
   - **F** sharp teeth and hooves
   - **G** flat teeth and hooves
   - **H** sharp teeth and claws
   - **J** flat teeth and claws

3. **Compare** Tundra ecosystems have little precipitation and long cold winters. Grasslands ecosystems have more precipitation than the tundra. Grasslands are found in temperate or tropical regions. How do you think the adaptations of organisms compare in the tundra and grasslands?

4. **Infer** Armadillos, anteaters, pangolins, aardvarks, and echidnas all eat ants and termites. They are not very closely related, and as you can see below, they live on five different continents. They have an obvious physical similarity. How do genetic variation and adaptation explain the similar features of these animals?

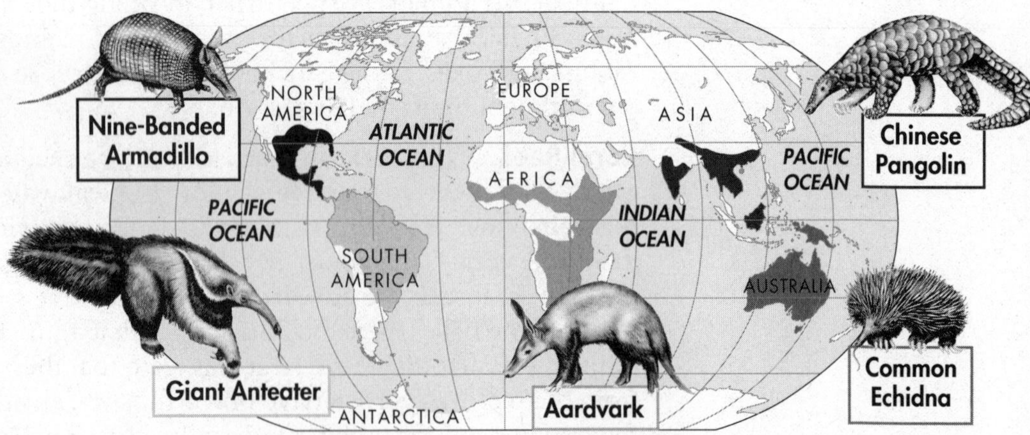

The Flow of Matter and Energy Through Trophic Levels

TEKS 12C

READINESS

Analyze the flow of matter and energy through trophic levels using various models, including food chains, food webs, and ecological pyramids.

Vocabulary
trophic level
producer
consumer
food chain
food web
ecological pyramid

How can you analyze the flow of energy through food chains and food webs?

In any ecosystem, organisms can be classified in **trophic levels** according to how they get food and by the feeding relationships that they engage in. The first trophic level consists of **producers**, which make energy-rich compounds that provide food for themselves and other organisms. Producers include plants and algae.

The next trophic levels consist of **consumers**, which get food by eating other organisms. All animals are consumers. First-level consumers, which eat plants, make up one trophic level. Second-level consumers eat the first-level consumers and are another trophic level. Ecosystems may support additional trophic levels, depending on the species present in that area.

Decomposers, which include bacteria and fungi, get food by breaking down wastes and the remains of dead organisms. Along with *scavengers*, which are animals that eat dead animals, they make up nature's "clean-up crew."

A **food chain** shows the feeding relationships in a community. A food chain always begins with producers. Then the energy of the producers passes to consumers. Food chains overlap because the same organism could be the prey or the predator of more than one animal. A **food web,** as shown in **Figure 1,** shows the overlapping food chains of an ecosystem.

Figure 1
A Food Web

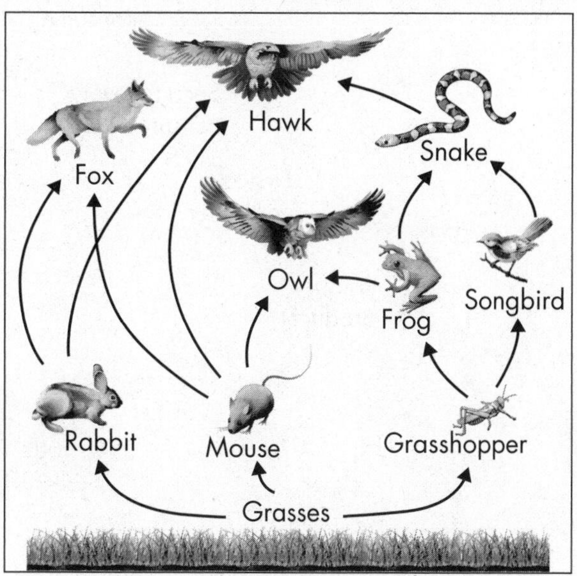

Study Tip

Remember that the arrows of a food chain or food web point in the direction in which matter and energy flow. They point from the producer to the consumer and from the prey to the predator.

In a food web, arrows show the flow of energy in an ecosystem. Animals that are the same number of steps removed from the producers are members of the same trophic level. An animal can occupy more than one trophic level. For example, a hawk occupies the second trophic level when it eats the rabbit that eats grass, but it occupies the fifth trophic level when it eats the snake that eats the songbird that eats the grasshopper that eats the grass. Regardless of what trophic level they occupy, animals depend on producers for food. In the food web shown in Figure 1, secondary and higher-level consumers eat animals and not plants. But the animals they eat depend on plants for their food.

You can also use food chains and food webs to predict the effects of changes to the ecosystem. For example, if a disease lowers the population of secondary consumers in the forest, then populations of primary consumers might increase.

How can you analyze the flow of matter and energy using ecological pyramids?

An **ecological pyramid** represents the producers and consumers of an ecosystem in a pyramid-shaped diagram. Producers usually represent the base of the pyramid, which is typically the most numerous and massive of the trophic levels. Above the producers are the first-level consumers, then the second-level consumers, and then the third-level consumers.

Figure 2 shows an *energy pyramid*, which is shaped to show the relative amounts of energy available in each trophic level. The energy always decreases from one level to the level above it, typically by about 90 percent. Only about 10 percent of the energy available within one trophic level is transferred to organisms at the next trophic level. When an animal consumes another animal, only a small amount of the energy from the prey is stored in the predator. The rest is used for the predator's life processes and lost to the environment as heat.

Figure 2
Energy Pyramid

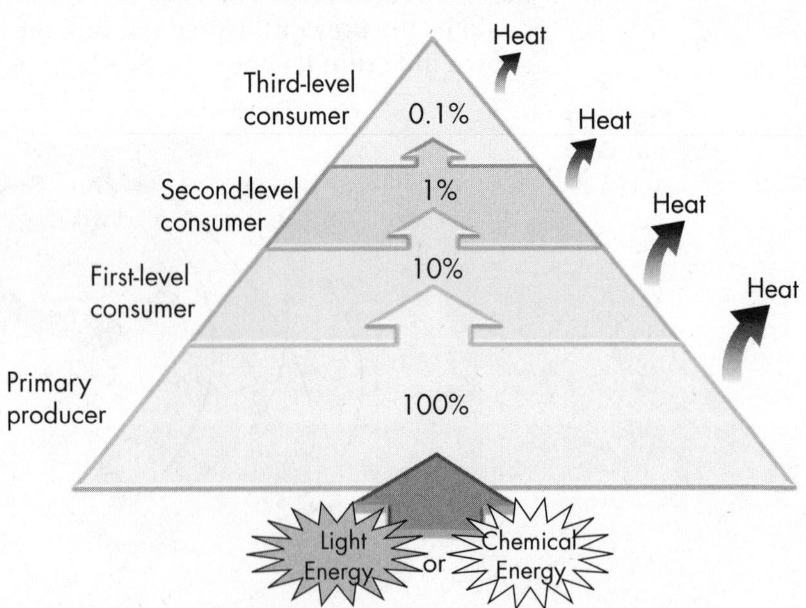

An energy pyramid helps explain the reason that ecosystems typically have a maximum of four or five trophic levels. Above a certain level, there is not enough energy left to sustain an animal population.

Other types of ecological pyramids show biomass and population. Biomass is the total mass of all the organisms in a given area. A *pyramid of biomass* shows the total biomass at each trophic level. A *pyramid of numbers* shows the total number of organisms at each trophic level. In most cases, both biomass and numbers also are lower at higher trophic levels.

TEKS End-of-Course Assessment Review

1. **Analyze** Which organism should be classified in more than one trophic level?

   A maple trees, which are producers

   B monarch butterflies, which feed on milkweed plants

   C brown bears that eat berries, fish, and other plants and animals

   D timber wolves that hunt and eat plant-eating animals

2. **Analyze** Which diagram would be most helpful in comparing the populations of trophic levels in an ecosystem?

   F food web diagram

   G energy pyramid

   H pyramid of biomass

   J pyramid of numbers

3. **Analyze** Which organism(s) in **Figure 1** should be classified in more than one trophic level? Explain. What are the second-level consumers in the food web?

4. **Explain** What might happen in the food web shown in **Figure 1** if there were a sudden decrease in the number of frogs?

5. **Evaluate** Could a forest animal survive by hunting and eating only wolves, owls, eagles, and other predators? Explain your reasoning using evidence from ecological pyramids.

Resources and the Survival of Species

TEKS 12D

Recognize that long-term survival of species is dependent on changing resource bases that are limited.

Vocabulary
resource
extinct
mass extinction
endangered

How is the long-term survival of species affected by their resource bases?

The long-term survival of species depends on the resources supplied by their environment. **Resources** are necessities, such as food, water, air, and space, that organisms need to survive and reproduce. In any environment, most resources are limited and their availability can change over time. Without enough resources, the species may die out, or become **extinct**.

The African savanna provides a good example of this concept. Some species have survived there in very similar forms for thousands of years because the resource bases have remained very similar. The grasses have provided food for zebras, wildebeests, and other grazers. Herds of zebras and wildebeests have provided food for lions, cheetahs, and other predators. For thousands of years, the climate was about about the same.

But now some parts of the savanna are becoming drier. Areas are being taken over by farms, ranches, and expanding cities. As resource bases of the African savanna become scarcer, it is very likely that long-term survival of the species living there will be in jeopardy.

No matter what ecosystem a species lives in, its population size is affected by the factors shown in **Figure 1.** Competition affects resource bases such as food, water, and space. Human activities and natural disasters can also influence a species' access to limited resource bases.

Figure 1
Factors Influencing Population Size

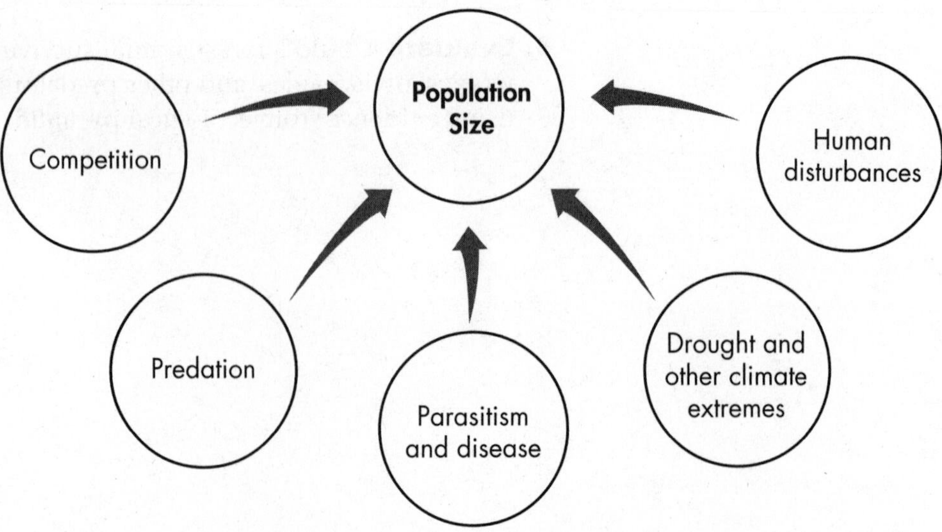

Study Tip

Remember that the long-term survival of a species depends on its environment. Individual organisms always die, but their offspring, and therefore the population and species, will survive if the environment continues to meet the species' needs.

What can change the resource bases of an environment?

The resources of an environment might remain similar for millions of years. But they also can change suddenly or drastically. A sudden change to the environment can cause a rapid extinction of many species. Dinosaurs, for example, thrived for millions of years in an environment that was warm and swampy. Thick forests provided food for plant-eating dinosaurs, which in turn provided food for the meat eaters.

Then, about 66 million years ago, a huge asteroid struck Earth. The fossil record shows that a mass extinction event occurred around this time. During a **mass extinction,** large numbers of species become extinct and whole ecosystems collapse. Some scientists hypothesize that the impact of the asteroid, possibly along with massive volcanic eruptions, caused a cloud of dust that surrounded the planet, blocked the sun, and killed most plants. Without producers, a huge number of animal species—including all the dinosaurs except for the ancestors of birds—became extinct. Other species, such as many early mammals, had adaptations that enabled them to survive the changes and thrive.

Changes to resource bases may also occur gradually. Over thousands of years, weathering and erosion flatten mountains and carve river valleys. The movement of tectonic plates builds mountains and shifts land masses. These actions change species' access to resources. Many factors gradually change climate. By chance, some species have adaptations that enable them to survive the changes. Some species move to a different area that supports their needs. Other species become extinct.

What currently affects the resource bases of species?

For about 150 years, since the Industrial Revolution, the resource bases of many species have been changing. All over the world, land that was once home to wildlife is now used for farms, ranches, and cities. Fresh water is diverted from wildlife habitats to areas where people grow crops and for use in homes and factories. As these resources are used for other purposes, fewer resources are available for wildlife.

Pollution also affects resource bases. In 2010, an oil rig explosion and huge oil spill in the Gulf of Mexico polluted the water and coastline. Many marine organisms were killed, and the oil residue that remains in the wetlands and coastline may impact species for many more years.

Many species are now **endangered**, meaning they could soon become extinct. Often this is caused at least partly by a dwindling natural habitat. Examples of endangered species include the Florida panther of the Everglades, the golden lion tamarin of the Amazon rain forest, and the giant panda of bamboo forests in China.

Conservation biologists have identified areas called "hot spots," which are concentrated areas that contain significant numbers of endangered species. Identifying these areas helps biologists determine where their efforts could save many species. **Figure 2** on the next page highlights these hot spots.

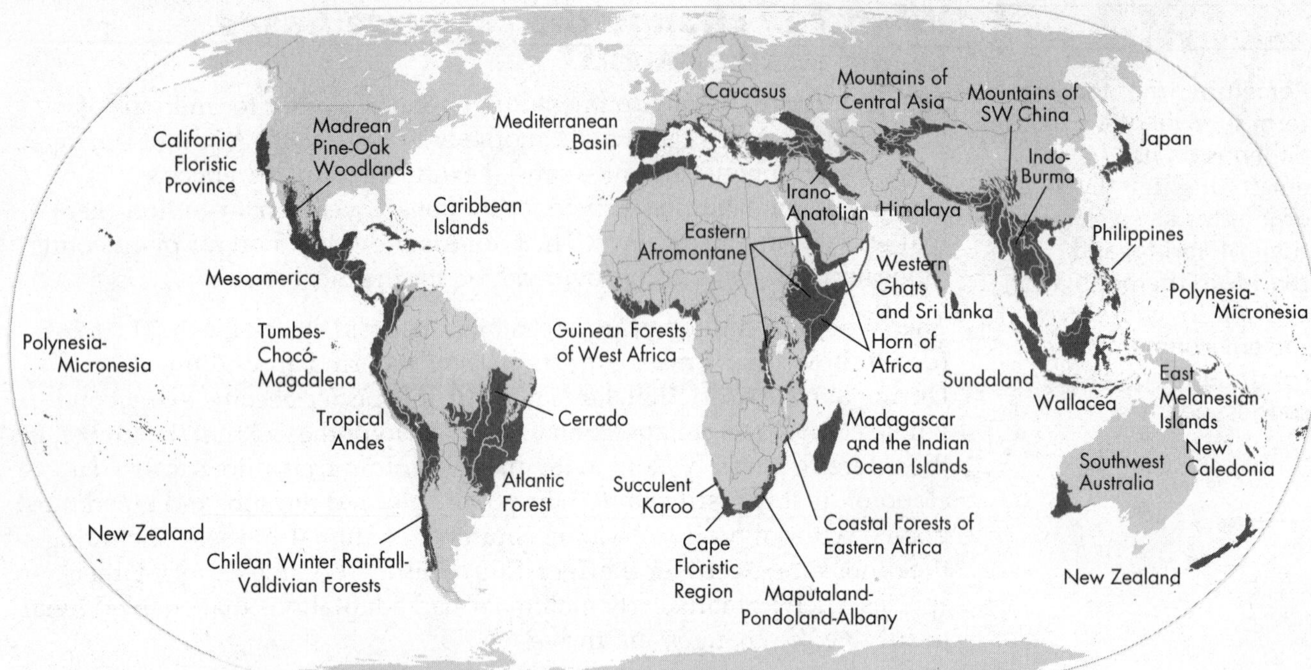

Figure 2
Ecological Hot Spots

TEKS End-of-Course Assessment Review

1. **Predict** A grasslands environment is home to grasses and other plants, grazing animals, and their predators. Which event or change to the grasslands would affect the long-term survival of the most species?
   A the death of one eagle, a predator of small grasslands animals
   B the reduction of yearly rainfall by 50 percent
   C a tornado or severe thunderstorm that strikes the grasslands
   D the flooding of a river that runs through the grasslands

2. **Predict** Which event would be likely to cause a mass extinction?
   F a severe earthquake
   G the flooding of a river
   H several major volcanic eruptions occurring at about the same time
   J the overfishing of popular food fish from the ocean

3. **Form a Hypothesis** All organisms need water to survive. Of a species of cactus, moss, or banana tree, which would you expect to best survive a reduction of its normal water supply by 50 percent? Explain.

4. **Apply Concepts** Choose a species and describe how its resource base has been changing. How have these changes affected the species?

Carbon and Nitrogen Cycles

TEKS 12E

Describe the flow of matter through the carbon and nitrogen cycles and explain the consequences of disrupting these cycles.

Vocabulary
nitrogen fixation
denitrifying bacteria
eutrophication

How does matter flow through the carbon cycle?

Carbon makes up less than 1 percent of Earth's crust and atmosphere. Yet all living things depend on carbon compounds. As shown in **Figure 1,** the carbon cycle is a set of processes that moves carbon between Earth's atmosphere, Earth's surface, and living things. In the atmosphere, carbon exists mostly as CO_2. Carbon dioxide leaves the atmosphere when it dissolves in water or is taken up by plants for photosynthesis. It is released to the atmosphere during cellular respiration, during geologic processes such as volcanic eruptions, and when fossil fuels or forests are burned.

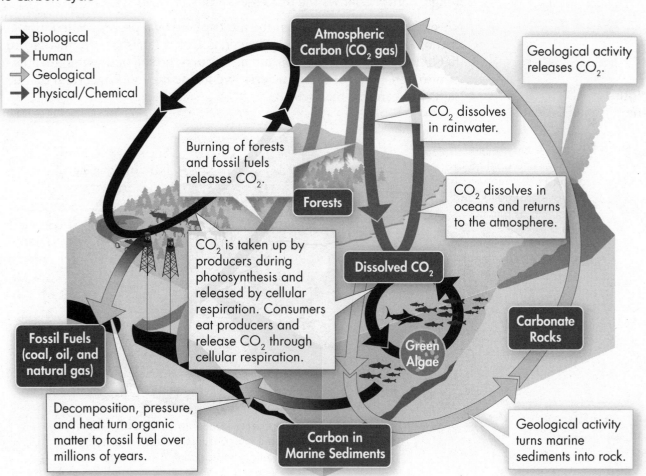

Figure 1
The Carbon Cycle

What are some consequences of disruptions to the carbon cycle?

Over the past 100 years, the levels of carbon dioxide in Earth's atmosphere have increased. Human activities such as burning fossil fuels and forests release carbon dioxide into the atmosphere faster than it can be removed by natural processes.

Most scientists cite increasing levels of carbon dioxide as a contributing factor to global climate change. Their reasoning is that carbon dioxide is a greenhouse gas that helps keep heat from leaving the atmosphere, and that the higher carbon dioxide levels are causing rising temperatures and climate change.

Rising carbon dioxide levels are also affecting the oceans. When carbon dioxide dissolves in water, carbonic acid forms. As more and more carbonic acid forms, ocean water is becoming more acidic—a process called *acidification.* This negatively affects the marine organisms that have a low tolerance for changing pH levels.

How does matter flow through the nitrogen cycle?

Nitrogen gas makes up 78 percent of Earth's atmosphere. In the nitrogen cycle, nitrogen moves between the atmosphere, Earth's surface, and living things. **Figure 2** shows the processes of the nitrogen cycle.

Nitrogen gas is removed from the atmosphere by a process called nitrogen fixation. In **nitrogen fixation**, nitrogen is "fixed," or changed into a form that living things can use. Certain bacteria in the soil and water are able to fix nitrogen. Some of these bacteria live inside the roots of certain plants. Lightning can also fix nitrogen.

Figure 2
The Nitrogen Cycle

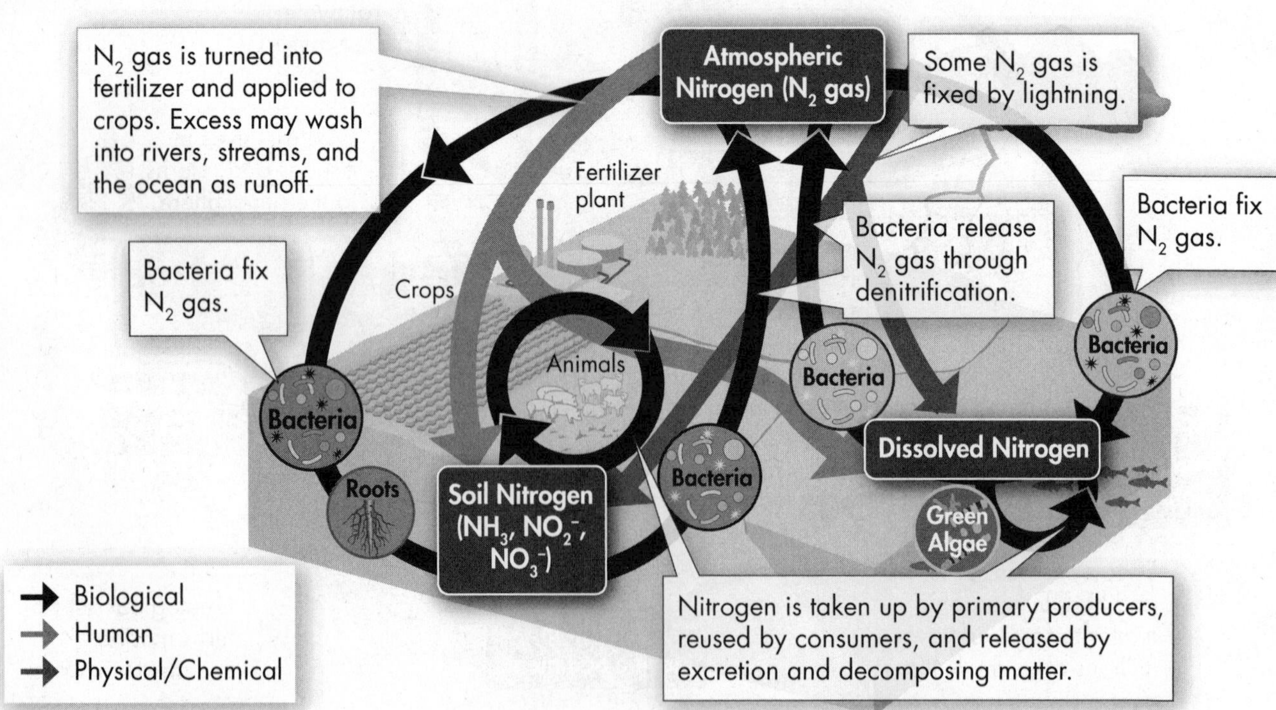

Study Tip

Remember that in nitrogen fixation, atmospheric nitrogen is converted, or "fixed," so that living things can use it. In denitrification, the process is reversed. The prefix *de-* means to reverse or undo.

In the soil, a variety of bacteria convert fixed nitrogen from one form to another. The result is a mixture of nitrogen compounds, including nitrites, nitrates, and ammonia compounds. Plants incorporate ammonia into amino acids, which are the building blocks of proteins.

Some bacteria in the soil break down the remains of dead plants and animals, providing more fixed nitrogen to the soil. While, the actions of **denitrifying bacteria** return nitrogen to the atmosphere.

What are some consequences of disruptions to the nitrogen cycle?

To increase plant growth, farmers and gardeners often mix nitrogen-containing fertilizer into the soil. But fertilizer runoff can affect the balance of nitrogen in bodies of water. In a process called **eutrophication**, nitrogen dissolves in a body of water and stimulates the growth of plants and algae. When the plants and algae die, bacterial populations that feed on the dead matter boom. These bacteria consume so much oxygen from the water that fish and other aquatic animals cannot survive.

Another consequence of disrupting the nitrogen cycle is acid precipitation. Acid precipitation can lead to the death of plants and animals by altering the pH levels of soil and water. It can also cause harmful metals to leach from pipes and enter drinking water.

TEKS End-of-Course Assessment Review

1. Predict Which change would most likely reduce the rate at which carbon dioxide is increasing in Earth's atmosphere?

A a decrease in the combustion of fossil fuels

B a decrease in total photosynthesis among Earth's plants and algae

C an increase in the population of denitrifying bacteria

D an increase in Earth's animal population

2. Sequence Which pathway shows how atmospheric nitrogen is converted into the nitrogen compounds that plants need?

A atmospheric nitrogen → denitrifying bacteria → plants

B atmospheric nitrogen → plants

C atmospheric nitrogen → nitrogen-fixing bacteria and other soil bacteria → plants

D atmospheric nitrogen → animals → denitrifying bacteria → plants

3. Infer Why are oceans important to the carbon cycle?

12F Ecosystem Stability

TEKS 12F

★ READINESS ★

Describe how environmental change can impact ecosystem stability.

Vocabulary
habitat fragmentation
invasive species

What is ecosystem stability?

Most ecosystems face environmental change on a regular basis. A stable ecosystem can cope with these alterations without undergoing much change. Despite a changing environment, the number of species, their population sizes, and the way they interact remains relatively the same. Ecosystems with high levels of biodiversity are more likely to be stable than ecosystems with less biodiversity.

How can environmental change impact the stability of an ecosystem?

Severe changes to the environment are likely to upset an ecosystem's stability. If individuals in a population cannot overcome the challenges of these changes and continue to reproduce, then their population size will decrease. Individuals also may leave an area if their needs are not being met. As an ecosystem's biodiversity changes, its ability to cope with further environmental changes is also affected. Several types of natural phenomena can negatively affect ecosystem stability.

Fire Fires can quickly kill all or most of the trees and other plants in a patch of forest. Many forest animals might also be killed or displaced by the fire. For the first few days after a severe forest fire, few animals live in the altered ecosystem.

But the changes aren't usually permanent. The topmost soil may be scorched and covered in ashes, but fertile soil survives underneath. Seeds of small grasslike plants will sprout. With the death of larger plants, grasses have ample space, sunlight, and other resources to grow. The grasses will provide food for newly arriving small animals. Later, bushes and shrubs will grow, as will young trees. Burnt trees will fall to the ground and decay, providing nutrients to support new trees. After many years, a stable forest ecosystem will return.

Storms Severe storms, such as tornadoes and hurricanes, can uproot trees and kill animals across a wide region. Floods can drown animals and deposit thick layers of silt or mud on the land. An avalanche can bury the land in soil and rocks. Yet after each of these events, the ecosystem is likely to recover and return to its previous condition unless there are additional disturbances.

Natural Climate Change Earth is always undergoing changes such as orbital changes, continental drift, and atmospheric changes. Over time, these changes can lead to extreme alterations to ecosystems. On the other hand, catastrophic events such as asteroid strikes can quickly affect worldwide ecosystem stability.

How can human activities cause environmental change and impact the stability of ecosystems?

Human activities impact ecosystems in many ways. In some cases, the change to an ecosystem is deliberate, such as replacing a forest or grasslands with a lawn, ranch, or farm. Other changes to ecosystems lead to unintended consequences.

Habitat Loss When people use land to grow food or to build new neighborhoods or highways, the species that live there either die off or are forced to live in a smaller area. When species are living in a small area of suitable habitat surrounded by areas of unsuitable habitat, this is called **habitat fragmentation** (**Figure 1**). The changes to biodiversity and the size of the habitat threaten the stability of the ecosystem.

Figure 1
Habitat Fragmentation

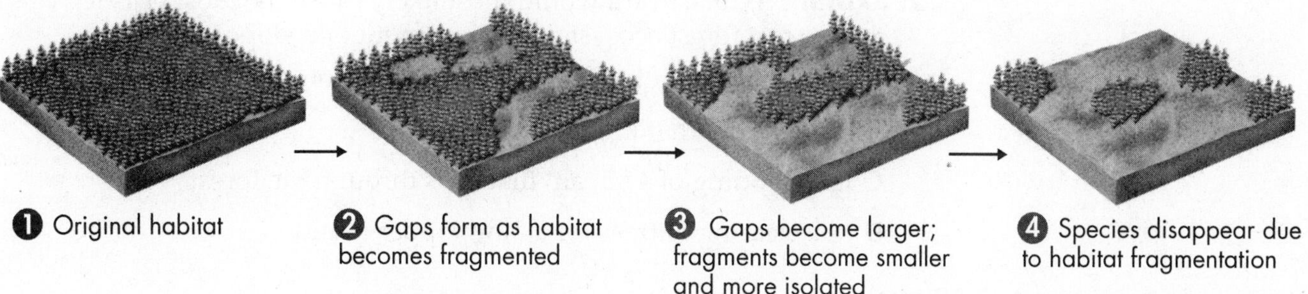

❶ Original habitat

❷ Gaps form as habitat becomes fragmented

❸ Gaps become larger; fragments become smaller and more isolated

❹ Species disappear due to habitat fragmentation

Pollution Pollution impacts land and water ecosystems in many ways. Some forms of pollution can travel far from their sources. Mercury, for example, is a toxic metal that is released into the atmosphere from coal-fired power plants. It can travel thousands of kilometers before falling to the surface in precipitation. Mercury can build up in the bodies of fish, making them unsafe to eat.

Pollution can also affect ecosystems very quickly. Spills in which oil or other harmful chemicals are released into the environment can quickly kill plants and animals and change the structure of an ecosystem for years or, even, permanently.

Study Tip

Remember that the stability of an ecosystem depends on factors that affect many or all members of the community, not just a few organisms or a single species.

Invasive Species In the late 1800s, a fast-growing Asian plant called kudzu was brought to the southeast United States. It was planted for livestock feed and erosion control. Unfortunately, kudzu proved to be an invasive species. **Invasive species** grow unchecked in a new ecosystem and harm the native species, often by consuming their resources. Some invasive species, such as kudzu, were introduced intentionally. Others were introduced unintentionally. For example, zebra mussels that attached to the hulls of ships traveling in Europe were carried to the Great Lakes. They thrived in their new environment and are now disturbing the Great Lakes ecosystem.

Global Climate Change Evidence shows that levels of carbon dioxide in the atmosphere have been increasing steadily for the past 100 years. The burning of fossil fuels, such as coal and oil, is contributing to the increase in the carbon dioxide levels. Many scientists agree with the hypothesis that the rising level of carbon dioxide is causing an increase in Earth's average temperatures, leading to worldwide climate change. As the climate changes, the stability of most ecosystems could be affected.

TEKS End-of-Course Assessment Review

1. **Describe** Which is the best definition for a stable ecosystem?
   - **A** an ecosystem in an environment that never changes
   - **B** an ecosystem that can respond to changes without significant effects to the ecosystem as a whole
   - **C** an ecosystem with high biodiversity
   - **D** an ecosystem that is unlikely to be affected by human activity

2. **Explain** Which event would most likely cause the most drastic change to a forest ecosystem along a mountain slope?
   - **A** a landslide that buries part of the forest in rocky soil
   - **B** a forest fire that kills most of the trees
   - **C** the flooding of a stream that runs through the forest
   - **D** the clearing of trees for a new copper mine

3. **Evaluate** Purple loosestrife is an Asian marsh plant that was introduced to North America as a garden plant. Unfortunately, it escaped into natural marshes, and it has replaced native marsh plants that animals rely on for food, shelter, and nesting. In some places, an insect parasite of purple loosestrife has been introduced to control its growth. List two potential pros and two potential cons of this plan.

Answers to End-of-Course Assessment Reviews

Sample answers have been provided to open-ended questions. Some questions have many correct answers. If you are unsure about the accuracy of your answer, review it with your teacher.

TEKS 1A

1. **C** Safety gloves would provide a barrier between your hands and the oils.
2. **H** Safety goggles would protect your eyes from splashing acid.
3. Use a fire blanket to smother the flames, or use the safety shower if it is nearby (and if you do not need to run to get to it).
4. His attitude could endanger his eyes. Safety goggles do much more than protect eyes from chemical splashes. They also protect the eye from exposure to powdered chemicals, explosions, and flying debris.

TEKS 1B

1. **B** The Petri dish was not exposed to chemical or biological contaminants and may be disposed of with other trash.
2. One should never flush a chemical substance (solid or liquid) down the drain without first knowing the approved disposal methods for that chemical. Many substances must not be flushed down the drain because they can contaminate a community's water supply.
3. Evan should have first checked with the teacher to confirm that the compound should be recycled. If so, he should then have asked if there was a designated recycling container for that compound.
4. Chemicals that may not be dangerous alone can be dangerous when combined with certain other substances. If a single waste container is used for all chemicals, there is the possibility of a hazardous reaction.

TEKS 2A

1. **D** The answer to this question involves people's judgment and opinions and is not testable or falsifiable.
2. **H** Technology is an application of science.
3. Although synthetic internal organs for human transplant may not be developed in the immediate future, it may eventually be possible to develop them. As new information is learned, previous scientific thoughts and explanations might be revised or discarded. The new information and ideas could be applied to develop new technology.
4. Answers will vary, but the answer should note a way of looking at the world that is not science, such as astrology. Answers should discuss that science is the study of physical phenomena and the process by which people attempt to understand those phenomena by constructing testable explanations and predictions about them and gathering data that support or falsify those expectations.

TEKS 2B

1. **C** An unsupported hypothesis is not useful for making predictions or understanding observations, so it should be modified and the new hypothesis should be tested.
2. **H** As new data and evidence become available, a hypothesis may need to be revised or even rejected altogether.
3. *Sample answers:* Hypotheses: The lettuce seeds didn't germinate because they needed warmer temperatures; the seeds didn't germinate because they were planted too close together, not deep enough, or too deep; the seeds didn't germinate because they needed more water. Explanation: Each statement qualifies as a hypothesis because each is a tentative explanation that is capable of being tested.
4. A hypothesis that is not supported by experimentation is never a failure. Valuable knowledge is gained. For example, if your hypothesis stated that the seeds needed more sun, and you tried several plots in different sunny spots but they still didn't germinate, your hypothesis would not be supported. However, this information is valuable because now you know that lack of sun was not the problem. Your next step might be to formulate another hypothesis about why the seeds didn't germinate and to test the new hypothesis.

TEKS 2C

1. **A** Remember that theories present well-established, highly reliable explanations.
2. **H** Scientists demand that theories be supported by evidence. When evidence amasses against a theory, the theory will be revised or replaced.
3. It cannot be a new theory. A scientific theory requires multiple independent researchers—not a single researcher; it also must be highly reliable—a single investigation cannot demonstrate reliability as an explanatory/predictability tool; it also must be well established—a single investigation cannot establish a theory.
4. A scientific theory involves an explanation; it is not a factual statement that can be proven true or false. A theory is powerful because it has undergone an immense amount of testing over time, and it has been applied to make valid predictions in many cases.
5. The friend's description involves a hypothesis, since he is giving a specific example in which he expects homeostasis would take place, but has not tested his example in real-world conditions. He also uses a theory—the theory of homeostasis—to formulate his hypothesis.

TEKS 2D

1. **B** This statement is a proposed explanation for a specific, narrowly defined situation, and you can gather objective data that support or refute it.
2. **G** This is the definition of a hypothesis.
3. **B** This is the definition of a theory.
4. Hypotheses are reasonable, testable explanations of an observation in nature. Theories are also reasonable and testable but much broader in scope. Theories are also well supported by evidence from many experiments.

TEKS 2E

1. **A** Pipettes are capable of measuring small amounts, such as milliliters with precision.
2. **H** Hypotheses need to be clearly stated so they can be tested.
3. **C** This hypothesis has very specific independent and dependent variables and therefore is testable.
4. This is a descriptive study. The biologist is collecting numerical data only during one month during which conditions are unlikely to change greatly. It is not a comparative study because there is no comparison. No variables are being manipulated so it is not an experimental study.
5. *Sample answer:* Hypothesis: Peppers on plants that are in direct sunlight are larger than peppers that are not in direct sunlight.; Independent variable: sunlight or shade; Dependent variable: length of peppers; Equipment: ruler in centimeters; Experiment: Choose two plants from the same kind of pepper. Place one plant in the shade and one plant in the sun. Give both equal amounts of water and keep both at the same temperatures. Record the length of the peppers in centimeters over a period of several weeks. Compare the results to evaluate the validity of the hypothesis.

TEKS 2F

1. **D** The measurements are not close to the actual mass, so they are not accurate, and they are not close to each other, so they are not precise.
2. **H** Properties such as color can be described but not easily quantified.
3. **C** Circle graphs are useful for presenting parts of a whole, such as the fractions of different types of ladybugs that the scientist observed.
4. Useful tools or pieces of equipment would include a hand lens for observing the film on the leaves; a microscope or stereoscope for observing the film and leaves at the cellular level, and potentially for observing the microorganisms that are infecting the plants; a Petri dish with growth medium for growing a culture of the microorganisms; and prepared slides of known microorganisms, which can be studied and compared to identify the microorganisms infecting the plants.

TEKS 2G

1. **A** The mean is the average value of a data set. Values greater than the mean are balanced by values less than the mean.
2. **H** Reviewing these details could help explain the unusual result.
3. There is no best-fit line because the 10 data points are scattered all over the graph.

TEKS 2H

1. **C** The abstract is a kind of summary that introduces a journal article.
2. **F** Direct communication with an audience is the key advantage of an oral report.
3. **C** This process, called peer review, helps ensure that the reports in science journals are accurate.
4. **F** Flowcharts are useful for showing a sequence of steps, such as the sequence of chemical reactions that break apart sugars.

TEKS 3A

1. **C** Empirical evidence comes from the results of science experiments.
2. **F** The more variables that affect an event, the more difficult it becomes for scientists to evaluate the role these variables play in the outcome.
3. *Sample answer:* The slogan suggests that the detergent will not allow red clothing dye to stain white clothes. It can be tested by taking photographs of red and white clothing before and after they are washed with the detergent. The experiment should involve several trials under different conditions, such as wash water temperature, presence of fabric softener or other additives, and type of washing machine used. Under all tested conditions, the amount of detergent used and articles of clothing should be kept constant.

TEKS 3B

1. **B** Scientists use journal articles to report the results and conclusions of their investigations, and they include data that support their conclusions.
2. **J** The law states that scientific information must be accurately presented. But marketing materials can be written in misleading ways.
3. People apply the scientific information they learn to make choices about diet, safety, lifestyle, and purchasing products. Because of the importance of these choices, people should carefully evaluate the source of the information for its reliability, and then apply critical thinking skills to draw proper conclusions.

TEKS 3C

1. **D** The term "best care" can be defined in many ways. Without data, drawing a reasonable inference about the claim is not possible.
2. **F** These data are objective and will give you a clear idea of an aspect of the service's performance that will be important to you.
3. **B** This statement has data that can be scientifically tested.
4. Companies are in business to sell products and services. While laws prevent them from making inaccurate statements, these laws do not prevent them from making statements that could mislead people who are not thinking critically.

TEKS 3D

1. **A** Identifying insects and other pests, and their relationships to crops is a common research topic for biologists.
2. **F** Though it saved many human lives, DDT caused unexpected harm; plastics have brought many unexpected benefits to society as well as drawbacks such as pollution.
3. *Sample answer:* Scientific research results in both benefits and drawbacks. For example, computers and the Internet help some people perform their jobs more efficiently and conveniently but take away other jobs, such as those of travel agents.

TEKS 3E

1. **C** A lily is three-dimensional, while a drawing is two-dimensional. Any drawing of a lily will simplify or misrepresent certain details of the lily's structure.
2. **H** A computer simulation could not accurately show the action of enzymes in the digestive system.
3. *Sample answers:* A drawing of a plant or animal may show many external structures or internal structures, but it cannot show all structural features. A diagram of a food web or energy pyramid may show only some, not all, of the organisms that have a role in the ecosystem.

TEKS 3F

1. **B** Fleming discovered penicillin in 1928.
2. **J** Rachel Carson helped launch the study of ecology, which examines the relationships between living things and their environment.
3. Possible answers include the development of cell theory, the germ theory of disease, and the theory of evolution by natural selection.

TEKS 4A

1. **A** The lack of a nucleus or membrane-bound organelles signifies a prokaryotic cell.
2. **F** All eukaryotes have nuclei.
3. **C** Since prokaryotes are unicellular, they cannot form tissues or organs.
4. Similarities: Both types of cells carry out the functions of life, such as growth, reproduction, and response to the environment. Both types have genetic material in DNA and have ribosomes and cytoplasm. Differences: Prokaryotic cells are significantly smaller; they lack nuclei and membrane-bound organelles; and they never form specialized tissues.

TEKS 4B

1. **C** Active transport is always necessary to move substances from regions of low concentration to high concentration.
2. **J** This change occurs during photosynthesis, which plants but not animals perform.
3. Ribosomes on rough ER follow instructions from DNA to make proteins → proteins are assembled in these ribosomes → assembled proteins enter ER where they are modified → modified proteins leave ER in vesicles that transport them to the Golgi apparatus → in Golgi apparatus, proteins are modified, stored, and prepared to be sent elsewhere in the body.

TEKS 4C

1. **A** Like cells, a virus uses DNA or RNA to contain genetic information.
2. **H** Viruses take over the cell processes for making proteins, and this leads to the production of copies of the virus.
3. **D** By infecting the immune system, HIV weakens the body system that has the job of fighting infections.
4. Both viruses are RNA viruses, and both quickly mutate and evolve, making the production of vaccines challenging (in the case of influenza) or to date impossible (in the case of HIV). They differ in that HIV attacks the immune system directly, and influenza attacks the respiratory system.

TEKS 5A

1. **B** Mitosis involves the separation of double-stranded chromosomes into individual chromatids. The replication of chromatids occurs during the S phase.
2. **G** During anaphase, the four double-stranded chromosomes are separated into four chromatids. Each of the two daughter cells has one set of four chromatids.
3. **B** In metaphase, the spindle apparatus has aligned the chromosomes along the center of the cell.
4. Yes. All of these cells formed from repeated mitotic divisions of the first cell of the organism, and therefore they have the same chromosomes and the same DNA.

TEKS 5B

1. **D** Smooth muscles control the movement of food through the digestive tract, the flow of blood through blood vessels, and the size of pupils in response to light.
2. **J** Parenchyma cells in roots store starch.
3. Red blood cells leaked from the cut. Platelets came to the site of the injury to stop the bleeding, and white blood cells fought infection from microorganisms that entered the cut. Eventually, new epithelial cells grew and repaired the cut.

TEKS 5C

1. **A** The process of RNA interference helps control gene expression by interfering with the translation of mRNA.
2. **H** Cell differentiation occurs when specific genes begin being transcribed and translated into proteins.
3. **C** The hours of daylight change in the same way every year and are a common environmental factor that triggers changes in plants.

4. *Sample answer:* Internal cell activities that affect cell differentiation include the activities of enzymes, other proteins, and hormones. External factors that affect cell differentiation include chemical exposure; nutrition; and environmental factors such as temperature, diurnal and seasonal cycles, and levels of oxygen.

TEKS 5D

1. **D** A disruption to the normal cell cycle is the cause of all types of cancer.
2. **H** At an early stage, the tumor is likely small and has not metastasized. It can be surgically removed.
3. If the tumor is detected early enough, it can be treated or surgically removed before the cancer metastasizes.
4. If the cells underwent apoptosis, the cells would die, and their cell cycle would not get out of control; so cancer would not occur.

TEKS 6A

1. **D** Guanine and cytosine are complementary base pairs.
2. **H** DNA strands have a sugar-phosphate backbone, and the nitrogenous base pairs are bound into a double helix.
3. ACGAAT. The complementary base pairs are C-G and A-T, so each nitrogenous base in the original sequence would be replaced with its complement in the opposing strand.

TEKS 6B

1. **B** Three nucleotides make up a codon, which codes for one amino acid.
2. **H** The removal of one nucleotide from a codon affects all the codons that follow it.
3. **C** Uracil is found in RNA but not DNA.
4. The order of nucleotides in a codon determines the amino acid that it codes for. For example, the codon ACG codes for threonine. But if the codon were read backward, as GCA, then it would code for alanine. The start and stop codons would also be misread if the RNA were translated in the wrong direction.
5. There is more than one possible answer because more than one codon codes for these amino acids. Each of the amino acids in the sample protein can be made up of two or more different codons.

TEKS 6C

1. **B** Translation takes place on ribosomes in the cytoplasm.
2. **J** RNA polymerase binds to the promoter and then moves along the DNA molecule to transcribe it into RNA.
3. Both DNA and RNA are made of strings of nucleotides with sugar-phosphate backbones and four possible nitrogenous bases. But the sugar in DNA is deoxyribose, and the sugar in RNA is ribose. Also, three of the nitrogenous bases are the same (adenine, guanine, and cytosine), but RNA has uracil instead of thymine. Finally, DNA has two strands and RNA has one strand.
4. The purpose of transcription is to build mRNA molecules that can leave the nucleus and be used as templates to produce proteins. The purpose of translation is to use the sequence of codons in mRNA to build the appropriate protein.
5. DNA in nucleus → (transcription) RNA polymerase → DNA strand opens → mRNA is built base by base → mRNA moves to cytoplasm → (translation) → mRNA associates with ribosome → tRNA picks up amino acids based on code carried in its anticodon → anticodon on the tRNA pairs with a codon on the mRNA → the protein is synthesized from amino acids on the tRNA → a completed protein and mRNA is released from the ribosome → ribosome ready for reuse.

TEKS 6D

1. **C** Transcription factors are proteins that bind to DNA and affect the transcription of a gene. In many cases, their presence allows RNA polymerase to attach to DNA and begin transcribing it.
2. **H** The organization of the operon allows the genes to be expressed only when lactose is present.
3. Multicellular organisms rely on a wide variety of cell types. Without proper regulation, a muscle cell might produce a protein that is specific to the function of a nerve cell, gland, or other type of cell. The production of unneeded proteins would waste energy and nutrients, and it could easily disturb the proper function of the cell.
4. The *lac* operon allows the cell to respond to environmental conditions. When lactose is present, the operon is expressed, allowing the production of the enzyme to digest lactose. When lactose is not present, the operon is not expressed and the cell doesn't use energy producing an enzyme that digests lactose.

TEKS 6E

1. **C** Two parts of the chromosome switched placement. This is an example of an inversion.
2. **F** Mutations that occur in cells that produce sperm and eggs are much more likely to be passed on to offspring.
3. Illustrations should be supported by material in the text. The addition of one or two nucleotides will cause an insertion, or frameshift, mutation. In both cases, the reading frame will shift for all codons after the inserted nucleotides. Because codons are read in groups of three nucleotides, however, the insertion of three nucleotides will not cause a frameshift mutation. Most likely, the inserted three nucleotides will code for an additional amino acid in the protein.

TEKS 6F

1. **C** This is a monohybrid cross that produces round peas (either *RR* or *Rr*) and wrinkled peas (*rr*) in a predicted ratio of 3:1. The actual ratio of the results may not be 3:1 exactly.
2. **G** In codominance, both alleles are expressed in the heterozygous genotype.
3.

	B	*b*
B	*BB*	*Bb*
b	*BB*	*bb*

Phenotypic ratio is 3 brown shells:1 cream-colored shell.

TEKS 6G

1. **C** This illustration shows chromatids separating during anaphase I.
2. **F** Because genes that are found on the same chromosome usually are inherited together, independent assortment occurs at the chromosome level.
3. Sexual reproduction involves the joining of two cells, one from each parent, to form the first cell of a new organism. If body cells joined together, the new cell would have double the number of chromosomes. Meiosis is essential to produce haploid gametes, which are cells with half the number of chromosomes that the body cells of the organism have.

TEKS 6H

1. **A** A karyotype would show one chromosome not paired with a homologous chromosome.
2. **H** The bacterial gene will produce one protein. If the scientist's goal is achieved, this protein will provide pest resistance.
3. DNA fingerprinting is a technology used to identify individuals by differences in the sequence of DNA segments between individuals. Chromosomal analysis studies the organization of the genome in chromosomes in order to determine abnormalities. Genetic modification is the insertion of a gene from one organism into a host genome, often with the goal of transferring a useful trait to the host.

4. DNA fingerprinting is able to positively identify individuals. It could be used to identify a victim, or could be used to find a match between a tissue sample from a crime scene and a suspect.

TEKS 7A

1. **A** Homologous structures show how anatomical structures of organisms can change over time.
2. **G** Scientists use molecular homologies (similarities among the molecules of organisms) to help identify common ancestry.
3. It's possible that the organisms lived in similar environments with similar selection pressures. By chance, the same adaptations evolved in the distantly related species.

TEKS 7B

1. **B** If the species evolved quickly, any intermediate forms might not have left fossils behind.
2. **F** Parts of the fossil record may be incomplete because geological activity such as seismic activity or erosion has confused or destroyed parts of it.
3. **A** Adaptive radiation involves a rapid increase in number and diversity of species that share a common ancestor.
4. Periods of stasis may be followed by the appearance of many new species in the fossil record. These periods can be evidence for the punctuated equilibrium model of evolution.
5. Gradualism suggests that evolution is constant, and that it occurs at a constant but slow rate. Punctuated equilibrium suggests that evolution occurs very rapidly in specific relatively short time intervals, preceded and followed by longer periods with few changes.

TEKS 7C

1. **C** This answer acknowledges that traits are genetically based and that traits that give a better chance of survival are more likely to be passed on to offspring than other traits.
2. **H** Disruptive selection has occurred because the population is divided into two distinct phenotypes, light tan and dark tan.
3. There would be increasingly more green grasshoppers after several rainy years. During rainy years the grass would most likely be green. More green grasshoppers would survive because they would blend in, which would protect them from predators and allow them to reproduce more successfully. During years of drought, the grass would be brown, and the brown grasshoppers would blend in, allowing them to survive and reproduce more successfully.

TEKS 7D

1. **B** As the environment changes, individuals without favorable alleles are less likely to survive and reproduce, so the frequency of the adaptive allele will increase.
2. **F** Over time the population will have a a higher frequency of alleles for phenotypes with a fitness advantage to find and eat seeds.
3. **B** Traits for increased fitness and survival to adulthood can determine the reproductive success of an individual.
4. Because of the scarcity of and competition for resources, many individuals in a population do not survive to reproductive age. By producing a large number of offspring, populations increase the likelihood that at least a few offspring survive to maturity and reproduce.

TEKS 7E

1. **A** The use of penicillin was a significant change to the environment of the bacteria. Bacteria that were resistant to penicillin became more likely to survive and reproduce.
2. **G** By chance, the population had a phenotype that allowed it to cope better with dry conditions. Over time, that phenotype became more prominent in the population. As a result, the population was largely unaffected by the drought.
3. Geographic isolation may have been important initially as populations of tortoises became separated on different islands because they would no longer share a common gene pool. Different traits provided advantages on the different islands.
4. When environmental conditions change, certain genetic variations may provide an advantage or disadvantage for survival that did not exist before. The frequencies of the variations change over time. Advantageous variations become more common, while variations that provide a disadvantage to an organism's reproductive success become less common.
5. For speciation to occur, two populations of a species need to be isolated so that mating does not occur. The separation could be geographical, behavioral, or temporal. The two populations would also have to be exposed to environmental pressures that would lead to an increase in frequency of different traits.

TEKS 7F

1. **C** Genetic drift is a process in which individuals have been randomly eliminated from the population. A dramatic reduction and alteration of genes in a population is called the bottleneck effect.
2. **F** The presence of a new trait is likely the result of a mutation, which is a change in the genetic information in an organism.
3. **C** Mutations contribute to the genetic diversity within a species.
4. A mutation in a gene can give an individual an adaptation that allows it to better survive and reproduce. If the mutation is passed on from generation to generation, it likely will become more common in the population.
5. A greater number of chromosomes allows for the genes to recombine in more ways in the offspring, producing a wider variety of genetic traits in a species.

TEKS 7G

1. **B** The first cells lived when Earth's atmosphere lacked oxygen. They obtained energy by breaking apart small molecules.
2. **H** Oxygen accumulated as a by-product of photosynthesis by bacteria.
3. **A** The engulfed cell gave the host an enhanced ability to obtain energy.
4. **J** Similar to free-living bacteria, mitochondria and chloroplasts contain their own DNA, reproduce by binary fission, and have ribosomes that closely resemble bacterial ribosomes. This suggests that at one time they lived independently.
5. According to endosymbiotic theory, eukaryotes acquired mitochondria and chloroplasts when a large host cell engulfed a smaller cell that remained within the host cell, and the organisms began living symbiotically.

TEKS 8A

1. **C** Taxonomy is the study of classifying and naming organisms.
2. **F** Scientists use binomial names because they are very specific and easily understood by other scientists.
3. **B** An order is a group of species within a class.
4. The upper three levels would change to show the correct family, genus, and species for the giraffe.

TEKS 8B

1. **B** Ferns develop from an embryo and have vascular tissues but develop no seeds or flowers.
2. **H** The appearance of a derived trait tells you in which groups a new trait arose.
3. **B** A dichotomous key is useful for finding the species of an organism.
4. X, Y, and Z are in the same clade because in this cladogram, they represent all the groups that descend from a common ancestor. Without X, however, Y and Z would not represent a clade, because all the groups descending from that ancestor would not be included.

TEKS 8C

1. **D** The eukaryotic cell is the feature that distinguishes all Protista, Fungi, Plantae, and Animalia from Eubacteria and Archaebacteria.
2. **F** Archaea do not have peptidoglycan in their cell wall; Eubacteria do.
3. **B** All protists are eukaryotes, and some are unicellular heterotrophs.
4. **J** These are all the kingdoms with autotrophic species.
5. Unlike plants, which are autotrophs, fungi are heterotrophs that obtain their nutrients by decomposing other organisms. In addition, the cell walls of fungi contain chitin, whereas the cell walls of plants contain cellulose.

TEKS 9A

1. **A** Carbohydrates are the body's main source of energy.
2. **G** Proteins act as catalysts for nearly all of the chemical reactions that occur in the cell.
3. All biomolecules are made of carbon atoms combined with atoms of certain other elements, including oxygen, hydrogen, nitrogen, and phosphorus. Lipids are not polymers.

TEKS 9B

1. **C** These molecules are either reactants or products of both processes.
2. **H** The reactants of photosynthesis come from the environment, and some of the reactants of cellular respiration are made in the cell.
3. In glycolysis, glucose is broken down into smaller molecules. These molecules are transported to the mitochondria, where they are converted into water and carbon dioxide in the Krebs cycle. Other products of the Krebs cycle enter electron transport, which concludes with a process in which hydrogen and oxygen are combined into water.
4. The products of photosynthesis are the reactants of cellular respiration, and the products of cellular respiration are the reactants of photosynthesis.

TEKS 9C

1. **C** Enzymes allow chemical reactions to occur very rapidly, at a speed necessary for life processes.
2. **F** Like a key fitting into a lock, a substrate must specifically fit the active site of an enzyme.
3. **A** All enzymes are sensitive to changes in pH and work optimally only at specific pH values.
4. By controlling the function of enzymes, organisms can respond to changes in their environment, such as the presence of food in the digestive system or the presence of a toxin in the blood. Enzymes also catalyze reactions that are important for the growth and development of organisms, and these reactions must be carefully timed and controlled because if reactions get out of control, illness could result.

TEKS 9D

1. **A** The experiment showed that small organic molecules could arise from gases in Earth's early atmosphere.
2. **J** With the ability to duplicate itself independently, RNA could have arisen as the first genetic material.
3. Scientists had a revised hypothesis about the gases in Earth's early atmosphere, and they wanted to see if they could replicate Miller and Urey's results with their new hypothesis.
4. The earliest cells must have been anaerobic.

TEKS 10A

1. **C** Keeping blood sugar within a certain range is an important part of homeostasis.
2. **H** The endocrine system stimulates digestive organs to release enzymes to break down food, and the nervous system can stimulate muscles that move food through the digestive system.
3. Illness and injury can strike any body part or body system, so multiple lines of defense are essential. Pathogens can enter the body through the respiratory, digestive, or integumentary system. The nervous system can help sense and avoid dangers.

TEKS 10B

1. **C** In xylem, water and nutrients are carried upward through the plant, from roots to stems and leaves. In phloem, sugars and other materials travel from the leaves to other plant parts.

2. **J** A plant's stem has negative gravitropism, meaning it grows upward (against the pull of gravity) regardless of the slope of the ground or other factors.

3. *Sample answers:* The production of food by photosynthesis in the leaves requires water to be absorbed in the root system and transported up stems to leaves by xylem. The food is then transported throughout the plant in phloem; the growth of new roots requires food to be transported from leaves to root tips by phloem.

TEKS 10C

1. **B** The levels of organization are cell, tissue, organ, organ system, and organism.

2. **J** Bones are made of many tissues that work together.

3. **D** Skeletal muscles are attached to bones. Movement occurs when muscles pull on bones.

4. *Sample answer:* Picking up a pencil involves muscles moving the arms and fingers, the circulatory and respiratory systems supplying the muscles with oxygen, and the nervous system processing information about the pencil's location and controlling the muscular movements necessary to pick it up.

TEKS 11A

1. **B** In a negative feedback mechanism, an increase in the level of a substance, such as glucose, leads to a reaction that will decrease the level of the substance.

2. **H** The hypothalamus stimulates actions that conserve heat in a cold environment and release heat in a warm environment.

3. Negative feedback mechanisms occur when a decrease in the product or the result causes an increase in the response, and vice versa. The feedback leads to an opposite response. Positive feedback mechanisms occur when an increase in the product or result causes an increase in the response. The feedback leads to an increase in the response.

4. This is a positive feedback mechanism because an increase in the product (more platelets) leads to an increase in the response (an increase in the number of platelets responding to the site of the injury). The response helps maintain homeostasis because it stops bleeding and seals a wound, maintaining blood pressure and keeping out pathogens.

TEKS 11B

1. **A** If the population of predators decreases, the population of their prey is likely to increase.

2. **J** As the milfoil grows, it uses water, sunlight, and growing space. Because fish cannot eat the milfoil, the fish population may decrease. All the populations of the lake will be affected.

3. *Sample answer:* Plant and animal populations will decrease if wetlands are being drained or woods are being cleared, or they might increase or remain stable if parks are being established. New roads can fragment communities when they cut through fields and woods. New businesses and industries can increase pollution and degrade communities, though food-service industries provide food for certain populations, such as rats, raccoons, and pigeons.

4. *Sample answer:* Feral hogs are causing declines in the populations of amphibians, birds, or other native Texas animals that are their prey; feral hogs are causing declines in the populations of hawks, eagles, or other native Texas predators because they are eating their prey.

TEKS 11C

1. **B** In parasitism, the parasite benefits and the host is harmed. In mutualism, both organisms benefit from the relationship.

2. **H** Parasites disrupt the health of their hosts.

3. Microorganisms can maintain the health of ecosystems by breaking down the organic matter of dead plants and animals and recycling nutrients that living organisms can use. They can disrupt the health of ecosystems by killing organisms that are important to the ecosystem.

TEKS 11D

1. **A** The hardened lava is barren, and no soil or organisms exist.
2. **J** This forest is an example of a climax community, in which species diversity and population sizes are at their greatest.
3. The ecological succession that will take place is secondary succession because the soil remains. Species such as wildflowers and grasses will grow in the soil. When they die, they will provide the soil with organic material. Larger plants such as shrubs will grow and continue to add nutrients to the soil. Next, trees will take root. As plant communities develop, animals such as insects, birds, and rodents and the animals that prey on them will move into the area. Over time, the ecosystem may become a climax community.

TEKS 12A

1. **C** Mutualism is a relationship between organisms in which both organisms benefit.
2. **G** The organisms are competing for the same resource.
3. The species that was less adapted to that niche would find a new niche, move out of the habitat, or die out. The principle is called the competitive exclusion principle.
4. *Sample answer:* The decline in water level will cause increased competition between fish for space. The decline in fish will also affect predation relationships, in that the predators that eat fish, such as raccoons and snapping turtles, will have fewer fish to eat.

TEKS 12B

1. **B** Although separated by distance, the birds should have similar adaptations, such as strong wings for flight in windy conditions and large bills for scooping up or spearing fish.
2. **G** Flat teeth and hooves are characteristic of large grassland herbivores, such as buffaloes, zebras, and llamas.
3. *Sample answer:* Organisms in the tundra would have to have adaptations to help them survive with little precipitation. They would also have to have adaptations for surviving the cold. For example, animals may have extra layers of fat compared to animals on the grassland. Organisms in the grassland, on the other hand, may have adaptations to help them handle warm conditions.
4. *Sample answer:* All of the animals shown have a long snout that is likely used to probe ant or termite nests. Genetic variations among populations of these organisms' ancestors included genes that allowed for some organisms to have longer snouts than others. Because this was a beneficial feature in their environment, the organisms with this adaptation were more likely to survive and reproduce. Over time, long snouts became a characteristic of all these organisms.

TEKS 12C

1. **C** Brown bears could be classified as both primary consumers (because they eat berries and other plant matter) and secondary or tertiary consumers (because they eat fish and other animals).

2. **J** A pyramid of numbers shows the population sizes of each trophic level.

3. The hawk and owl both participate in two different trophic levels; the hawk is a second-level consumer and (rabbit→hawk; mouse→hawk) and fourth-level consumer (grasshopper→frog→snake→hawk; grasshopper→songbird→snake→hawk), and the owl is a second-level consumer (mouse→owl) and a third-level consumer (grasshopper→frog→ owl). The frog, songbird, owl, hawk, and fox are the second-level consumers in the food web.

4. *Sample answer:* The snake and owl would be most severely affected, because both rely on the frog and only one other animal for food, but the owl likely would be affected more than the snake. The snake might experience a boom in the population of its other food source, the songbird, due to a boom in the songbird's food source, the grasshopper, because its predator, the frog, has declined. The hawk's food supply could decline if the snake's population dropped, because snakes are one of the hawk's three sources of food.

5. The forest animal likely could not survive on a diet of predators exclusively. As shown by an energy pyramid, very little energy is concentrated in the bodies of predators. As shown in a pyramid of numbers, there are relatively few predators, and an animal would need to eat a large number of predators to gain the energy it needed.

TEKS 12D

1. **B** All plants and animals depend on water. If the available water on the grasslands is reduced drastically, then species that could not survive in the altered environment or relocate would become extinct.

2. **H** Many volcanic eruptions at the same time could send soot and ash into the skies, blocking sunlight and killing plants worldwide. Many species could die out quickly.

3. The cactus species is most likely able to survive drier than normal conditions. Cactuses are adapted to live in dry, desert climates, where water is limited. The other plants live in wetter environments and are not adapted to dry conditions. They likely would die with substantially reduced water supplies.

4. Answers will vary based on the choice of species, but will likely include the effect of some human activities on the habitat of the animal, such as the following: Land that was once home to the species is now used to raise farm crops and livestock; dams, wells, and irrigation systems have diverted water resources; forests have been cut down for lumber. Answers should also include any natural changes to the species environment (such as the die-off of the giant panda's bamboo).

TEKS 12E

1. **A** Combustion of carbon compounds adds carbon dioxide to the atmosphere. Decreasing combustion should decrease the rate at which carbon dioxide levels are rising in the atmosphere.

2. **H** Nitrogen-fixing bacteria convert, or "fix," atmospheric nitrogen into a useful form. Other soil bacteria then convert the fixed nitrogen into forms that plants can use to make amino acids.

3. Carbon dioxide from the atmosphere dissolves in ocean water. Algae that live in the ocean take in carbon dioxide for photosynthesis. Without these actions, atmospheric carbon dioxide levels would increase significantly.

TEKS 12F

1. **B** Similar to a body that can maintain homeostasis, a stable ecosystem can respond to changes without significant effects.

2. **J** Because the new mine would likely remove all the soil as well as all the plants and animals and because the disruption would continue, it would not only change the area but prevent it from recovering.

3. Sample answer: Pros: the insects will kill enough of the loosestrife, and the marshes will recover; the insects will keep the loosestrife under control; Cons: the insects could have unintended ecosystem effects (kill other plants, etc.) or become invasive; the insects may not kill enough of the loosestrife.

Glossary

abiotic factor: a nonliving factor that shapes an ecosystem, 148

accuracy: the closeness of a measurement to the true value of what is being measured, 23

active site: area of an enzyme that can bind with a specific substrate or substrates, 130

active transport: the process by which cells use energy to transport molecules through the cell membrane from areas of low concentration to areas of high concentration, 53

adaptation: a heritable characteristic that improves an individual's ability to survive and reproduce in its environment, 100

adaptive radiation: process by which a single species evolves into several different forms that live in different ways, 97

allele: one of a number of different forms of a gene, 85

animal: a heterotrophic multicellular eukaryote whose cells lack cell walls, 123

anticodon: a group of three bases on a tRNA molecule that are complementary to the three bases of an mRNA codon, 77

archaea: single-celled prokaryotes that do not have peptidoglycan in their cell walls and may have histones, 122

autotroph: organism that captures energy from sunlight or chemicals and uses it to produce its own food from inorganic compounds; also called a producer, 122

bacteria: prokaryotes with cell walls that contain peptidoglycan, 122

behavioral isolation: form of reproductive isolation in which two populations develop differences in behaviors that prevent them from breeding, 107

binary fission: a type of asexual reproduction in which a cell replicates its DNA and divides in half, producing two identical daughter cells, 58

binomial nomenclature: a classification system in which each species is given a two-word scientific name, 115

biogeography: the study of past and present distribution of organisms, 95

biohazard: a biological substance that poses a threat to the health of organisms, primarily humans, 5

biomolecule: large organic molecule that consists of a chain of carbon atoms that bond with some combination of hydrogen, nitrogen, oxygen, and phosphorus, 124

biotic factor: a living part of the environment with which an organism might interact, 148

bottleneck effect: a change in allele frequency following a drastic reduction in the size of a population, 109

cancer: a group of diseases characterized by cells that lose the ability to control growth, 68

capsid: a protein coat that surrounds a virus, 55

carbohydrate: macromolecule made of carbon, hydrogen, and oxygen, 124

catalyst: a substance that increases the speed of a chemical reaction, 130

cell cycle: the set of stages of growth and reproduction for a cell, 58

cell differentiation: the process that transforms developing cells into specialized cells with different structures and functions, 64

cellular respiration: a series of reactions that release energy by breaking down glucose and other food molecules in the presence of oxygen, 127

chlorophyll: pigment in plants and other photosynthetic organisms, 127

chromosomal analysis: the detailed study of the chromosomes of a cell, 91

chromosome: a threadlike structure of DNA and protein that contains genetic information, 70

clade: a group of organisms that includes a single ancestor and all of its descendants, 119

cladogram: a diagram that shows evolutionary relationships among selected groups, 118

codon: a set of three nucleotide bases that codes for a particular amino acid during protein synthesis, 73

commensalism: a symbiotic relationship in which one organism benefits and the other organism is not affected, 158

community: a group of different populations that interact with each other, 148

companion cell: in plants, phloem cell that surrounds sieve tube elements, 61

competition: the struggle between organisms for the same limited resources in a particular area, 158

competitive exclusion principle: principle that states that no two species can occupy the same niche in the same habitat at the same time, 158

consumer: an organism that relies on other organisms for its energy and food supply, 163

control: group in an experiment that is exposed to the same conditions as the experimental group except for one independent variable, 19

crossing-over: process in which a section of one chromosome exchanges places with the complementary section on its homologous chromosome, 89

cytokinesis: division of the cytoplasm to form two separate daughter cells, 58

decomposer: an organism that breaks down and obtains energy from dead organic matter, 163

decontamination: the removal of hazardous compounds, 4

denitrifying bacteria: bacteria that convert nitrogen compounds to nitrogen gas, 171

dependent variable: variable that changes in response to the independent variable, 19

derived character: trait that appears in a new species but not in the ancestral species, 119

dichotomous key: a guide that compares pairs of observable traits to help the user identify an organism, 119

diffusion: the process by which particles move from an area of higher concentration to an area of lower concentration 53

dihybrid cross: the mating of two organisms that differ for two traits, 86

directional selection: form of natural selection in which individuals at one end of a distribution curve have higher fitness than individuals in the middle or at the other end of the curve, 101

disruptive selection: form of natural selection in which individuals at the upper and lower ends of the curve have higher fitness than individuals near the middle of the curve, 101

DNA fingerprinting: tool used by biologists that analyzes an individual's unique collection of DNA restriction fragments; used to compare specific sections of two or more DNA samples, 92

DNA replication: process of copying DNA prior to cell division, 65

domain: the largest, most inclusive taxonomic category into which biologists classify organisms, 121

ecological pyramid: illustration of the relative amounts of energy or matter contained within each trophic level in a given food chain or food web, 164

ecological succession: the natural process of predictable changes that occur in a community following a disturbance, 154

ecosystem: all of the living (biotic) and non-living (abiotic) aspects of an environment, 148

endangered: an organism at serious risk of extinction, 167

endoplasmic reticulum: internal membrane system found in eukaryotic cells; place where lipid components of the cell membrane along with proteins and other materials exported from the cell are assembled, 54

endosymbiotic theory: theory that proposes that eukaryotic cells formed from symbiotic relationships among several different prokaryotic cells, 113

enzyme: a protein catalyst that increases the rate of a specific biological reaction, 53, 130

epithelial cell: a cell that lines the outside of the body, a body cavity, or organs, 63

eukaryotic cell: a cell that has a nucleus, 49

eutrophication: the process in which nutrients, such as nitrogen and phosphorus, dissolve in a body of water and stimulate the growth of plants and algae, 171

extinct: referring to a species that has died out, 166

facilitated diffusion: type of diffusion in which molecules cross a cell membrane through protein channels, 53

fermentation: process by which cells release energy from glucose in the absence of oxygen, 128

fitness: an organism's ability to survive, attract a mate, and reproduce in a particular environment, 100

food chain: a diagram that shows the feeding relationships in a community of organisms, 163

food web: a diagram that shows the overlapping food chains of an ecosystem, 163

fossil: preserved remains or traces of ancient organisms, 94

founder effect: change in allele frequencies as a result of the migration of a small subgroup of a population, 109

frameshift mutation: mutation that changes the "reading frame" of codons due to the addition or deletion of a nucleotide, 83

fungi: heterotrophic eukaryotes whose cell walls contain chitin, 122

gene: a sequence of DNA that includes instructions for producing a particular protein; factor passed from parent to offspring, 70

gene expression: a process that controls and regulates the assembly of a protein, 65, 79

gene flow: the movement of genes from one population to another population, 110

genetic drift: an evolutionary mechanism in which allele frequencies randomly change in a population, 109

genetic modification: the scientific alteration of the genome of an organism; also called genetic engineering, 92

genome: the entire set of genetic information that an organism carries in its DNA, 91

genotype: the genetic makeup of an organism, 85

genus: a taxonomic group that includes closely related species, 115

geographic isolation: form of reproductive isolation in which two populations are separated by geographic barriers, such as rivers, mountains, or bodies of water, leading to the formation of two separate subspecies, 107

Golgi apparatus: cell organelle that modifies, stores, and prepares proteins and other materials from the endoplasmic reticulum for destinations inside or outside of the cell, 54

gradualism: the evolution of a species by gradual accumulation of small genetic changes over long periods of time, 98

gravitropism: response of a plant to the force of gravity, 141

guard cell: a specialized plant cell that controls the opening and closing of stomata and protects the plant from water loss, 62, 139

habitat fragmentation: splitting of ecosystems into separate areas, 173

heterotroph: organism that obtains food by consuming other living things; also called a consumer, 122

heterozygous: having two different alleles for a single trait, 85

homeostasis: the regulation of relatively stable internal conditions despite changes to the environment 52, 145

homologous structures: structures that are similar in different species of common ancestry, 95

homozygous: having two identical alleles for a single trait, 85

hormone: chemical produced in one part of an organism that affects another part of the same organism, 131

hypothalamus: structure at the base of the brain that acts as a control center for recognition of and response to hunger, thirst, fatigue, anger, and body temperature, 146

hypothesis: a tentative statement or explanation for an observation in nature, 10

independent variable: the factor in an experiment that is deliberately changed, 19

index fossil: a fossil that is used to compare the relative age of other fossils, 97

inference: a logical interpretation based on prior knowledge and experiences, 25

internal feedback mechanism: trigger within a system in which the result of the process controls the process itself, 145

interphase: the period of the cell cycle between cell divisions, 58

invasive species: a non-native species that grows unchecked in a new ecosystem and harms the native species, often by using resources that native species need, 173

karyotype: a visual display of all the chromosomes in an organism's genome, grouped by pairs and arranged in order of decreasing size, 91

kingdom: the largest and most inclusive group in traditional taxonomic classification system, 121

law of independent assortment: scientific law stating that the alleles for two traits, such as pea color and pea shape, segregate independently of one another during the formation of gametes, 86

law of segregation: scientific law stating that two alleles segregate, or separate, during gamete formation, 85

lipid: macromolecule made up of mostly carbon and hydrogen; includes fats, oils, and waxes, 125

lysogenic cycle: type of infection in which a virus embeds its DNA into the DNA of the host cell and is replicated along with the host cell's DNA, 56

lytic cycle: type of infection in which a virus enters a cell, makes copies of itself, and causes the cell to burst, 56

malignant: cancerous, having the ability to spread to other parts of the body, 67

mass extinction: an event during which many species become extinct during a relatively short period of time, 167

meiosis: process in which the number of chromosomes per cell is cut in half through the separation of homologous chromosomes in a diploid cell, 88

messenger RNA (mRNA): type of RNA that carries the genetic information of DNA from the nucleus to ribosomes in the cytoplasm, where it is translated into a protein, 76

metastasis: spread of cancerous cells from one area of the body to other areas, 67

microorganism: any organism that cannot be seen without the aid of a magnifying glass or microscope, 151

mitosis: part of eukaryotic cell division during which the cell nucleus divides, 58

monohybrid cross: mating of two organisms that differ in one trait, 85

monomer: small chemical unit that makes up a polymer, 124

mutation: a change to the genetic material of a cell, 82

mutualism: a symbiotic relationship in which both organisms benefit, 159

natural selection: the process by which individuals that are best suited to their environment survive and reproduce the most successfully, 100

niche: the full range of conditions and resources an organism needs for survival and how it obtains these resources, 157

nitrogen fixation: process of converting nitrogen gas into nitrogen compounds that plants can absorb and use, 170

nucleic acid: macromolecule containing hydrogen, oxygen, nitrogen, carbon, and phosphorus, 126

nucleotide: subunit of which nucleic acids are composed; made up of a 5-carbon sugar, a phosphate group, and a nitrogenous base, 70, 126

nucleus: membrane-enclosed structure that contains the cell's genetic material in the form of DNA, 49

operon: groups of genes that are controlled by the same regulatory sections of DNA, 79

organ: group of tissues that work together to perform closely related functions, 143

organ system: group of organs that work together to perform closely related functions, 143

organelle: specialized structure that performs important cellular functions within a eukaryotic cell, 50

organic molecule: a molecule that contains bonds between carbon atoms, 133

osmosis: diffusion of water through a selectively permeable membrane, 53

parasitism: a symbiotic relationship in which one organism lives on or inside another organism and harms it, 158

passive transport: the movement of a substance across the cell membrane without the use of energy, 53

pathogen: disease-causing agent, 152

phenotype: the physical traits of an organism, 85

phloem: vascular tissue in plants that transports sugars and other nutrients throughout the plant, 140

photosynthesis: the process used by plants and other autotrophs to capture light energy and use it to power chemical reactions that convert carbon dioxide and water into oxygen and energy-rich carbohydrates such as sugars and starches, 127

phototropism: tendency of a plant to grow toward a light source, 141

pioneer species: first species to populate an area during succession, 154

plant: an autotrophic eukaryote whose cell walls contain cellulose, 122

platelet: a cell fragment released by bone marrow cells that clings to wounds and is part of the blood clotting process, 63

point mutation: a gene mutation that affects or changes one base pair of a gene, 82

polymer: a large molecule made of small, repeated units called monomers, 124

polypeptide: long chain of amino acids that makes proteins, 73

population: a group of individuals of the same species that live in close vicinity and interbreed with one another, 100

precision: the closeness, or reproducibility, of a set of measurements taken under the same conditions, 23

predation: a relationship in which one organism (the predator) captures and eats another organism (the prey), 158

primary succession: ecological succession that occurs on bare rock or hardened lava on which no soil or organisms exist, 154

principle of dominance: principle which states that some alleles are dominant and others are recessive, 85

producer: an organism that makes its own food from light energy and inorganic compounds, 163

prokaryotic cell: a cell that does not have a nucleus, 49

protein: macromolecule that is a polymer of amino acids; contains carbon, hydrogen, oxygen, and nitrogen, 125

protist: a single-celled eukaryote that is not a fungus or plant, 122

punctuated equilibrium: a pattern of evolution in which long stable periods are interrupted by relatively short periods of rapid change, 98

qualitative data: observations that do not include precise measurements, 22

quantitative data: observations that involve measurements of a specific property, 22

recombination: a source of heritable variation that results from independent assortment and crossing-over during meiosis, 110

reproductive isolation: separation of a species or population so that they no longer interbreed and thus evolve into two separate species, 107

resource: a material, such as food, water, air, and space to live and grow, that organisms need to survive and reproduce, 166

retrovirus: a type of RNA virus, in which genetic information is copied from RNA to DNA rather than from DNA to RNA, 56

ribosomal RNA (rRNA): type of RNA that combines with proteins to form ribosomes, 76

ribosome: cell organelle containing RNA and protein that is found in the cytoplasm; the site of protein synthesis, 54

RNA interference (RNAi): the blockage of gene expression by means of microRNA, 65

scavenger: animal that consumes the carcasses of other animals, 163

scientific theory: a well-established, highly-reliable explanation of a natural or physical phenomenon, 13

secondary succession: type of ecological succession that occurs after an event in which the ecosystem is not completely destroyed, 154

sexual reproduction: type of reproduction in which cells from two parents unite to make the first cell of a new individual, or offspring, 88

sister chromatid: one of two distinct strands in a chromosome, 59

speciation: the formation of a new species, 106

species: a group of organisms that can breed with each other and produce fertile offspring, 115

stabilizing selection: form of natural selection in which individuals near the center of a distribution curve have higher fitness than individuals at either end of the curve, 101

stem cell: an unspecialized cell that can differentiate into one or more types of specialized cells, 64

stoma (pl.: stomata): small opening in the epidermis of a plant that allows carbon dioxide, water, and oxygen to diffuse into and out of the leaf, 139

substrate: a reactant in an enzyme-catalyzed reaction, 130

symbiosis: a relationship in which two species live close together, 158

taxonomy: the scientific system of naming organisms and assigning them to groups, 115

temporal isolation: form of reproductive isolation in which two or more species reproduce at different times, 107

tetrad: structure containing four chromatids that forms during meiosis, 89

thigmotropism: response of a plant to touch, 141

tissue: group of similar cells that perform a particular function, 142

transcription: the process in which a gene serves as a template for the assembly of an RNA molecule, 72, 77

transfer RNA (tRNA): type of RNA that attaches to individual amino acids and transfers them to ribosomes, 76

translation: the process in which mRNA codons are decoded into a series of amino acids that will make up a protein, 72, 77

trophic level: each step in a food chain or food web, 163

tumor: mass of rapidly growing, abnormal cells, 67

vestigial structure: a structure that is inherited from ancestors but has lost much or all of its original function, 96

virus: a nonliving particle made of proteins, nucleic acids, and sometimes lipids, 55

xylem: vascular tissue in plants that transports water and dissolved minerals upward from the roots and throughout the plant, 139

Test-Taking Tips

Multiple-choice questions make up the entire end of course assessment tests. So you need to become an expert at deciphering multiple-choice questions. We have included a variety of strategies that will help you. You will not need to use all of these strategies for every question.

In a multiple-choice question, several possible answers are given to you, and you need to figure out which one of those answers is best. The first part of the question is called the stem. The stem can be a question or an incomplete statement. Read the stem carefully before you look at the answer choices.

The answer choices are indicated by letters, A, B, C, and D. One answer choice is correct. The other answer choices, called distractors, are incorrect.

Anticipating the Answer

A useful strategy for answering multiple-choice questions is to come up with your own response before you look at the answer choices. After you come up with your own response, compare it with the answer choices. You will then be able to identify the correct choice quickly. This technique is especially useful for questions that test vocabulary.

Sample Question

A scientist investigates the rate at which uracil in the cell nucleus is assembled into larger molecules. The results from this investigation would help explain which process?

A DNA replication

B the transcription of DNA to make RNA

C the translation of RNA to make proteins

D mitosis

The correct answer is **B**. If you remember that uracil is the nucleotide found in RNA but not DNA, then you can conclude that the scientist is studying the synthesis of RNA, which occurs during transcription. Because neither DNA nor proteins contain uracil, **A** and **C** must both be incorrect. Because mitosis does not involve RNA, **D** must be incorrect.

Using the Process of Elimination

Suppose you are not sure of the correct answer. You may be able to determine the correct answer through the process of elimination. Look at each answer choice and eliminate the choices that are least likely to be correct.

Sample Question 1

Which material in a host cell would indicate an infection from an RNA virus, not a DNA virus?

A viral mitochondria

B viral proteins

C reverse transcriptase

D viral capsids

The correct answer is **C**. If you remember that reverse transcriptase is involved in the production of RNA viruses but not DNA viruses, you can choose **C** quickly. Alternatively, you can eliminate the other answer choices. Viruses do not have mitochondria or other organelles, so you know that **A** is incorrect. Both DNA and RNA viruses contain proteins and a capsid (the outer coat of the virus), so **B** and **D** are incorrect too.

Sample Question 2

Down syndrome is a genetic disorder caused by cells receiving three copies of chromosome 21. Which event typically leads to Down syndrome?

F crossing over during prophase I of meiosis

G nondisjunction during anaphase I of meiosis

H a substitution mutation during DNA replication

J a frameshift mutation during DNA replication

The correct answer is **G**. Choice **F** is incorrect because crossing over, which is an event of normal meiosis, does not lead to a gamete receiving three copies of a chromosome. Choices **H** and **J** describe causes of gene mutations, not chromosome mutations.

Identifying What Is Being Asked

In some questions, you must be careful to distinguish between background information and the question itself. In the following sample question, the first paragraph presents background information. The question asks for evidence that supports the scientist's conclusion.

Sample Question

On an island, a scientist observes that the native lizards are different from similar species that live on the nearby mainland. The scientist concludes that the common ancestors of the lizards began developing into different species when the island separated from the mainland.

Which evidence, if it existed, would support the scientist's conclusion?

A Fossils of the same lizard species on both the island and mainland.

B The appearance of a mainland lizard living on the island.

C The appearance of an island lizard living on the mainland.

D Geologic evidence that the island arose from a volcanic eruption.

The correct answer is **A**. The matching fossils would suggest that the same lizard species once lived on both the island and mainland, which is consistent with the scientist's conclusion. The evidence described in **B** and **C** could be explained in many ways; for example, the lizards could be pets. These choices neither support nor contradict the scientist's conclusion. Choice **D** contradicts the scientist's conclusion that the island separated from the mainland.

Identifying an Event's Place in a Sequence

Some questions ask you to identify the correct place of an event in a sequence of events. For example, the question may ask you which event comes first or last, which event precedes another event, or which event occurs at the same time as another event.

Before you answer this kind of question, try to recall as much of the entire process as you can. Then look at all the answer choices. Begin by eliminating those that you know to be incorrect. For example, if you are asked to identify the last event in a series, eliminate the answer choices that indicate steps that occur early in the process.

Some multiple-choice questions that involve sequence will not ask you about where an event falls in a sequence, but rather ask about the correct sequence of events or steps in a process.

Sample Question

In the process of cellular respiration, a molecule of glucose is sequentially combined with oxygen to form carbon dioxide and water. In which stage of cellular respiration is carbon dioxide produced?

A the Krebs cycle

B electron transport

C the initial reactions of glycolysis

D the last reaction of glycolysis

The correct answer is **A**. Remember that cellular respiration occurs in three stages, which are sequentially glycolysis, the Krebs cycle, and electron transport. In animal cells, glycolysis alone produces the waste product of lactic acid, not carbon dioxide, so **C** and **D** cannot be correct. Electron transport concludes with the joining of hydrogen and oxygen to form water, not carbon dioxide, so **B** is incorrect.

Interpreting Line Graphs

A line graph enables you to see patterns in data and to make predictions. You must understand what the *x*- and *y*-axes represent and how to interpret the slope, or shape, of the line. In the line graph below, the *x*-axis represents temperature, and the *y*-axis represents percent enzyme activity, with 100 percent representing maximum activity. This information, as well as the title, tells you that the line relates the temperature in humans and thermophiles (heat-loving archaea) to enzyme activity.

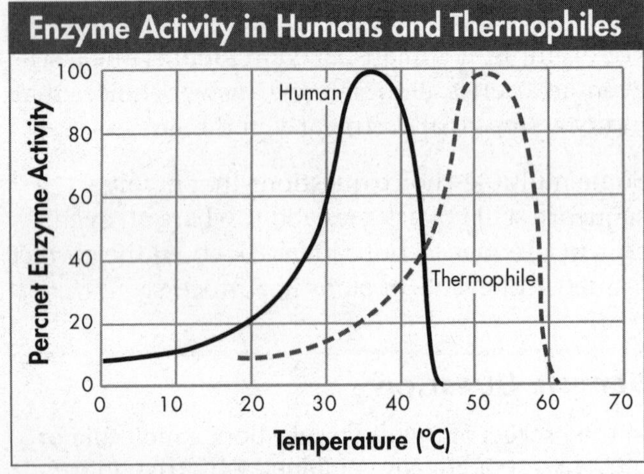

Sample Question 1

According to the graph above, at about what temperature do thermophiles demonstrate maximum enzyme activity?

A 37°C

B 42°C

C 50°C

D 60°C

The correct answer is **C**. As the dotted line in the graph shows, the maximum enzyme activity for thermophiles occurs at about 50°C.

Sample Question 2

What statement best describes a difference between humans and thermophiles shown in the graph?

F The temperature of maximum activity is lower for human enzymes than for thermophile enzymes.

G A temperature increase causes human enzymes to become more active and thermophile enzymes to become less active.

H A temperature increase from 42°C causes human enzymes to become more active and thermophile enzymes to become less active.

J The enzymes of humans and thermophiles are equally active at a temperature of 42°C.

The correct answer is **F**. The two lines in the graph have the same shape, but the line for human enzymes is at its peak at a lower temperature than the line for thermophiles. Notice that **J** is an accurate statement, but it does not answer the question.

Interpreting Data Tables

Data tables are one way in which scientists present the results of experiments. Before answering a question about a data table, look at the table to get a general sense of what kind of information it contains. If the table has a title, it usually indicates what the experiment was about. If a table does not have a title, you can often infer information about the experiment by examining the headings of the columns and rows.

Concentrations of Pollutants Along Cobb River

Location	Mercury (ng/L)	Lead (µg/L)	PCBs (ng/L)
1	3.0	0.17	0.15
2	3.2	0.25	0.24
3	3.8	0.31	0.31
4	3.9	0.38	0.35

Sample Question 1

A scientist took water samples from four locations along Cobb River. She measured the concentrations of three pollutants in each sample. In the data table, the locations are numbered in order of their positions along the river, with Location 1 farthest upstream and Location 4 farthest downstream.

Which conclusion can be drawn from the data in the table?

A Industries are polluting the water at three or more locations along Cobb River.

B Lead and PCB have approximately equal concentrations along Cobb River.

C Mercury is a greater health hazard than lead or PCB for communities along Cobb River.

D Pollutants tend to flow downstream with the river water.

The correct answer is **D**. For each pollutant, the concentration in the water increases as the river flows downstream, which suggests that pollutants flow with the water. **A** is incorrect because there is no information about the source of the pollutants. **B** is incorrect because the unit of measurement is different for lead than for mercury and PCBs. **C** is incorrect because there is no information about the levels of these pollutants that constitute a hazard to human health.

Sample Question 2

A scientist suggests that the sources of mercury in Cobb River are the airborne emissions of coal-fired power plants. Which activity would be most likely to provide data to test this scientist's hypothesis?

F Measuring the mercury concentration in the water of four other rivers.

G Measuring the mercury concentration in the soil of the banks of the river.

H Measuring mercury concentration in collected rainwater that falls near the river.

J Comparing the mercury content of coal and other fossil fuels.

The correct answer is **H**. For the mercury emissions of power plants to pollute a river, they must travel through the atmosphere and fall to the surface as rain or snow.

Interpreting Diagrams

Scientists use diagrams to clearly show the parts of objects or the steps of a process. Often, a diagram is much larger than the object it represents, as is the case for diagrams of microscopic objects such as cells. In other cases, a diagram is much smaller than the object, as in the case of many human organs.

In a multiple-choice test, begin by looking at a diagram to get an overall sense of what it shows. Then look for labels with lines connected to parts of the diagram. If you didn't immediately recognize the subject of the diagram, the labels should help. Then read the question. After you choose an answer, recheck the diagram to make sure that your answer is correct.

Sometimes you will be asked to interpret a set of related diagrams. For example, each part of a diagram could represent a different part of an investigation or step of a process, such as a chemical reaction.

To interpret a set of diagrams, make sure that you understand the meanings of arrows and other symbols. You should also compare and contrast the different diagrams. Determine their common and different features. Then read the question and answer choices carefully.

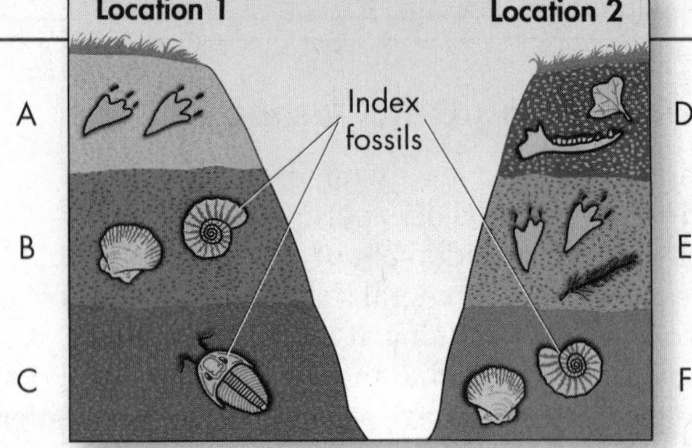

Sample Question 1

The diagram above shows matching index fossils in rock layers B and F, and that layer F is farther below the surface than layer B. From these observations, what conclusion can be drawn about the rock layers?

A Rock layer B formed long before rock layer F.

B Rock layer B formed long after rock layer F.

C Rock layers B and F formed at about the same time.

D Rock layers C and F formed at about the same time.

The correct answer is **C**. Index fossils are the remains of organisms that lived during a specific span of time and that lived across a wide region. Here, the matching fossils in layers B and F indicate that these two layers are about the same age, despite the fact that layer F is farther below the surface.

Sample Question 2

Which of the following features does the diagram represent most accurately?

F the distance between Location 1 and Location 2

G the number of index fossils in the rock layers

H examples of index fossils in the rock layers

J relative sizes of the index fossils in the rock layers

The correct answer is **H**. Remember that all diagrams and models have limitations, meaning they represent some features accurately and others less accurately. The purpose of a diagram is often the key to identifying its limitations. Here, the purpose is to identify and describe index fossils. The accuracy of the features described in **F**, **G**, and **J** was sacrificed to help meet this purpose in the space allowed.

Sample Question 3

A bacteriophage is a virus that infects bacteria. The diagram below shows two cycles of viral reproduction: the lytic cycle and the lysogenic cycle. In the lytic cycle, the bacterial cell actively reproduces viral particles. In the lysogenic cycle, the viral DNA is incorporated into bacterial DNA but viral particles are not produced.

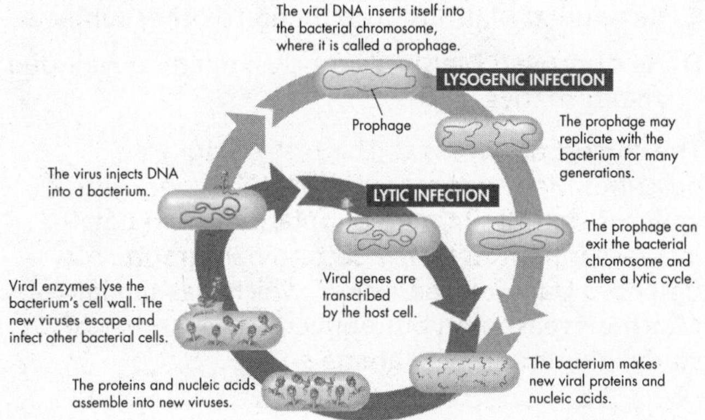

The viral DNA inserts itself into the bacterial chromosome, where it is called a prophage.
LYSOGENIC INFECTION
Prophage
The prophage may replicate with the bacterium for many generations.
The virus injects DNA into a bacterium.
LYTIC INFECTION
The prophage can exit the bacterial chromosome and enter a lytic cycle.
Viral enzymes lyse the bacterium's cell wall. The new viruses escape and infect other bacterial cells.
Viral genes are transcribed by the host cell.
The bacterium makes new viral proteins and nucleic acids.
The proteins and nucleic acids assemble into new viruses.

In the lysogenic cycle, how many cell divisions occur before the cell enters the lytic cycle?

A exactly 1

B either 1 or 2

C either 1, 2, or 3

D an indeterminate number

The correct answer is **D**. The part of the diagram that shows the lysogenic cycle indicates that when the bacterial cell divides, the viral DNA is replicated along with the bacterial DNA. The label indicates that it may occur for many generations.

Sample Question 4

In the lytic cycle,

F the prophage replicates with the bacterium.

G the prophage can exit the bacterial chromosome.

H viruses infect other bacteria.

J the viral DNA inserts itself into the bacterial chromosome.

The correct answer is **H**. According to the diagram , all the other processes occur only as part of the lysogenic cycle.

Interpreting a Text Passage

Sometimes you will be asked to read a text passage consisting of one or more paragraphs and then to answer questions about the passage. Always read the entire text passage before answering any questions.

The order of the questions may be different from the order of information in the text passage. For instance, the first question may ask about something found in the last paragraph of the text, and the last question may relate to information in the first sentence of the text.

When you have chosen an answer, check the text passage to make sure your answer is correct. If you are unsure of an answer to a question, skim the passage again to see whether you can find the information you need. The answer may not be stated directly; you may need to make inferences about what you have read or apply a concept that is not stated in the text.

Sample Questions 1 and 2 refer to the following passage.

> In developing his ideas, Charles Darwin incorporated the work of many scientists and other experts. The work of economist Thomas Malthus was especially important. Malthus observed that babies were being born at a faster rate than people were dying. Malthus reasoned that because Earth's resources were limited, this increase in the human population could not continue indefinitely.
>
> Darwin recognized that this reasoning applied even more strongly to plants and wild animals. A mature oak tree, for example, produces thousands of acorns every summer. A frog might lay hundreds of eggs at the same time. Darwin concluded that in nature, only a small fraction of offspring must survive and become adults.

Sample Question 1

How did Darwin apply the work of Thomas Malthus to develop his own ideas?

A He tested Malthus's explanations with an experiment.

B He explained Malthus's evidence with new reasoning.

C He applied Malthus's reasoning to other subjects.

D He disproved Malthus's conclusion and developed an alternative.

The correct answer is **C**. The first paragraph describes Malthus's reasoning and its conclusion, which is that the human population could not increase indefinitely. The second paragraph describes Darwin's reasoning, which was similar to Malthus's reasoning but applied to new areas of study: plants and wild animals.

Sample Question 2

When a species is introduced into an ecosystem, its population may increase quickly. Such a species is called an *invasive species*. According to Darwin's ideas as discussed in the passage, how might the population of an invasive species change over time in an ecosystem?

F It eventually will reach a stable maximum.

G It will rise and fall in a natural cycle.

H It will continue to increase indefinitely.

J It will rise briefly and then suddenly crash.

The correct answer is **F**. Notice that invasive species are not mentioned in the passage. However, Darwin's ideas about limited population growth apply to invasive species just as they apply to any other wild species.

Griddable Items

Some questions involve writing answers on a bubble grid that has a decimal point. Begin by figuring out the correct number (the answer) and where the decimal point goes. Then, write the number in the spaces at the top of the grid, with the decimal point in the correct place. Finally, fill in the correct bubble beneath each numeral.

Here are important points to remember about the bubble grid used in the end-of-course assessment.

- If the answer is a negative number, you must enter a negative sign. Otherwise, the answer will be recognized as a positive number.
- If the answer is a decimal number, enter a decimal point in the proper location.
- If you are taking the test online, enter numbers into the boxes. If you are taking the printed version of the test, write the numbers in the boxes and then fill in the bubbles.
- You do not need to use all of the boxes. You may place an answer in any set of consecutive boxes.
- You may fill in extra zeros either before or after the answer, so long as the extra zeros do not change the answer. An entry of "20" is the same as "00020", but not "2000".

Sample Question

What is the volume of liquid shown in the graduated cylinder?

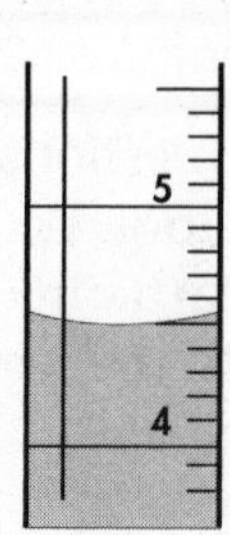

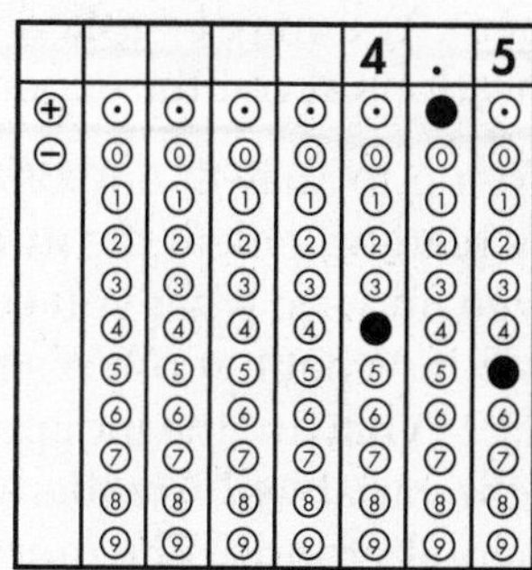

To solve, look at the bottom of the curve, called the meniscus, shown in the graduated cylinder. It is halfway between the 4 and 5 markings on the graduated cylinder, so the volume is 4.5 mL. Enter the symbols 4, decimal point, and 5 into the boxes. Then fill in the appropriate bubbles below the grid.

Interpreting Experiments

A problem may include a description of an experiment, an illustration of a lab setup, or a graph or table showing the results of an experiment. You may be asked to answer one or more questions about the experiment.

Before trying to answer any of the questions, carefully read or look at the information you have been given and see what you can learn directly or infer from it. What hypothesis might the scientist be testing? What are the independent and dependent variables? Are there control and experimental groups? The more you can understand about the experiment, the easier it will be to answer the questions.

Sample Question 1

A scientist uses radioactive phosphorus to label the DNA of bacteria. Then she allows the bacteria to undergo one cycle of DNA replication under normal conditions, with no additional radioactive phosphorus present.

Where is the radioactive phosphorus after DNA replication occurs?

A in one strand of each DNA molecule

B in both strands of half of the DNA molecules

C dispersed evenly among both strands of the DNA molecules

D in the cytoplasm of the bacterial cells

The correct answer is **A**. Remember that DNA has two strands, each containing repeated units of ribose (a sugar) and a phosphate group. By labeling the phosphorus, the scientist is able to track the changes to the strands during DNA replication. The experiment tests the process of DNA replication, in which each of the two strands of a DNA molecule serves as a model for a complementary strand.

Sample Question 2

A scientist performs an experiment to investigate the effect of temperature on the function of Enzyme A. Her setup includes three aqueous solutions, each containing identical concentrations of Enzyme A and the reactants but maintained at different temperatures. What is the dependent variable of the scientist's experiment?

F The temperature at which the reaction occurs.

G The initial concentrations of Enzyme A and the reactants in the solutions.

H The final concentrations of Enzyme A, reactants, and products in the solutions.

J The active site of Enzyme A.

The correct answer is **H**. The final concentration of Enzyme A, reactants, and products in the solution is the dependent variable, or variable that is affected by the independent variable.

Texas End-of-Course Assessments
Biology

Practice Tests

End-of-Course Assessment
Biology Practice Test A

1 While looking at a microscope slide, a student observes a cell similar to the diagram below. The student forms the hypothesis that the cell is a prokaryote. Which of the following cell characteristics supports the hypothesis?

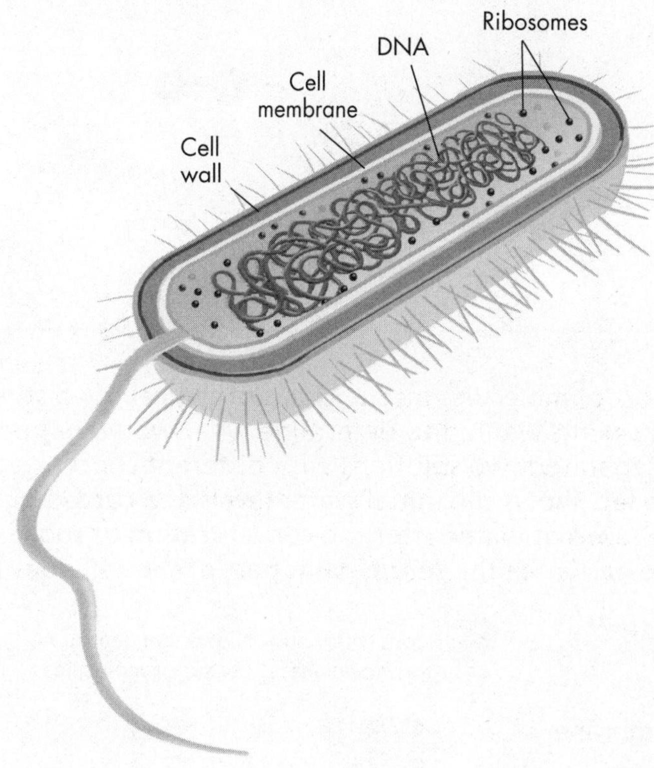

A Presence of a cell wall

B Presence of a cell membrane

C Presence of a flagellum

D Absence of a nucleus

2 The molecule in the diagram plays what role in the body?

F Releasing energy

G Forming part of the sugar-phosphate backbone of DNA

H Storing fat

J None of the above

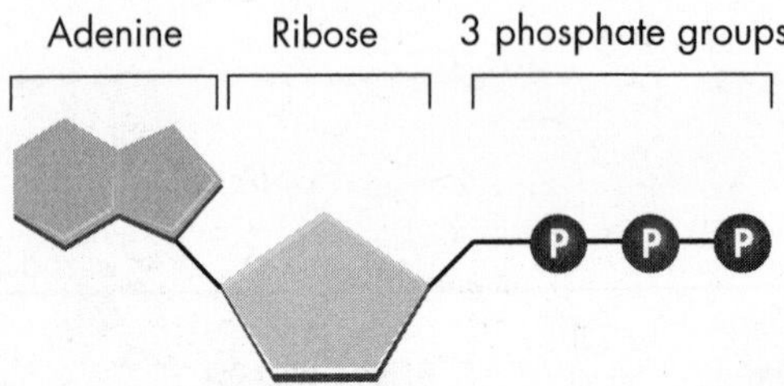

---

3 To study the transport of molecules into and out of the cell, two students set up the following investigation. The students wanted to determine what would happen if a selectively permeable barrier separated two solutions with different concentrations of sugar molecules. The diagram on the left shows the initial water levels in a curved glass tube. The diagram on the right shows the levels of water after the concentration of sugar molecules was the same on both sides of the barrier. In the setup, what part of the cell does the barrier represent?

A The cell membrane

B The cell wall

C The nuclear membrane

D The cytoskeleton

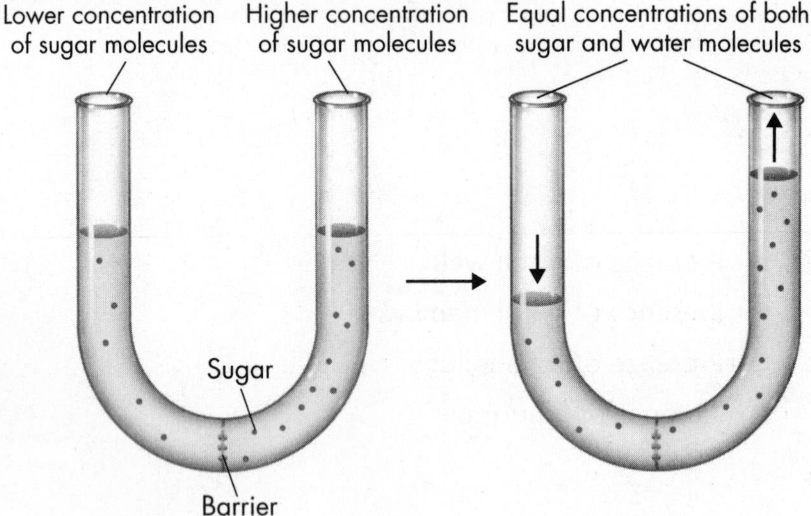

4 What is the typical sequence of events in lytic viral reproduction?

F Penetration; attachment to receptor proteins; replication; reassembly

G Attachment to receptor proteins; reassembly; replication; penetration

H Attachment to receptor proteins; penetration; replication; reassembly

J Reassembly; attachment to receptor proteins; replication; penetration

---

5 Unlike cells, viruses —

A can reproduce only by infecting living cells

B do not have proteins

C do not have nucleic acids

D obtain and use energy

6 The diagram represents the cell cycle in graphic form. What is one limitation of this graphic model?

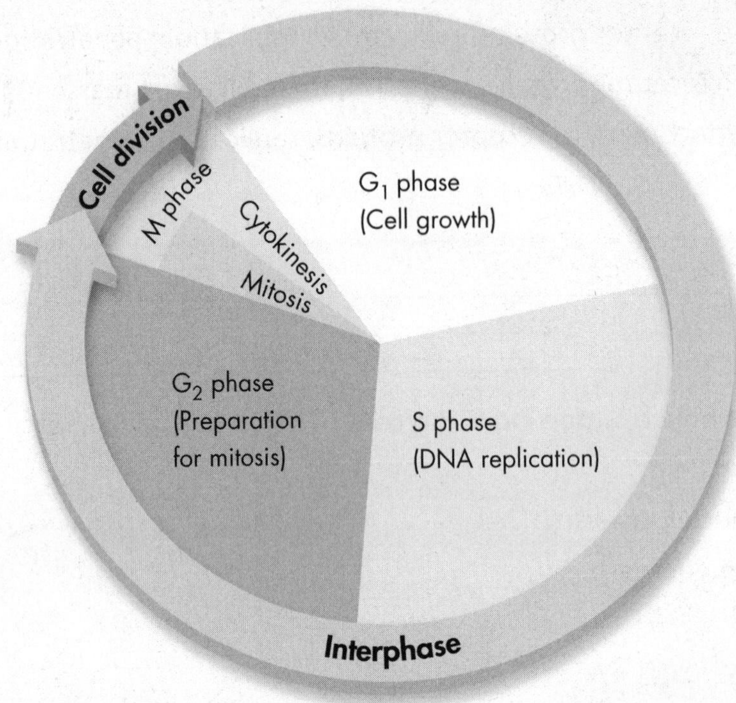

F It does not differentiate between the division of chromosomes and the division of the cytoplasm.

G It cannot be used to predict the length of the cell cycle for any specific organism.

H The sequence of the four phases is inaccurate.

J It does not indicate where in the cell cycle new DNA is synthesized.

---

7 What stage of mitosis is represented in this illustration?

A Telophase

B Prophase

C Anaphase

D Metaphase

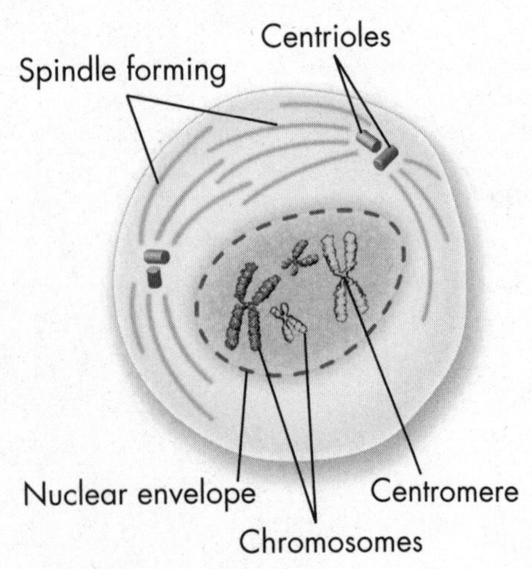

8 A scientist wants to investigate the effect of high acidity on the epithelial cells that line the digestive system of a frog. Which pieces of laboratory equipment would be most useful to the scientist?

F A probe that measures pH and a metric ruler

G A microscope and a probe that measures pH

H Electrophoresis apparatus and a Celsius thermometer

J A lab incubator and a Celsius thermometer

---

9 A research team is trying to find the specific cause of Cancer Z. Which of the following might be a hypothesis that the team is investigating?

A Cancer Z can be cured using a combination of chemotherapy and radiation.

B Cancer Z cannot be treated without knowing the exact mutation that is causing the cancer.

C A mutation in a gene on chromosome 5 is disrupting the cell cycle, causing Cancer Z.

D All cancers will someday be curable.

---

10 The biomolecule shown below is a —

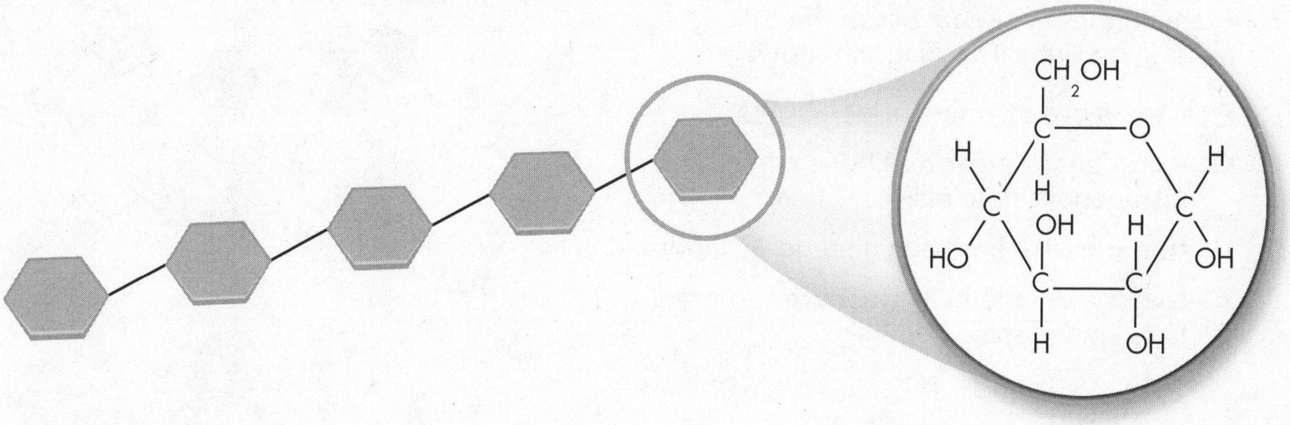

F carbohydrate

G lipid

H protein

J nucleic acid

11 Which of the following correctly describes lipid molecules and the cell membranes that they form?

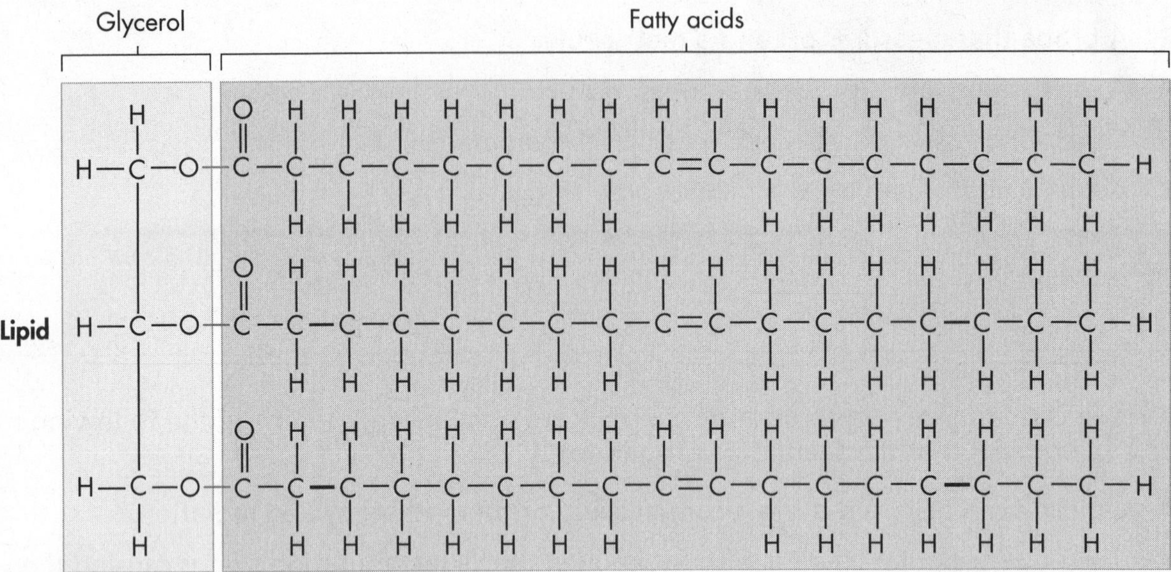

A Lipid molecules contain carbon, hydrogen, and oxygen atoms

B A lipid bilayer provides a flexible, strong barrier between the cell and its surroundings

C The fatty acid tails form an oily layer inside the cell membrane that keeps water out

D All the above

---

12 Examine the DNA sequence in the diagram at right. This diagram shows —

F a sequence of amino acids

G a phosphate-sugar backbone with nitrogenous base pairs

H that the DNA has been genetically modified

J that the double-helix structure turns in a left-handed spiral

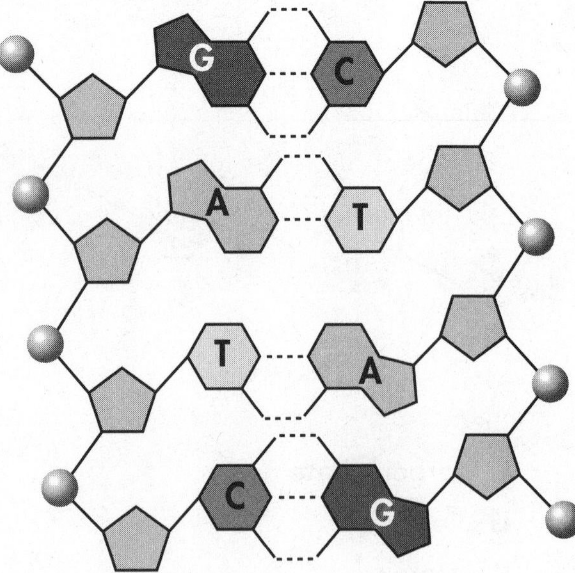

13 Study the segment of DNA shown below. What would be the complementary sequence of bases in the other strand of DNA that makes up the double helix?

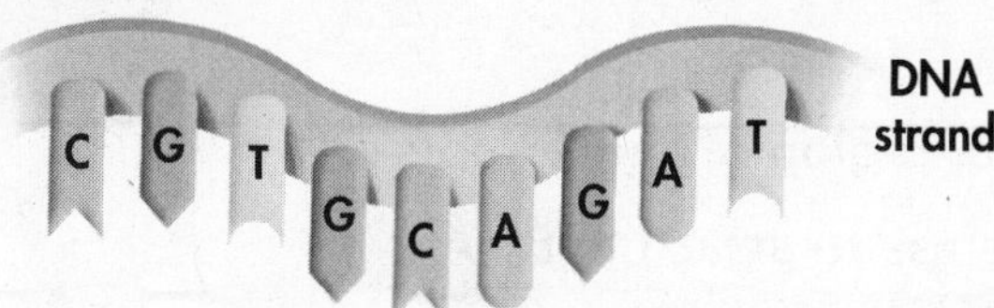

A GCACUGCUA

B CGTGCAGAT

C ATUUATCTA

D GCACGTCTA

---

14 DNA molecules, which store the genetic code, are found in —

F animals but not plants

G eukaryotes but not prokaryotes

H viruses but not cells

J all organisms

---

15 During protein synthesis, the translation process —

A takes place in the nucleus

B does not always involve mRNA

C involves tRNA molecules that each carry only one kind of amino acid

D All of the above

16 In eukaryotic cells, some transcription factors regulate the expression of genes by —

F removing a base from a DNA molecule

G transferring amino acids to ribosomes

H activating the operator region of the *lac* operon

J enabling RNA polymerase to attach to DNA

---

17 A geneticist wants to determine what mutation in a DNA molecule changed the structure of a specific protein. What would the scientist need to know *before* planning the investigation?

A The total number of bases in the DNA molecule

B Whether the DNA was part of an operon

C Whether the mutation was a substitution, an insertion, or a deletion

D The normal sequence of bases that code for the protein

---

18 Look at the diagram of the two chromosomes below.
To produce the mutant chromosome,

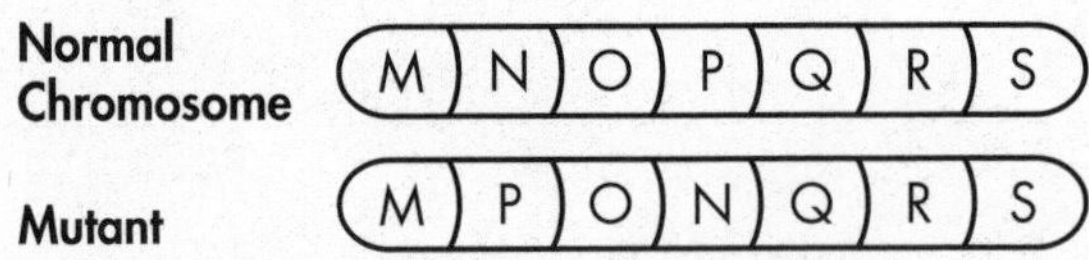

F part of the normal chromosome has been duplicated

G part of the normal chromosome has become inverted

H part of the normal chromosome has been deleted

J part of another chromosome has attached to the normal chromosome.

19 In peas, round shape *(R)* is dominant over wrinkled shape *(r)*, and yellow color *(Y)* is dominant over green color *(y)*. Look at the cross shown in the Punnett square below. What is the genotype that is missing in the bottom row?

RrYy × *RrYy*

	RY	*Ry*	*rY*	*ry*
RY	*RRYY*	*RRYy*	*RrYY*	*RrYy*
Ry	*RRYy*	*RRyy*	*RrYy*	*Rryy*
rY	*RrYY*	*RrYy*	*rrYY*	*rrYy*
ry	*RrYy*	*Rryy*	*rrYy*	

F_2 Generation

A *RrYy*

B *RRyy*

C *rrYY*

D *rryy*

---

20 In the nineteenth century, Gregor Mendel crossed true-breeding tall pea plants with true-breeding short pea plants. This cross (P) and its results (F_1) are diagramed at right. When two F_1 plants are crossed, what percentage of the offspring will probably be short?

F 0 percent

G 100 percent

H About 25 percent

J About 50 percent

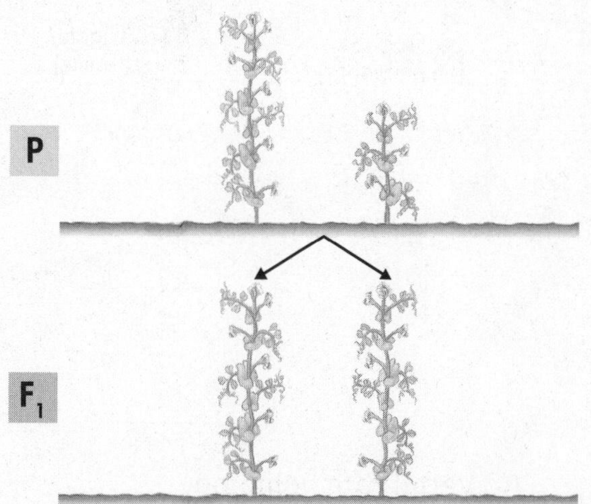

21 During meiosis, genetic recombination results because —

A gene mutations occur more frequently than at other times

B chromosome mutations occur more frequently than at other times

C chromosomes assort independently and crossing-over occurs

D genetic drift occurs

---

22 A genetic counselor hypothesizes that a certain individual has an extra chromosome. What is the best evidence she could use to test her hypothesis?

F A gel electrophoresis analysis

G A family pedigree

H A computer program that sequences the bases in a DNA molecule

J A karyotype

---

23 The diagram below shows an example of what type of homology?

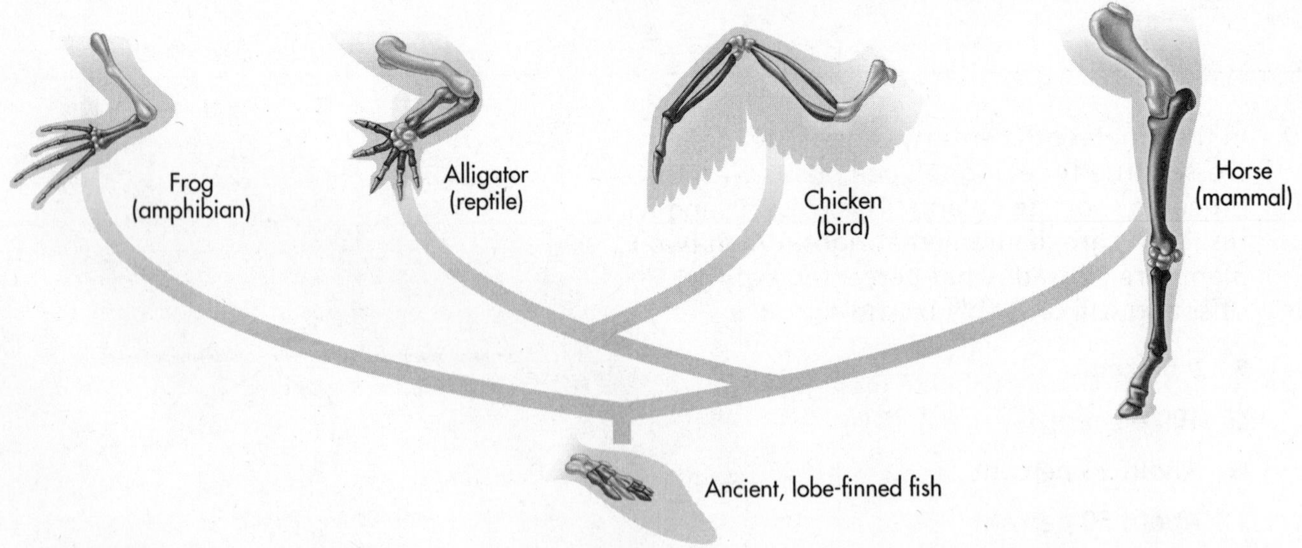

A Vertebrate homology

B Molecular homology

C Biogeographical homology

D Anatomical homology

24 A scientist compared the sequence of bases in a region of the same gene, *Hoxc8,* in a mouse, a baleen whale, and a chicken. Look at the base sequences in the table below. Which of the following statements is probably true?

Animal	Sequence of Bases in Section of *Hoxc8*
Mouse	C A G A A A T G C C A C T T T T A T G G C C C T G T T T G T C T C C C T G C T C
Baleen whale	C **C** G A A A T G C C **T** C T T T T A T G G C **G** C T G T T T G T C T C C C T G C **G** C
Chicken	**A** A **A** A A A T G C C **G** C T T T T A **C** **A** G C **T** C T G T T T G T C T C **T** C T G C T **A**

F The mouse is more closely related to the baleen whale than to the chicken.

G The chicken is more closely related to the mouse than the baleen whale is.

H The *Hoxc8* genes of the three animals are very different from one another.

J *Hoxc8* genes are not suitable for determining molecular homologies.

---

25 Many paleontologists hypothesize that present-day whales evolved from ancient ancestors that had four legs and walked on land. Evidence for that hypothesis would be a sequence of whale-like fossils —

A in which the oldest fossils had flipperlike appendages and the most recent fossils had four limbs

B in which the oldest fossils had four limbs and the most recent fossils had flipperlike appendages

C that indicate that the ancestors of present-day whales were wiped out during a mass extinction

D that indicate that whales evolved before animals with four legs

---

26 A farmer uses a chemical pesticide to kill insects that destroy the corn planted in a field. At first, the chemical kills 95 percent of the insects. After a few years, the pesticide kills only about 50 percent of the insects. Which of the following is the best inference about what caused the change in the pesticide's effectiveness?

F Some of the corn plants were able to change themselves so that they resisted the effects of the pesticide.

G After the first application of the chemical, some of the insects migrated to a different field. The allele frequency in the remaining population changed.

H In the beginning, a few insects were able to survive the pesticide. Over time, the frequency of the allele for pesticide resistance increased in the population.

J After the first application of the pesticide, the farmer switched to a different pesticide that killed a higher percentage of the insects.

27 The graph shows the relationship between beak size and survival for the medium ground finch, *Geospiza fortis,* during a drought on one of the Galápagos Islands. The graph shows that —

A when conditions are not dry, *Geospiza fortis* prefers small seeds

B all finches with beak sizes greater than 11 mm survived

C heritable variation accounts for the difference in beak size

D during a drought, large beak size is an adaptive advantage in *Geospiza fortis*

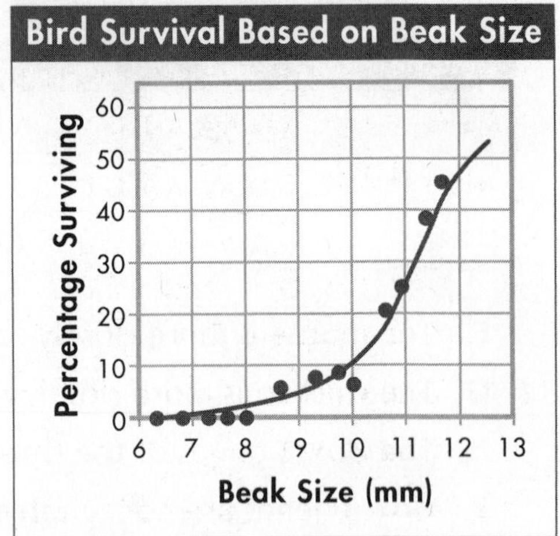

---

28 Researchers are trying to find new antibiotics to treat bacterial diseases. Why is the search for new antibiotics urgent?

F New antibiotics are needed to treat emerging diseases that have previously been unknown in the developed world.

G New antibiotics are needed to treat a variety of symptoms.

H Over time, more and more bacteria have become resistant to the antibiotics currently available.

J Each antibiotic kills only one kind of bacteria.

---

29 By chance, a few acorns from an oak tree are carried by a river for hundreds of miles to a new environment. Most of the acorns germinate and grow. After two or three generations, the new population of oak trees has some traits that are significantly different from those of the original population. What probably led to the difference in traits?

A Together, the acorns carried away by the river had allele frequencies that were different from those in the original population.

B The river water altered the acorns, giving those acorns greater fitness than the acorns in the original population.

C More mutations occurred in the new population than in the original population.

D The trees in the old environment had less genetic variation than the trees in the new environment.

30 Scientists use binomial nomenclature to name species because —

F a standardized naming system is critical in scientific classification

G it indicates where a species is found

H it is the only logical system of classification

J Latin is the only accepted scientific language

---

31 A dichotomous key is used to —

A make cladograms

B identify derived characteristics

C trace evolutionary development

D identify the species of an organism

---

32 A journal article contains the cladogram shown below. To communicate information that the cladogram shows, a student could report that —

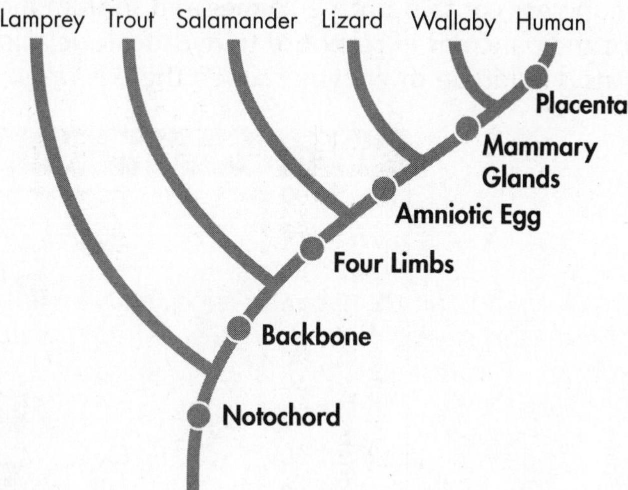

F wallabies lack mammary glands

G all the groups have four limbs

H the amniotic-egg trait appeared before the backbone trait

J all the groups have notochords

33 What process does the following equation describe?

$$6CO_2 + 6H_2O \xrightarrow{\text{light}} C_6H_{12}O_6 + 6O_2$$

A Greenhouse gas emissions
B Photosynthesis
C Cellular respiration
D None of these

---

34 Why is maintenance of a constant blood pH critical for body processes?

F Enzymes work best within a narrow pH range.
G Blood with a high pH helps prevent cancer.
H The production of vitamin C by skin cells requires low pH values.
J Some bacteria thrive in very acidic conditions.

---

35 The secretions of the pancreas contain both enzymes and sodium bicarbonate. The graph shows the secretions of the pancreas in response to hydrochloric acid, protein, and fat. What percentage of secretions is made up of enzymes when there is fat in the semi-digested food?

A 80 percent
B 20 percent
C 50 percent
D 40 percent

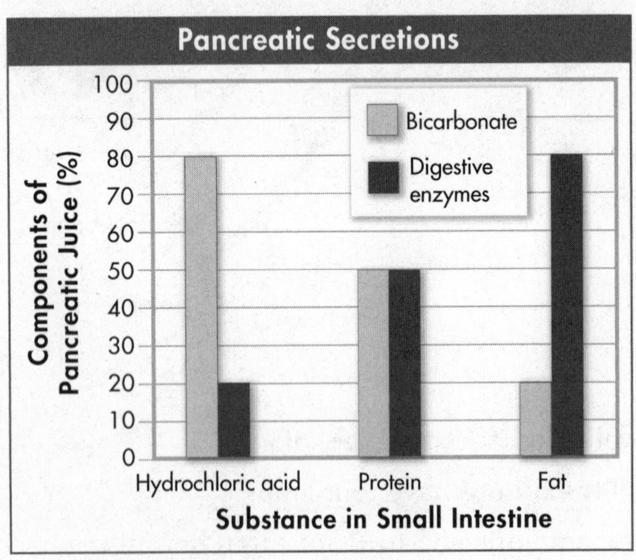

36 The diagram shows the human digestive system. In which structures do the digestive and muscular systems work closely together?

F 4, 5, and 6

G 1, 3, and 8

H 5, 6, and 8

J 4, 7, and 8

The Human Digestive System

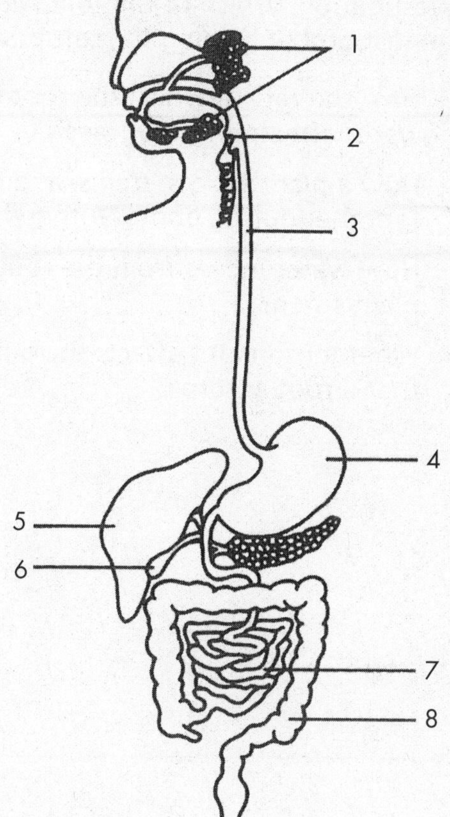

---

37 The body regulates blood pressure in a process in which nerves sense the blood flow resistance associated with higher blood pressure; the nerves relay this message to the brain; the brain then slows down the heart rate and dilates the blood vessels, lowering the blood pressure. This process is an example of —

A action potential

B positive feedback

C negative feedback

D atherosclerosis

---

38 Puberty begins when the hypothalamus signals the pituitary to release follicle-stimulating hormone (FSH) and luteinizing hormone (LH). During this process, which are the primary body systems that are interacting?

F The immune, reproductive, and nervous systems

G The circulatory, integumentary, and excretory systems

H The reproductive, endocrine, and nervous systems

J The excretory, reproductive, and endocrine systems

39 The diagram at right shows the setup for an investigation. Which of the following was the scientist probably using the setup to investigate?

A How the rate at which the root system absorbs water affects photosynthesis

B How a plant's roots, stems, and leaves work together during photosynthesis

C How water moves from the root system into the plant's stem

D Whether sunlight affects the amount of water that a root absorbs

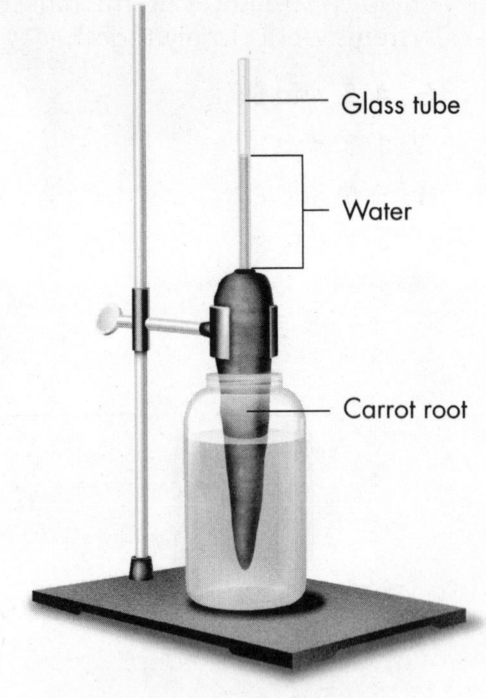

---

40 The diagram at right shows how hormones produced by a fully developed flower inhibit the development of a bud, temporarily preventing the bud from maturing. Which two systems are interacting in the diagram?

F Reproductive and support

G Reproductive and response

H Support and transport

J Response and photosynthetic

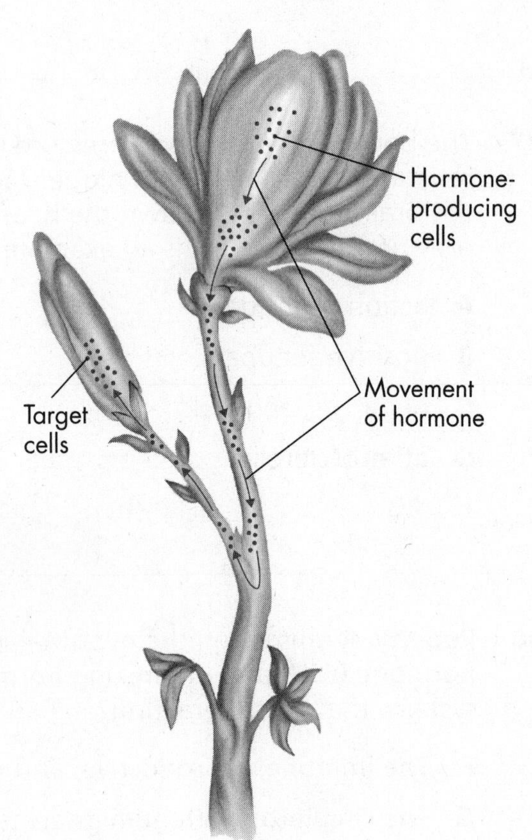

41 In a villus, what kinds of tissue work together to absorb nutrients and transport them throughout the body?

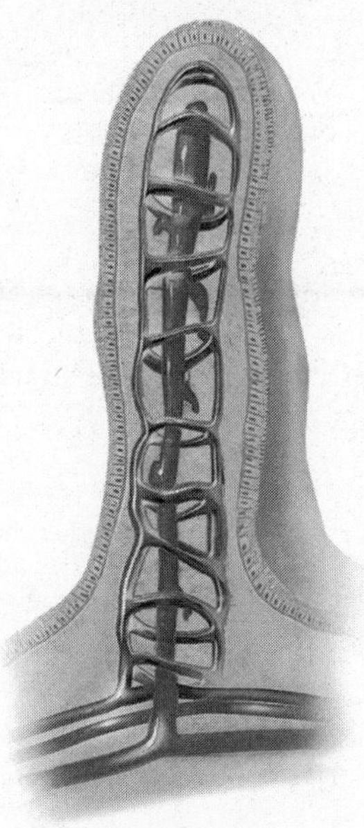

A Epithelial tissue and connective tissue

B Nerve tissue and muscle tissue

C Epithelial tissue and muscle tissue

D Artery tissue and vein tissue

---

42 Which interaction of body systems is an example of homeostasis maintenance?

F When you watch a scary movie, you feel your heart racing.

G During the movie, you eat and digest candy. As a response, your body's hormones stimulate cells to take up sugar from your blood.

H After the movie, your nervous system stimulates the muscles in your legs so you can walk out of the theater.

J Your brain enables you to remember a funny moment from the film and you laugh.

43 A scientist is writing a report and wants to include the following diagram. Which is the best title for this diagram?

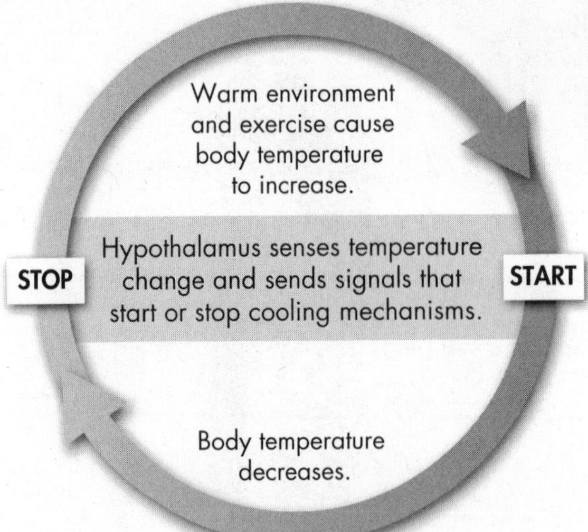

A Body Temperature Control Through Negative Feedback

B Body Temperature Control Through Positive Feedback

C Body Temperature on a Hot Summer Day

D The Function of the Hypothalamus

---

44 Scientists at a fertilizer-manufacturing company performed an experiment to determine whether a nitrogen-containing fertilizer (*NitroPro*) increased the height to which grass would grow. The scientists added the fertilizer to one plot of grass; another plot of grass, which acted as a control, received no nitrogen fertilizer. The graph, which shows the results of the experiment, was used in the company's advertising. Which of the following statements is justified by the data shown on the graph?

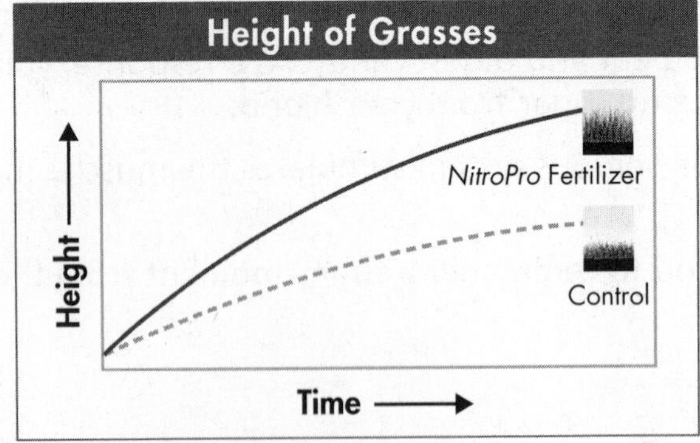

F *NitroPro* promotes the growth of grass.

G *NitroPro* makes your garden grow.

H With *NitroPro*, your gardening problems will be solved.

J *NitroPro* lawns are the greenest lawns in the neighborhood.

45 Mycorrhizae are symbiotic associations between some fungi and plant roots. The graph below shows the growth rate of three species of trees—spruce, lemon, and aspen—when mycorrhizae are present and when they are not. Based on the graph, what would probably happen if mycorrhizae were removed from the soil?

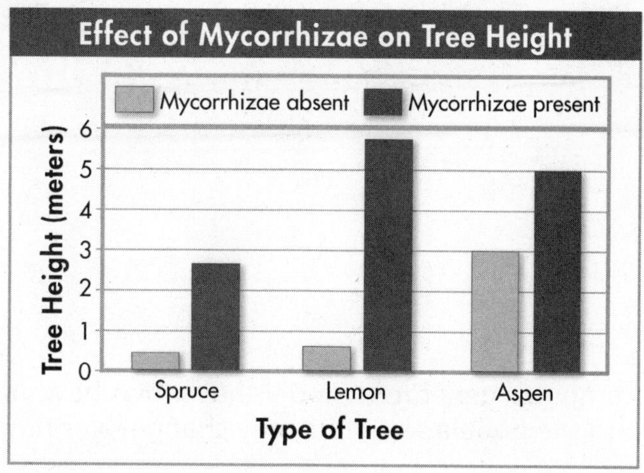

A The aspens will do better without the mycorrhizae.

B The effect on the aspens will be greater than on the lemon trees.

C The growth of all three kinds of trees will slow down.

D All three kinds of trees will die within a year after the mycorrhizae are removed.

---

46 Students are observing primary succession in an area that has just experienced a volcanic eruption. The students formulated several hypotheses. Which of the following hypotheses will probably be supported by evidence?

F Lichens will be the pioneer species.

G Raccoons will be the pioneer species.

H Nesting birds will colonize the area before grasses do.

J Maple trees will appear before mosses do.

---

47 In which of the following areas would secondary succession most likely occur?

A A lava flow

B An area with a well-balanced, well-established ecosystem

C A previously forested area devastated by fire

D A rock ledge exposed by the melting of the glacier that covered it

48 Remora fishes have an adhesive disk on their heads that they use to attach themselves to whales. When food floats away from the whale's mouth, unused, the remora unhitches itself from the whale and eats the food the whale let float away. The relationship between the remora and the whale is an example of —

F parasitism

G commensalism

H mutualism

J competition

---

49 The graph below is a computer-generated model that shows how, in general, the sizes of a predator population and the population of its prey change over time. What is one limitation of this model?

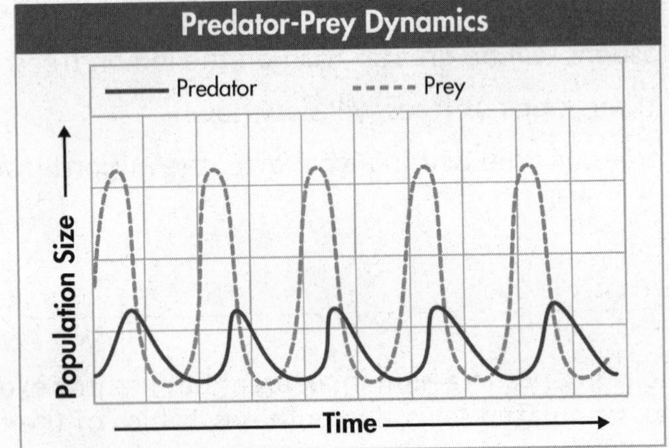

A The difference between the sizes of the two populations is exaggerated.

B In reality, the sizes of the populations of a predator and its prey change very little as time passes.

C The graph does not show actual population data.

D The graph is based on inaccurate data.

50 In the food chain shown here, which organism or organisms are autotrophs?

F The algae

G The flagfish

H The largemouth bass

J All of these

---

51 In the diagram below, the percentages refer to —

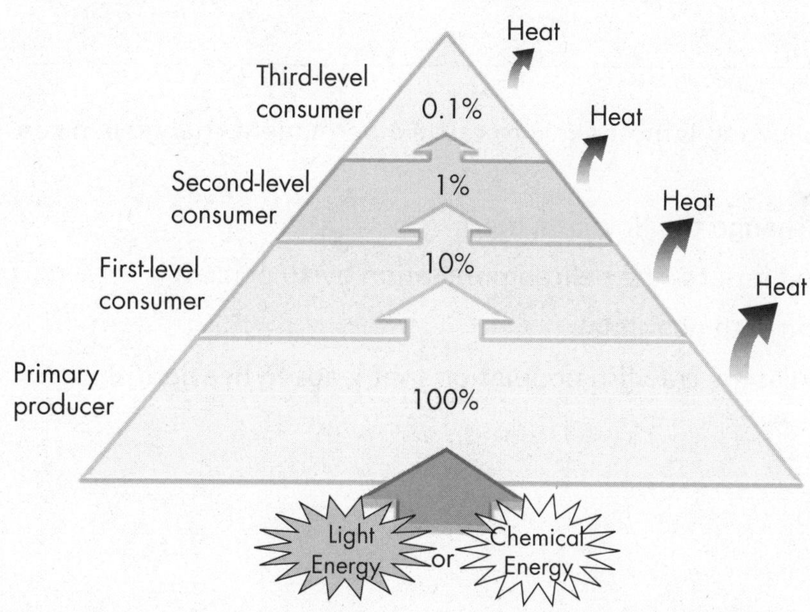

A the matter that gets transferred to the next higher trophic level

B the organisms that get consumed by organisms in the trophic level above

C the energy that gets transferred to the next higher trophic level

D the organisms at each level that are autotrophs

52 What two agents convert nitrogen gas into forms that organisms can use?

F Nitrogen-fixing bacteria and lightning

G Denitrifying bacteria and nitrogen-fixing bacteria

H Fertilizer and denitrifying bacteria

J Enzymes and ammonia

---

53 Excess algae are growing in a waterway near some farmland. Which is the most logical explanation for this observation?

A Fertilizer runoff polluted the water with nitrogen and phosphorus.

B Pesticide runoff polluted the water with carbon and oxygen.

C An invasive species caused the algal growth.

D Acid rain caused the algal growth.

---

54 Which of the following is most likely to cause a permanent change in a coastal wetland ecosystem?

F Levees that change the flow of water

G A disease that reduces the pelican population by 10 percent

H A long period with no rainfall

J An explosion in the crawfish population that leads to heavier fishing

Name ______________________ Date __________ Class ______________

Biology Practice Test A

Answer Sheet

1.	Ⓐ	Ⓑ	Ⓒ	Ⓓ
2.	Ⓕ	Ⓖ	Ⓗ	Ⓙ
3.	Ⓐ	Ⓑ	Ⓒ	Ⓓ
4.	Ⓕ	Ⓖ	Ⓗ	Ⓙ
5.	Ⓐ	Ⓑ	Ⓒ	Ⓓ
6.	Ⓕ	Ⓖ	Ⓗ	Ⓙ
7.	Ⓐ	Ⓑ	Ⓒ	Ⓓ
8.	Ⓕ	Ⓖ	Ⓗ	Ⓙ
9.	Ⓐ	Ⓑ	Ⓒ	Ⓓ
10.	Ⓕ	Ⓖ	Ⓗ	Ⓙ
11.	Ⓐ	Ⓑ	Ⓒ	Ⓓ
12.	Ⓕ	Ⓖ	Ⓗ	Ⓙ
13.	Ⓐ	Ⓑ	Ⓒ	Ⓓ
14.	Ⓕ	Ⓖ	Ⓗ	Ⓙ
15.	Ⓐ	Ⓑ	Ⓒ	Ⓓ
16.	Ⓕ	Ⓖ	Ⓗ	Ⓙ
17.	Ⓐ	Ⓑ	Ⓒ	Ⓓ
18.	Ⓕ	Ⓖ	Ⓗ	Ⓙ
19.	Ⓐ	Ⓑ	Ⓒ	Ⓓ
20.	Ⓕ	Ⓖ	Ⓗ	Ⓙ
21.	Ⓐ	Ⓑ	Ⓒ	Ⓓ
22.	Ⓕ	Ⓖ	Ⓗ	Ⓙ
23.	Ⓐ	Ⓑ	Ⓒ	Ⓓ
24.	Ⓕ	Ⓖ	Ⓗ	Ⓙ
25.	Ⓐ	Ⓑ	Ⓒ	Ⓓ
26.	Ⓕ	Ⓖ	Ⓗ	Ⓙ
27.	Ⓐ	Ⓑ	Ⓒ	Ⓓ
28.	Ⓕ	Ⓖ	Ⓗ	Ⓙ
29.	Ⓐ	Ⓑ	Ⓒ	Ⓓ
30.	Ⓕ	Ⓖ	Ⓗ	Ⓙ
31.	Ⓐ	Ⓑ	Ⓒ	Ⓓ
32.	Ⓕ	Ⓖ	Ⓗ	Ⓙ
33.	Ⓐ	Ⓑ	Ⓒ	Ⓓ
34.	Ⓕ	Ⓖ	Ⓗ	Ⓙ
35.	Ⓐ	Ⓑ	Ⓒ	Ⓓ
36.	Ⓕ	Ⓖ	Ⓗ	Ⓙ
37.	Ⓐ	Ⓑ	Ⓒ	Ⓓ
38.	Ⓕ	Ⓖ	Ⓗ	Ⓙ
39.	Ⓐ	Ⓑ	Ⓒ	Ⓓ
40.	Ⓕ	Ⓖ	Ⓗ	Ⓙ
41.	Ⓐ	Ⓑ	Ⓒ	Ⓓ
42.	Ⓕ	Ⓖ	Ⓗ	Ⓙ
43.	Ⓐ	Ⓑ	Ⓒ	Ⓓ
44.	Ⓕ	Ⓖ	Ⓗ	Ⓙ
45.	Ⓐ	Ⓑ	Ⓒ	Ⓓ
46.	Ⓕ	Ⓖ	Ⓗ	Ⓙ
47.	Ⓐ	Ⓑ	Ⓒ	Ⓓ
48.	Ⓕ	Ⓖ	Ⓗ	Ⓙ
49.	Ⓐ	Ⓑ	Ⓒ	Ⓓ
50.	Ⓕ	Ⓖ	Ⓗ	Ⓙ
51.	Ⓐ	Ⓑ	Ⓒ	Ⓓ
52.	Ⓕ	Ⓖ	Ⓗ	Ⓙ
53.	Ⓐ	Ⓑ	Ⓒ	Ⓓ
54.	Ⓕ	Ⓖ	Ⓗ	Ⓙ

End-of-Course Assessment
Biology Practice Test B

1 Which structure in the cell diagram below is found in animal cells but not plant cells?

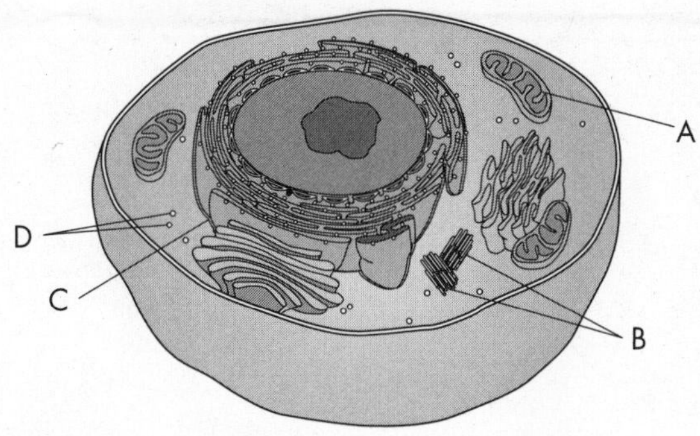

A Structure A—mitochondria

B Structure B—centrioles

C Structure C—endoplasmic reticulum

D Structure D—ribosomes

2 The diagram on the left below shows the appearance of a red blood cell under a microscope. The diagram on the right shows the same cell after a drop of solution is added to the microscope slide. What can be concluded about the solution in which the cell has been placed?

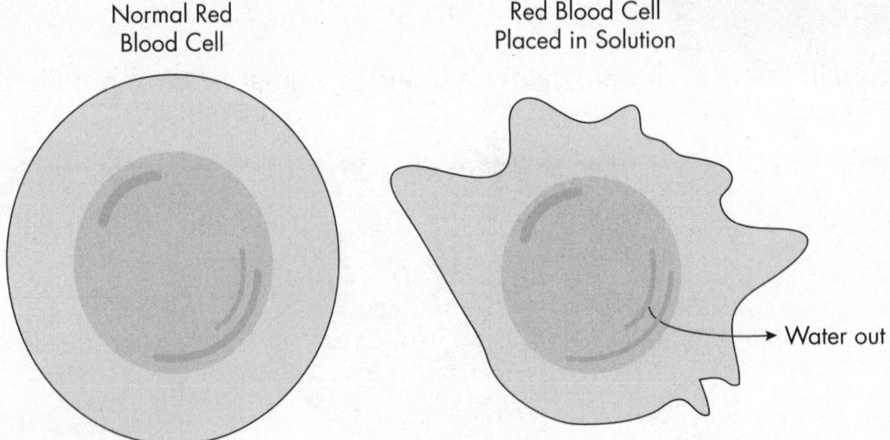

F The solution is isotonic.

G The solution is hypotonic.

H The solution is hypertonic.

J The solution did not cause the change in the cell's appearance.

---

3 Cells in the thyroid gland have concentrations of iodine that are much higher than concentrations of iodine in the blood. By which process does iodine from the blood enter the thyroid cells?

A Osmosis

B Facilitated diffusion

C Active transport

D None of these

4 Plants and other producers form the base of food webs. In these producers, the reactions of photosynthesis occur in the chloroplasts, as illustrated below.

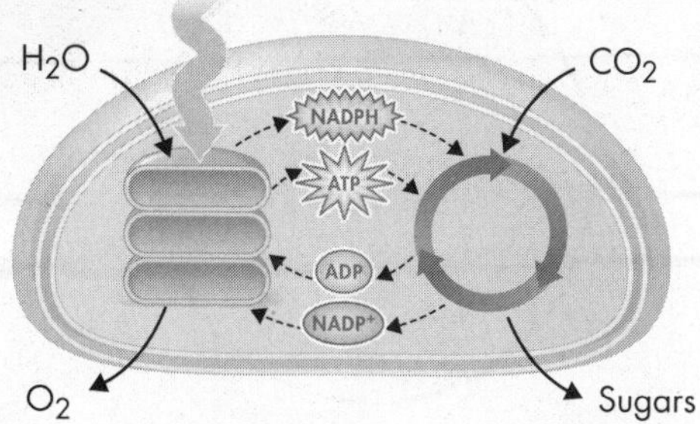

The source of carbon in the resulting glucose molecules is —

F carbon dioxide from the atmosphere

G light-dependent reactions

H the electron transport chain

J thylakoid membrane

---

5 The enzyme reverse transcriptase synthesizes DNA from a RNA template. During which of the following events does reverse transcriptase play a major role?

A The separation of chromosomes during anaphase of the cell cycle

B DNA synthesis during the S phase of the cell cycle

C The translation of DNA into proteins

D An infection of human immunodeficiency virus (HIV), the retrovirus that causes AIDS

---

6 In domestic dogs, the diploid (2N) number of chromosomes is 78. With the aid of an electron microscope, a scientist observes a canine cell that contains 78 single-stranded chromosomes enclosed in a nucleus. What can be concluded about the cell?

F The cell is a sperm or egg cell.

G The cell has lost the ability to divide into daughter cells.

H The cell is in the G_1 phase of the cell cycle.

J The cell is in the G_2 phase of the cell cycle.

7 A student prepares a microscope slide of cheek cells. She identifies the cell shown below.

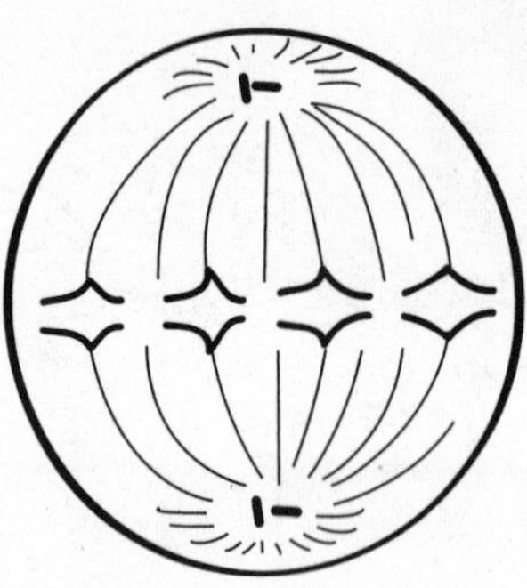

The stage of the cell cycle represented is —

A prophase

B metaphase

C anaphase

D telophase

---

8 To determine blood type, a drop of anti-A serum and a drop of anti-B serum are placed at either end of a microscope slide. A drop of blood is then added to each drop of serum. Clumping may occur, as shown below.

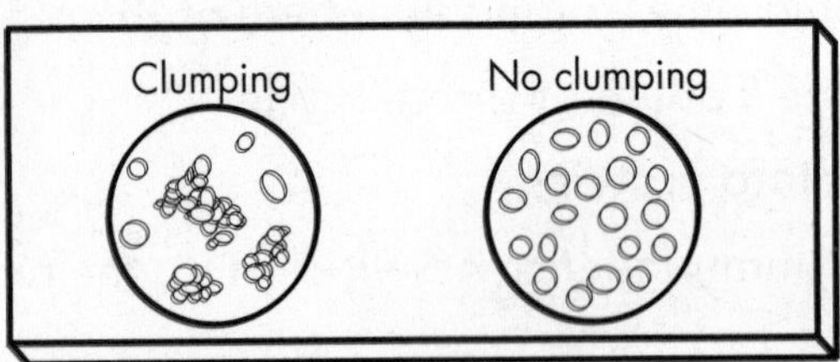

Clumping in anti-A serum or anti-B serum indicates the presence of antigen A or antigen B, respectively. The following slide represents the blood of a person whose blood type is —

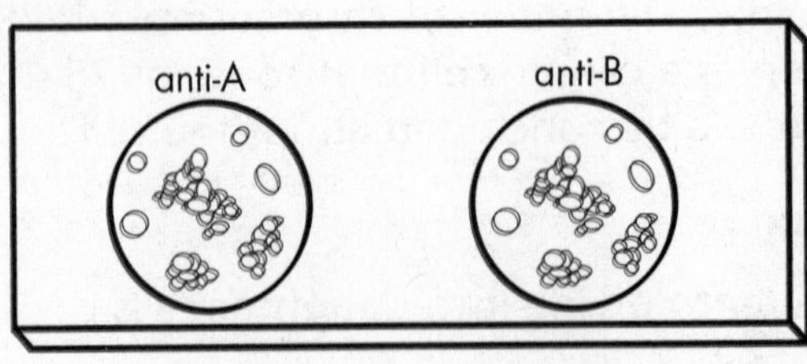

F A

G B

H AB

J O

9 Within a multicellular organism, the appearance and functions of cells may differ widely among different tissues, such as muscle and nerve tissue in animals, or leaf and root tissues in plants. What accounts for the differences among cells?

A Differences in the cells' genetic code

B Differences in DNA structure

C Differences in the sections of DNA that are replicated

D Differences in the genes that are transcribed and translated

---

10 All forms of cancer are characterized by —

F an abnormal, unregulated production of cells

G the aggregation of cells into a mass called a tumor

H the spreading of abnormal cells to tissues across the body

J All of these

---

11 Which of the following molecules represents the subunit of a polypeptide?

A

base

P

sugar

C

H, H, H, O

N—C—C

H, R, OH

B

CH_2 — O — C(=O) — R

CH — O — C(=O) — R

CH_2 — O — C(=O) — R

D

CH_2OH

H, C — O, H

C, H, OH, C

HO, H, OH

C — C

H, OH

12 A biological supply company is advertising the synthesis of a new compound. Scientists note that when the compound is added to a particular chemical reaction, the reaction rate increases dramatically. The compound is likely a —

F carbohydrate

G protein

H nucleic acid

J None of the above

---

13 A scientist isolates all the double-stranded DNA from the cells of a particular species of echinoderm. She breaks down the DNA and determines the percentage of each nucleotide. The table below shows the results for adenine (A) and guanine (G). What are the likely approximate percentages for cytosine (C) and thymine (T)?

Base	A	C	G	T
% of Total DNA	32		18	

A C = 32; T = 18

B C = 18; T = 32

C C = 18; T = 18

D C = 32; T = 32

14 In the structure of DNA, hydrogen bonds exist between —

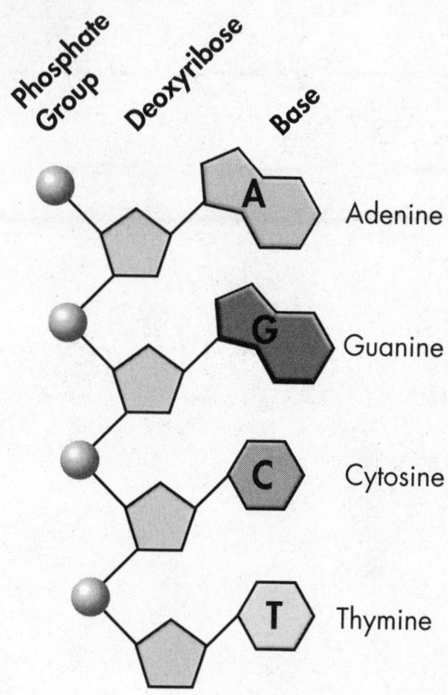

F the sugar of one nucleotide and the phosphate group of the next

G the bases along the center of the double-stranded molecule

H deoxyribose and base

J phosphate group and deoxyribose

---

15 In the translation of mRNA to proteins, the ratio of nucleotide bases to amino acids is approximately —

A 1 nucleotide base to 1 amino acid

B 1 nucleotide base to 3 amino acids

C 3 nucleotide bases to 1 amino acid

D 3 nucleotide bases to 2 amino acids

16 In the synthesis of a polypeptide, which tRNA molecule contains the correct anticodon to the next codon shown in the diagram?

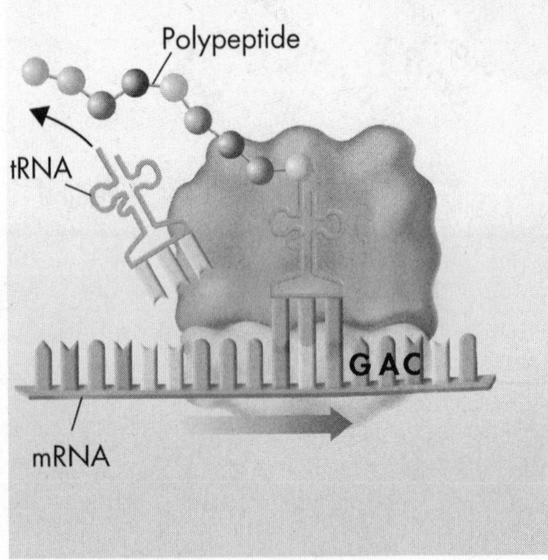

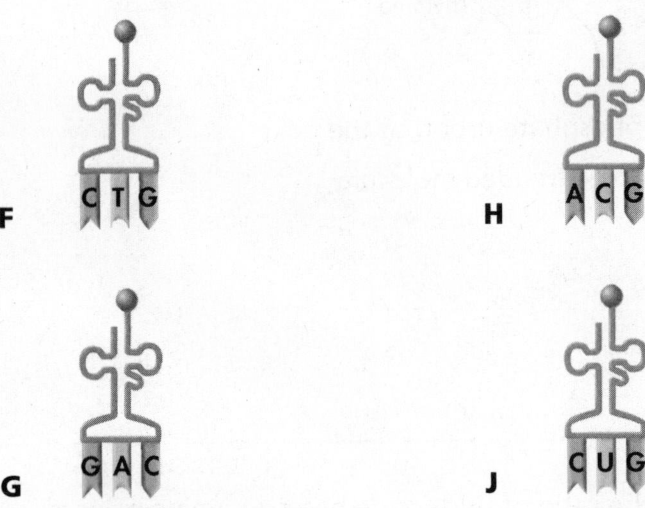

17 The compound lactose is composed of two simple sugars, glucose and galactose. The *lac* operon in *E. coli* consists of three genes, *lacZ, lacY,* and *lacA*, which code for proteins that transport lactose across the cell membrane and break the bond between galactose and glucose. *Lac* genes must be transcribed when lactose is the only food source available. Which of the following statements describes how the *lac* operon is regulated when glucose is available as a food source?

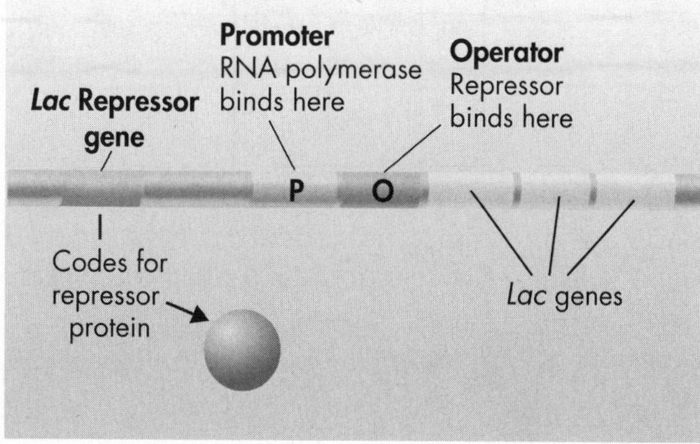

A The repressor protein binds to the O region, blocking transcription.

B Lactose binds to the repressor protein, turning on transcription.

C Glucose binds to the promoter, blocking transcription.

D Only one of the three *lac* genes is transcribed.

---

18 Following the start codon, the gene for a certain protein begins with the DNA sequence ACGTTGGTAAT. How would the protein most likely be altered if cytosine (C) was removed from this sequence?

F Only the first amino acid would be different.

G Only the first two amino acids would be different.

H All or nearly all of the amino acids would be different.

J Every other amino acid would be different.

---

19 Which change to a gene is likely to have the least effect on the protein that it codes for?

A An insertion mutation near the beginning of the gene

B A substitution mutation to the first nucleotide of a codon

C A substitution mutation to the second nucleotide of a codon

D A substitution mutation to the third nucleotide of a codon

20 In a particular plant, the allele for white flowers *(W)* is dominant and the allele for purple flowers *(w)* is recessive. Several generations of this plant have been grown in a greenhouse. The current generation consists of approximately 50% white flowers and 50% purple flowers, shown in the Punnett Square below.

	W	*w*
w	*Ww*	*ww*
w	*Ww*	*ww*

What are the likely genotypes of the original cross that resulted in the previous generation that consisted of about 75% white flowers and 25% purple flowers?

F *Ww* × *Ww*

G *WW* × *ww*

H *Ww* × *ww*

J *ww* × *ww*

---

21 A chicken that is homozygous for black feathers (*BB*) is crossed with a chicken that is homozygous for white feathers (*bb*). If the alleles for black and white feathers are codominant, what feather colors will be observed among the offspring?

A Gray feathers

B A mixture of black and white feathers on each offspring

C Black feathers among half of the offspring, white feathers among the other half

D Black feathers among one fourth of the offspring, white feathers among one fourth, and gray feathers among half

22 The diagram below shows seven stages that occur during meiosis. Using the appropriate numbers, place the stages of meiosis in their proper order.

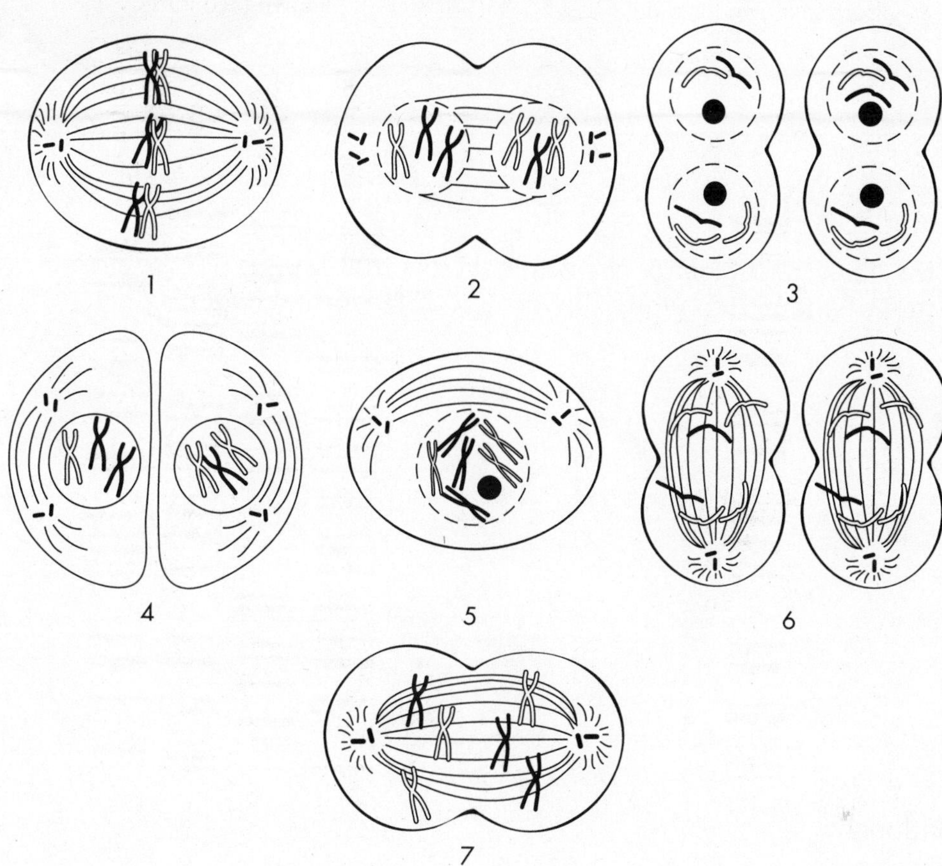

F 5, 1, 7, 2, 4, 6, 3

G 7, 1, 2, 6, 3, 5, 4

H 4, 5, 7, 1, 3, 6, 2

J 5, 3, 7, 2, 6, 1, 4

23 Gel electrophoresis of elephant DNA samples produced the fingerprints below. From which elephant population did the illegally obtained tusk originate?

DNA fingerprint of elephant tusk obtained from unknown location

DNA fingerprints of elephant droppings from known locations

Population 1 Population 2 Population 3 Population 4

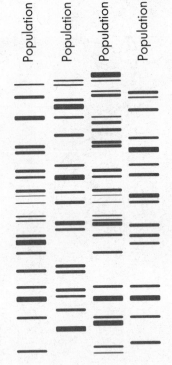

A Population 1

B Population 2

C Population 3

D Population 4

---

24 Cytochrome c is a small protein involved in cellular respiration, consisting of 104 amino acids. Based on the cytochrome c data, which pair of these organisms probably shares the most recent common ancestry?

F Dog and penguin

G Moth and yeast

H Chimpanzee and dog

J Chimpanzee and penguin

Organism	Number of Amino Acids That Are Different From Chimpanzee Cytochrome c
Dog	10
Moth	24
Penguin	11
Yeast	38

25 A paleontologist discovers a set of fossilized tracks at Location 1. Later, similar tracks were found at Location 2. The diagram below shows the appearance of fossils in rock layers A through F. What inference about the age of fossils in the region can be made based on these findings?

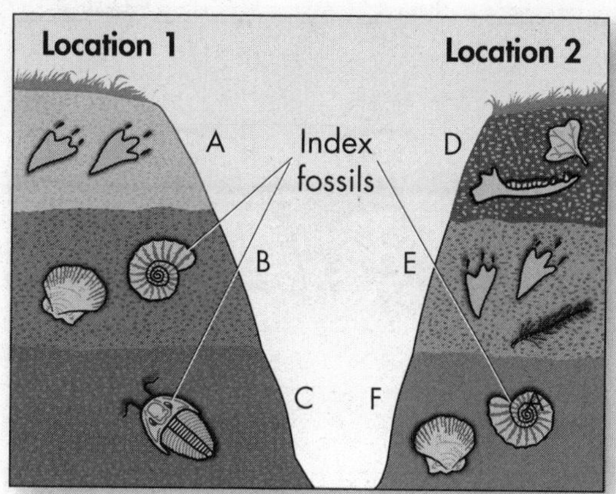

A Layer C consists of the oldest rocks.

B Layer A consists of the youngest rocks.

C Layers B and E are the same age.

D Layers C and D are the same age.

---

26 Long periods of stasis in the fossil record, followed by short periods of significant evolutionary change, are explained by which model of evolution?

F Evolution by genetic drift

G Evolution through geographic isolation

H Gradualism

J Punctuated equilibrium

27 A population of field mice displays coat color varying from light to dark. A group of researchers reports that they have identified several mutations in a gene that seem to be responsible for the color differences. Over time, how might natural selection result in differential reproductive success of members of the mice population?

A Light-coated mice and dark-coated mice are equally preyed upon by owls.

B Dark-coated mice migrate out of the population.

C Light-coated and dark-coated mice produce equal numbers of offspring.

D Mice with a coat color better adapted to their environment survive and reproduce.

---

28 You visit a natural history museum and study an exhibit on mammals around the world that feed on termites and ants. You read that these mammals, shown in the diagram below, evolved independently five times. The species are unique, but have evolved similar adaptations useful for hunting and eating insects—powerful front claws, a long hairless snout, and a long sticky tongue. Which of the following best describes the mammals' evolutionary relationship?

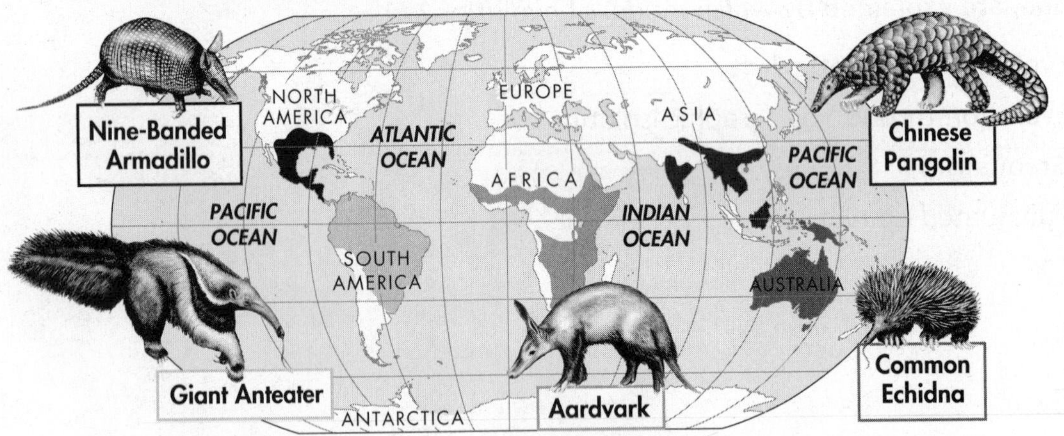

F They developed similar traits due to a shared gene pool.

G They have coevolved in different regions of the world.

H Facing similar environmental pressures, they developed similar adaptations through convergent evolution.

J The original population of mammals from which they descended passed through a genetic bottleneck.

29 A new species of vine is inadvertently introduced into a forest by campers. The vine grows quickly up the trunks of native trees, gradually killing them by interrupting the growth of branches and leaves. What best describes how natural selection will affect the population of trees in this forest?

A New adaptations will appear in adult trees that allow them to outcompete the vine.

B Trees that are best adapted to compete with the vine will survive and pass their existing adaptations to offspring.

C Offspring of the trees will be genetically identical.

D The vines and trees will interbreed to produce a new species.

---

30 Cephalexin is an antibiotic with a structure called a beta-lactam ring that disrupts the cell walls of bacteria, essentially destroying them. Some bacteria produce beta-lactamase enzymes, which break open the ring, rendering the antibiotic ineffective. A group of researchers have identified mutations in the enzyme that make bacteria even more resistant to cephalexin. A strain of resistant bacteria is grown on a Petri dish containing disks soaked in four different antibiotics. Which disk most likely represents cephalexin?

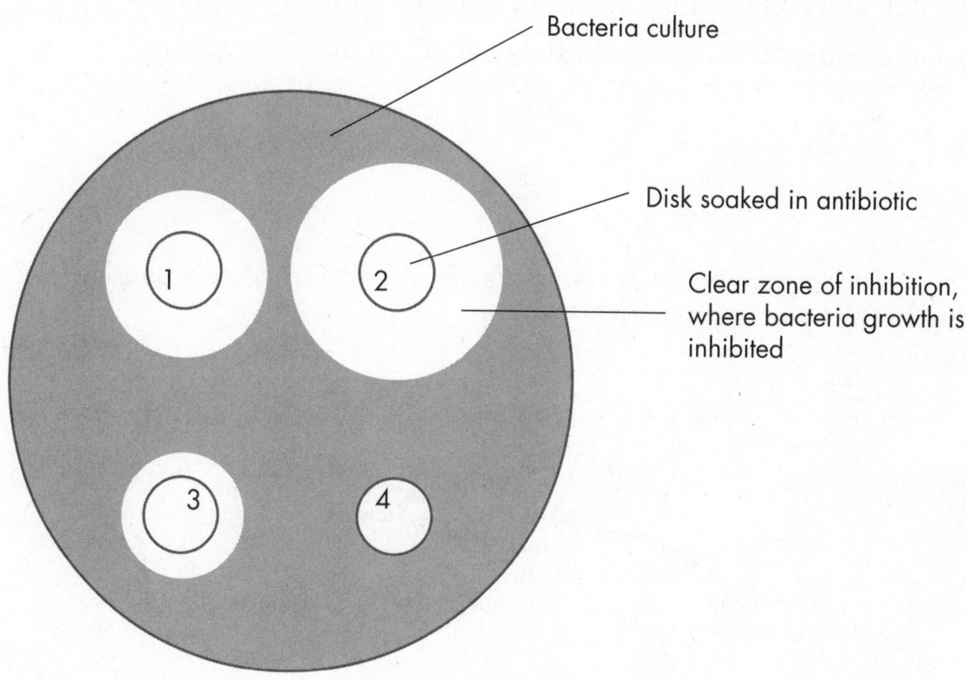

F Antibiotic 1

G Antibiotic 2

H Antibiotic 3

J Antibiotic 4

31 Endosymbiotic theory helps explain the complexity of eukaryotic cells. The idea that eukaryotic cells may have formed from symbiotic relationships among prokaryotes was first suggested over a century ago. Decades later, the theory was substantiated by many lines of observational and experimental evidence. Evidence supporting endosymbiotic theory includes which of the following?

A The variable number of chromosomes per cell among species

B The universal genetic code among species

C Unique features of mitochondria and chloroplasts that are similar to prokaryotes

D The symbiotic relationship between fungi and photosynthetic organisms in lichens

---

32 The Coho salmon *(Oncorhynchus kisutch)*, gila trout *(Oncorhynchus gilae)*, and brown trout *(Salmo trutta)* all belong to the family Salmonidae in order Salmoniformes. The two fish most closely related to each other are the —

F gila trout and brown trout because they are both called trout

G Coho salmon and brown trout because they belong to the same species

H Coho salmon and gila trout because they belong to the same species

J Coho salmon and gila trout because they belong to the same genus

---

33 As shown in the cladogram below, what characteristic do ferns, cone-bearing plants, and flowering plants all have in common?

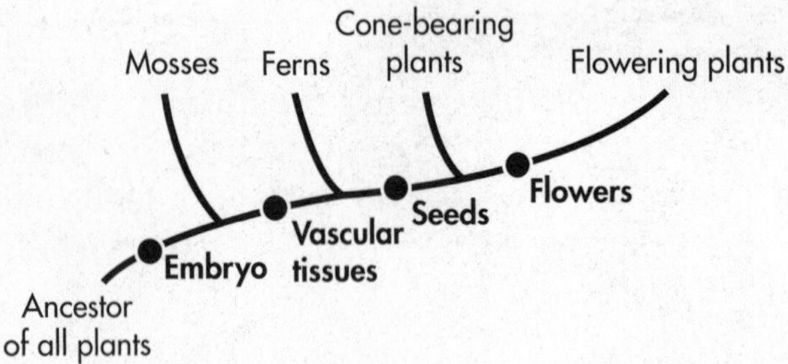

A Vascular tissues

B Seed production

C Flower production

D All the above

34 The table shows derived characters used to construct a cladogram of vertebrates. According to the table, the most closely related pair of organisms are the —

	Turtle	Lamprey	Salamander	Trout	Rabbit
Hair	No	No	No	No	Yes
Amniotic egg	Yes	No	No	No	Yes
Four legs	Yes	No	Yes	No	Yes
Jaw	Yes	No	Yes	Yes	Yes
Vertebrae	Yes	Yes	Yes	Yes	Yes

F lamprey and turtle

G trout and rabbit

H salamander and turtle

J lamprey and salamander

---

35 The table compares some molecular characteristics of organisms in the three domains.

Molecular Characteristic	Domain		
	Bacteria	Archaea	Eukarya
Introns (parts of genes that do not code)	Rare	Sometimes present	Present
RNA polymerase	One type	Several types	Several types
Histones found with DNA	Not present	Present	Present
Lipids in cell membrane	Unbranched	Some branched	Unbranched

A scientist studies the cell of a newly discovered organism and observes several types of RNA polymerase present and histones associated with its DNA. She also determines the presence of some branched lipids in the cell membrane. The organism likely belongs to which taxonomic group?

A Archaea

B Bacteria

C Protists

D Plants

36 What is the role of carbon dioxide (CO_2) in cellular respiration and photosynthesis?

F It is a reactant in both processes.

G It is a product of both processes.

H It is a reactant in cellular respiration and a product of photosynthesis.

J It is a product of cellular respiration and a reactant in photosynthesis.

---

37 The enzyme amylase is found in human saliva. In a laboratory investigation, two students studied the effect of amylase on starch. They measured the time it took 10 mL of a starch solution to break down when varying amounts of an amylase solution were added. The results are shown in the chart below.

Amylase Solution	Reaction Time
.5 mL	20 min
1 mL	10 min
2 mL	5 min
4 mL	150 s
8 mL	75 s

What conclusion can be drawn from the data?

A Amylase is involved in the digestion of proteins.

B Starch will not break down in the absence of amylase.

C Amylase is a catalyst for the reaction that breaks down carbohydrates.

D The time required for starch to break down is unrelated to the amount of amylase.

38 In the process of nutrient absorption, at which point do the nutrients processed by the digestive system enter the circulatory system?

F At the mucosal lining of the stomach

G At villi, finger-like projections along the wall of the small intestine

H Along the wall of the large intestine

J Inside the pancreas, liver, and other digestive glands

---

39 Which of the following body systems would mostly likely be affected by a disease that impaired the development of all the smooth muscle cells in an animal's body?

A Digestive system

B Circulatory system

C Excretory systems

D All of the above

---

40 A pharmaceutical company advertises its discovery of a new antigen that can be used to develop a highly effective vaccine against a certain bacterial infection. The company cites data showing a strong immune response elicited by the antigen. A person injected with the vaccine would likely show which of the following responses?

F The triggering of passive immunity

G Stimulation of white blood cell activity

H Increase in hemoglobin production

J Stimulation of osteoblasts

41 In plants, the hormones known as auxins stimulate cell elongation among other roles they play. The diagram at right shows the response of a houseplant on a windowsill to incoming sunlight. In which location on the plant is the concentration of auxins the greatest?

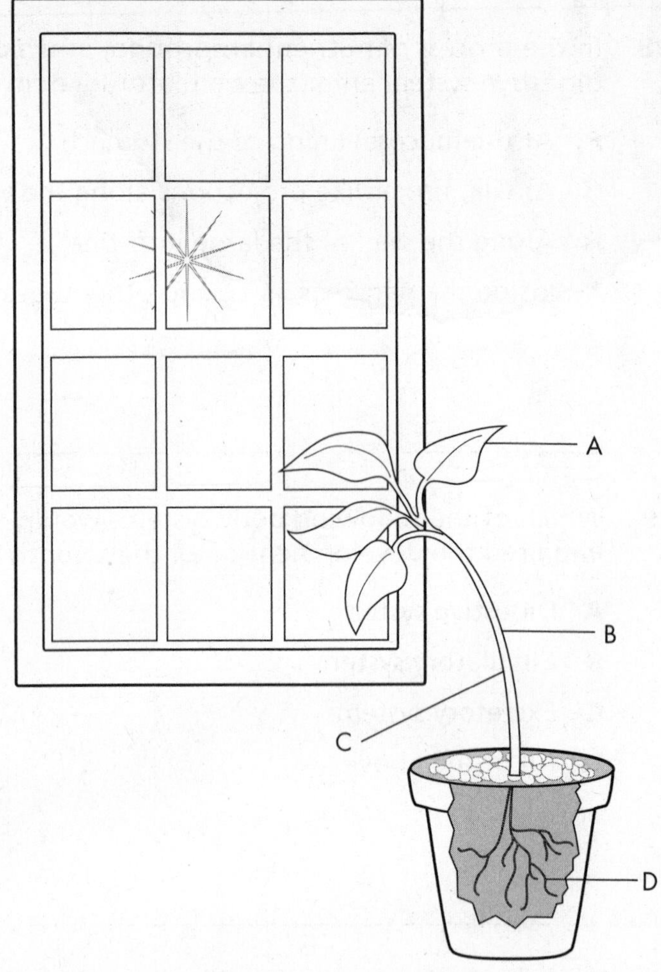

A Location A

B Location B

C Location C

D Location D

---

42 A student designs an experiment to demonstrate the presence of openings in the walls of xylem cells in plants. He takes a long-stemmed, white chrysanthemum and carefully cuts the stalk halfway up. He places each half of the stalk in a glass cylinder filled with water. Red dye is added to one cylinder; blue dye is added to the other. What observations would you expect to make over the next few days?

F The flower remains white.

G The flower turns blue, then changes to red.

H The flower turns red, then changes to blue.

J Initially part of the flower will be blue and part will be red, but eventually both colors will appear in all parts of the flower.

43 Maintaining a stable level of glucose in the body is an important part of homeostasis. What occurs between meals, when blood sugar drops?

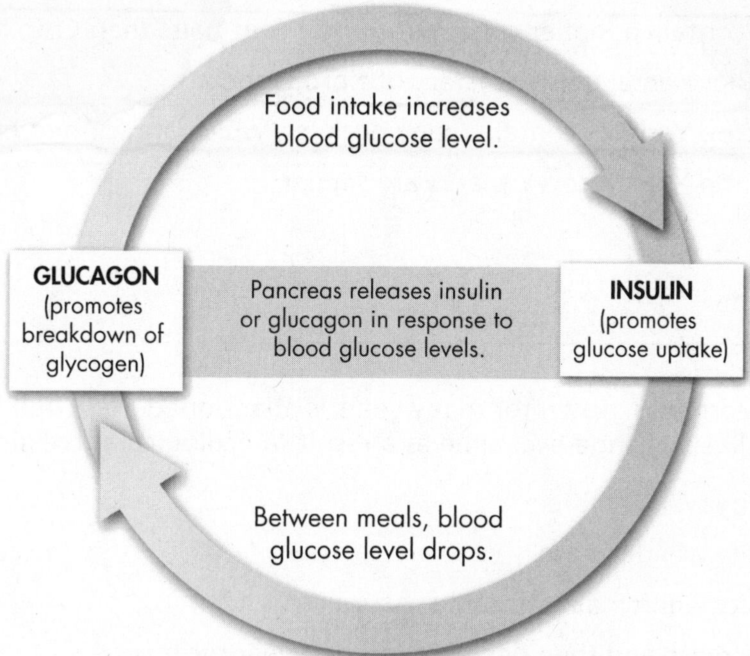

A Insulin is released, targeting fat tissues to convert glucose to lipids.

B Insulin is released, targeting skeletal muscles to convert glucose to lipids.

C Glucagon is released, stimulating the liver and skeletal muscles to break down glycogen into glucose.

D Glucagon is released, inhibiting glucose uptake by cells.

---

44 Which event would most likely cause the greatest changes to a pond community?

F A storm that damages the trees surrounding the pond

G The hatching of a clutch of frog eggs in the pond

H A severe drought that reduces the pond's water supply by one half

J The death of the largest member of the fish population

45 On a farm that practices crop rotation, Crop X is planted one year and Crop Y is planted the next year. This alternating cycle of planting is continued for several years. Crop Y increases the availability of nitrogen to plants in the soil. The roots of both crop plants are studied under a stereomicroscope. What observation would you expect to make?

A Crop X plants contain a higher concentration of root hairs than Crop Y plants.

B Crop Y plants have an extensive system of fibrous roots.

C The roots of Crop Y plants contain many nodules, which are formed by symbiotic bacteria.

D The roots of Crop X and Crop Y plants are similar.

---

46 A field on which corn was grown for many years is abandoned. How will the species diversity of the field most likely change over time as a result of ecological succession?

F Species diversity will increase.

G Species diversity will decrease.

H Species diversity will remain the same.

J Species will increase and then decrease in a ten-year cycle.

---

47 A severe wildfire has been reported in a densely forested region of the state. The forest ecosystem sustained extensive damage; for much of the forest, only soil and charred remnants of the once towering trees remain. What predictions can you make about how the ecosystem will change over time?

A Primary succession will occur.

B Lichens will be the predominant species in the forest for the next 20 years.

C Large mammals will migrate in to claim the newly available territory.

D Grasses and small shrubs will appear in the next few years, eventually followed by taller vegetation.

48 The ocellaris clownfish (*Amphiprion ocellaris*) lives in close association with the magnificent sea anemone (*Heteractis magnifica*). The sea anemone can grow up to 1 meter in diameter and provides the clownfish with protection and shelter, as well as food left over from its meals. The highly territorial clownfish chases away predators that feed on anemones and clean their host anemones of dead tissues and parasites. The relationship between the clownfish and sea anemone represents which of the following?

F Commensalism

G Mutualism

H Predation

J Parasitism

---

49 A wildlife preserve reports that its population of red foxes has increased while the coyote population has decreased. Which relationship between foxes and coyotes would help explain this observation?

A Coyotes and red foxes live near one another, but do not compete for resources.

B Coyotes and red foxes fill exactly the same niche in the forest.

C Coyotes are predators of red foxes.

D Red foxes parasitize coyotes.

---

50 Zebras are grazing animals that are native to the grasslands of Africa. Which animal can be predicted to have the most similar adaptations to those of a zebra?

F A predator of zebras that is native to the African grasslands

G An microorganism that lives in a symbiotic relationship with zebras

H An animal that competes with zebras for water or other resources

J A grazing animal native to the grasslands of North America

51 The diagram below illustrates the feeding relationships within an ecosystem. Approximately what percentage of the original amount of energy from producers is stored in the tissues of the frog?

A Food Web in an Area Around a Farmhouse

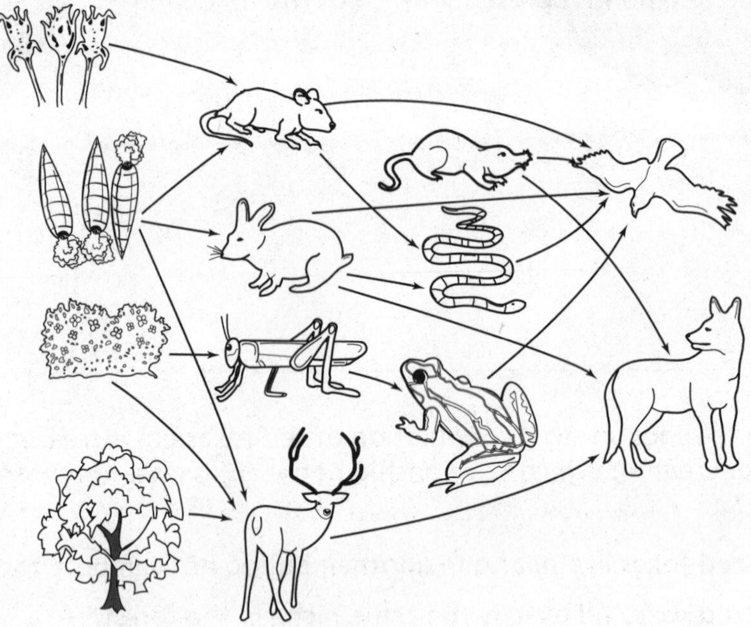

A 0.1%

B 1%

C 10%

D 100%

---

52 A new invasive beetle has been discovered in a farmland community. The beetle bores into and destroys the roots of entire fields of crops. The beetle was accidentally imported from abroad, and does not have predators in its new habitat. To control the destructive beetle, a group of researchers has proposed the use of nematodes that burrow into the soil and feed exclusively on the larvae of the beetle. Which best describes the beetle control method suggested by the researchers?

F Allowing the beetle population to crash as a result of density-independent limiting factors

G Using predation as density-dependent limiting factor

H Allowing the nematode population to reach carrying capacity

J Enabling the beetle population to grow exponentially

53 When fertilizers wash off farmland into streams and ponds, the nitrogen content of the water increases. This can lead to rapid growth of algae in a process called eutrophication. What effect does the dramatically increased growth of algae have on the freshwater ecosystem?

A The algae deplete nutrients in the water, reducing the resources available to other organisms.

B The algae provide increased food for fish, increasing fish populations.

C The algae increase the oxygen content in the water.

D The algae form symbiotic relationships with other producers in the ecosystem.

---

54 A keystone species is a species that is not usually abundant in a community yet has a strong impact on the structure of the community. In one coastal community, mangroves are keystone species. The roots of these trees provide food and shelter for many organisms, and keep sand, mud, and organic matter in place, preventing soil erosion and local flooding. Which of the following environmental changes would have the greatest impact on the coastal community?

F A severe hurricane that uproots most of the mangroves

G The planting of marsh grasses near the mangroves

H The reintroduction of native fish to the community

J A period of unusually high rainfall

Name ______________________ Date __________ Class ______________

Biology Practice Test B

Answer Sheet

1.	Ⓐ	Ⓑ	Ⓒ	Ⓓ
2.	Ⓕ	Ⓖ	Ⓗ	Ⓙ
3.	Ⓐ	Ⓑ	Ⓒ	Ⓓ
4.	Ⓕ	Ⓖ	Ⓗ	Ⓙ
5.	Ⓐ	Ⓑ	Ⓒ	Ⓓ
6.	Ⓕ	Ⓖ	Ⓗ	Ⓙ
7.	Ⓐ	Ⓑ	Ⓒ	Ⓓ
8.	Ⓕ	Ⓖ	Ⓗ	Ⓙ
9.	Ⓐ	Ⓑ	Ⓒ	Ⓓ
10.	Ⓕ	Ⓖ	Ⓗ	Ⓙ
11.	Ⓐ	Ⓑ	Ⓒ	Ⓓ
12.	Ⓕ	Ⓖ	Ⓗ	Ⓙ
13.	Ⓐ	Ⓑ	Ⓒ	Ⓓ
14.	Ⓕ	Ⓖ	Ⓗ	Ⓙ
15.	Ⓐ	Ⓑ	Ⓒ	Ⓓ
16.	Ⓕ	Ⓖ	Ⓗ	Ⓙ
17.	Ⓐ	Ⓑ	Ⓒ	Ⓓ
18.	Ⓕ	Ⓖ	Ⓗ	Ⓙ
19.	Ⓐ	Ⓑ	Ⓒ	Ⓓ
20.	Ⓕ	Ⓖ	Ⓗ	Ⓙ
21.	Ⓐ	Ⓑ	Ⓒ	Ⓓ
22.	Ⓕ	Ⓖ	Ⓗ	Ⓙ
23.	Ⓐ	Ⓑ	Ⓒ	Ⓓ
24.	Ⓕ	Ⓖ	Ⓗ	Ⓙ
25.	Ⓐ	Ⓑ	Ⓒ	Ⓓ
26.	Ⓕ	Ⓖ	Ⓗ	Ⓙ
27.	Ⓐ	Ⓑ	Ⓒ	Ⓓ
28.	Ⓕ	Ⓖ	Ⓗ	Ⓙ
29.	Ⓐ	Ⓑ	Ⓒ	Ⓓ
30.	Ⓕ	Ⓖ	Ⓗ	Ⓙ
31.	Ⓐ	Ⓑ	Ⓒ	Ⓓ
32.	Ⓕ	Ⓖ	Ⓗ	Ⓙ
33.	Ⓐ	Ⓑ	Ⓒ	Ⓓ
34.	Ⓕ	Ⓖ	Ⓗ	Ⓙ
35.	Ⓐ	Ⓑ	Ⓒ	Ⓓ
36.	Ⓕ	Ⓖ	Ⓗ	Ⓙ
37.	Ⓐ	Ⓑ	Ⓒ	Ⓓ
38.	Ⓕ	Ⓖ	Ⓗ	Ⓙ
39.	Ⓐ	Ⓑ	Ⓒ	Ⓓ
40.	Ⓕ	Ⓖ	Ⓗ	Ⓙ
41.	Ⓐ	Ⓑ	Ⓒ	Ⓓ
42.	Ⓕ	Ⓖ	Ⓗ	Ⓙ
43.	Ⓐ	Ⓑ	Ⓒ	Ⓓ
44.	Ⓕ	Ⓖ	Ⓗ	Ⓙ
45.	Ⓐ	Ⓑ	Ⓒ	Ⓓ
46.	Ⓕ	Ⓖ	Ⓗ	Ⓙ
47.	Ⓐ	Ⓑ	Ⓒ	Ⓓ
48.	Ⓕ	Ⓖ	Ⓗ	Ⓙ
49.	Ⓐ	Ⓑ	Ⓒ	Ⓓ
50.	Ⓕ	Ⓖ	Ⓗ	Ⓙ
51.	Ⓐ	Ⓑ	Ⓒ	Ⓓ
52.	Ⓕ	Ⓖ	Ⓗ	Ⓙ
53.	Ⓐ	Ⓑ	Ⓒ	Ⓓ
54.	Ⓕ	Ⓖ	Ⓗ	Ⓙ